Praise for Teresa Nicholas's *Buryin' Daddy*:

"An astonishingly beautiful and potent memoir about a mother and daughter each coping in their own way with the oppressive and domineering patriarch of the family, who remains unknowable until his death. Teresa Nicholas's eloquent prose pulled me squarely into her living room, and I, too, felt the tension when Daddy entered the room. The weight of his presence drives the author away from home and the mother into silence, until his death, when his secrets are revealed and intimacy is made possible between mother and daughter, and between a daughter and her dead father."

—Ann Fessler, author of *The Girls Who Went Away*

"*Buryin' Daddy* vibrates with honesty of feeling and thought, of eye and ear. Nicholas writes with compelling immediacy about her family—the pains a difficult father brought to an intelligent, sensitive daughter, the uncovering of secrets he had concealed from his family throughout his life, and the sense she and her mother eventually make of it all. An intimate story of simple moments and quiet truths, *Buryin' Daddy* is always moving but never sentimental—heartbreaking at times but ultimately uplifting."

—JoAnne Prichard Morris, author of *Barefootin': Life Lessons from the Road to Freedom*

"What is a normal family? What is love? In *Buryin' Daddy*, Teresa Nicholas takes us on a mesmerizing journey into the conflicted heart of her family. The power of her story lies in Nicholas's crystalline prose and unflinching courage in telling the truth. It is a revelation of family, love and forgiveness that is fast paced and thrilling."

—Ruth Williams, author of *Younger Than That Now*

"*Buryin' Daddy* is a stunningly beautiful memoir written with exceptional grace and eloquence. Teresa Nicholas wrenches the reader's heart as she struggles to first escape and then to understand her oppressive father and her childhood. The book is a classic portrait of how the American South both nurtures and haunts each generation."

—William Ferris, co-editor of the *Encyclopedia of Southern Culture*

Buryin' Daddy

Buryin' Daddy

Putting My Lebanese, Catholic, Southern Baptist Childhood to Rest

TERESA NICHOLAS

University Press of Mississippi Jackson

Willie Morris Books in Memoir and Biography

www.upress.state.ms.us

The University Press of Mississippi is a member

of the Association of American University Presses.

Manufactured in the United States of America

The names and identifying details of some characters in this book have been changed.

First printing 2011

∞

Library of Congress Cataloging-in-Publication Data

Nicholas, Teresa.

Buryin' daddy : putting my Lebanese, Catholic, Southern Baptist childhood to rest / Teresa Nicholas.

p. cm. — (Willie Morris books in memoir and biography)

ISBN 978-1-60473-970-1 (cloth : alk. paper) —ISBN 978-1-60473-971-8 (ebook) 1. Nicholas, Teresa. 2. Mississippi—Biography. 3. Fathers and daughters—Mississippi. I. Title.

CT275.N558A3 2011

976.2'063092—dc22

[B] 2010033289

British Library Cataloging-in-Publication Data available

For Gerard Marion Helferich

Part I

"Home Again, Home Again, Jiggedy-Jig"

One

I stand on Grendaddy's reclining chair in the center hall and let the yellow morning sunlight fall across my face. Arms outstretched, I reach toward the transom of the front door to catch the sunbeams. There are so many today! But as soon as I cup my small hands around them and pull them toward me, I open my fists and see that they are gone.

Every morning before breakfast, everybody goes outside. The old house quiet. I am the last one up, except for Mama. I jump from the recliner and head for Grandma's closet. Rows upon rows of shoes. I choose the black pair with the medium heels and slip my feet into them, filling them only partway. The hem of my cotton nightgown catches as I clomp toward the front of the old house. Out the screen door, across the porch, down the concrete steps.

The yard shimmers in the green summer, and I squint, then see Grandma crouching under the pecan trees, lopper in hand. Pruning. I sneak toward her, pulling at my nightgown to keep it from tangling in her shoes. I stand beside her. She looks up, startled, then smiles and calls my name. Treesa. I am her favorite. The camera is brought out, photos taken, and I wander about in a dreamy morning state.

"Time for breakfast," Grendaddy says. Grandma and I go into the kitchen, a big, bright room with two floor-to-ceiling windows and a metal table in front of them. We have three places to eat in Grandma's house—kitchen, breakfast room, and dining room. We always have breakfast and supper in the kitchen and dinner in the breakfast room. We only eat at the mahogany table in the dining room every other Sunday, when Grandma's brother, Hop, and his wife, Janice, come from Holmes County. This is also the only time we are allowed to sit on the prickly mauve couch in the living room. Then we can see Grandma's thrilling knickknack collection on the shelves next to the gas fireplace. A wooden backscratcher in the shape of a miniature rake, a set of tiny pink and green glasses Daddy calls shots. A dainty vase like a long-necked lady wearing a rhinestone choker.

Grendaddy is bumbling about the house, from his bedroom to the bathroom. Running water. Loud noises like thunder! "What is that?" I want to know. "Why, that's just your grendaddy," Grandma says, making her camel lips. The strong, black smell of coffee fills the kitchen. Grandma is putting the bacon on to fry. Debbie, my big sister, sits at the table and fiddles with the spoon in the fig preserves. I am standing next to Grandma at the stove, still in my nightgown and her shoes. Then Mama and Daddy come in, and Daddy rushes me to the table, shoes falling off, knees hitting the edge. Grandma tells him to watch out for my knees, but it is too late. The eggs are scrambled. We are just waiting for Grendaddy.

Grendaddy takes his place at the head of the table. Nubbin follows him, sits at his feet, face upturned, waiting. I reach out to touch his nose, but Grandma hands me a sandwich, white bread with the crust on, wrapped around two slices of bacon. I take it from her and start mashing it, making the bread fit around the meat, making it smaller and smaller. That's how I like it. "Eat your food," Daddy says. When Grandma isn't looking, Grendaddy reaches down and lets Nubbin lick bacon bits off his fingers. His eyes meet mine. We smile.

After breakfast, Grendaddy and Daddy leave for the grocery store on West Broadway, the Nicholas Cash Gro. Mama goes to her bedroom to lie down. She always lies down during the day. Debbie is going out to play with the neighborhood boys. First she straps on her guns, then puts on her cowboy hat. Grandma tells her to stay out of the trees. Two days ago, she jumped out of the pear tree and broke off her front tooth. She thinks she can fly.

Grandma and I are alone with the dishes now. "Want some coffee, Treesa?" she asks. Of course I do. We both love coffee. She hands me a big green cup and saucer and fills it partway with the coffee, then pours milk in the rest of the way. I curl my forefinger and thumb through the handle, let my little finger stick out like hers. Soon Aunt Pauline comes in from next door and has coffee with us. It is already hot, and Grandma gets up to pull the window shades. Pauline's arms rest on top of the table, bare. They are talking about a new roof.

Then Clemmy comes. She calls herself my black grandmother. She leans over and draws my face into her waistless body, and I smell her foreign smell. "Why you let this child drink coffee?" she asks Grandma and Pauline. "This child ain't even four years old and shouldn't oughta be drinkin' no coffee." She starts to take my cup from me, and we tug it back and forth, spilling the light brown liquid on the table. When I see her sixth finger protruding next to the pinky on her big black hand, I let the cup go.

It is the day for washing clothes. We all get up and move out of Clemmy's way so she can reach the washer in the corner of the kitchen. Aunt Pauline leaves, and Grandma steps over to the sink and begins to do the breakfast dishes. She tells me to go out to the back screened porch and play with Nubbin. We sit on the glider and swing for a while, but soon he steps off with a thud. He is a fat dog and not much fun. Mama calls out to me from her bedroom window, "Stop makin' so much noise on that thang!" And then Grandma comes out and asks if I want to sweep the front porch with her. I love it when we sweep.

She takes the broom from the nail on the back porch, and we walk through the house, quiet except for the low singing of the washing machine. Clemmy is separating piles of clothes in the kitchen. Mama is still in her bedroom. We walk down the center hall to the front door. Grandma opens the heavy wooden door, then the screen door.

Outside, we stand still for a moment in the sun and heat, waiting for our eyes and bodies to adjust. Then she goes to the far corner of the porch and starts to sweep, slowly, carefully, the broom touching every plank, removing the long, brown threads of pollen that have blown onto the open porch overnight. I watch carefully, standing next to her. When she is done, she has a small, neat pile. She begins to push it down the steps, collecting more and more. She works it to the concrete walkway, then pushes the growing pile toward the street.

Once in the yard, I lose interest and run to play on the roots of the linden tree. I imagine that two of them are like the scales in front of the Black and White Department Store downtown. I pretend to put coins in the deep crevices of the trunk and see my weight and fortune revealed in the tree's dark hide. Finally, Grandma pushes the pile into Grand Avenue, where it will wait for the street sweeper. Her face is sweaty, and her eyeglasses are having trouble staying up on her nose. She notices me standing on the tree roots and says we should go inside for a cool drink.

The old house is darker now without the sunlight coming

through the transom. I skip down the center hall barefoot and still in my nightgown. I hear sounds from the bathroom. Mama has gotten up and is taking her bath. I go to the door and tell her I want to come inside with her, but there is no answer. I say it over and over again, and I hear her shout, "No!" I begin to cry, sink down against the door, and then Grandma takes me in her lap in Grendaddy's chair. I am too much child for her, and my long legs flop to the side as I squirm and cry. She starts to sing and tap her foot. Her voice is low, slow. Like the sweeping, it lulls me. She sings:

Old frog
Sittin' on a log,
Cryin' for his daughter.
He cried all night,
His hair turned white—
Then he jumped off into the wa-ter.

I stop crying, am calm again. We get up, walk into the kitchen, where Clemmy has laid out the makings of our dinner.

Pork chops from the grocery, partly unwrapped from the brown butcher paper, sit on the counter. Big red tomatoes and black-eyed peas from Clemmy's garden. The peas need to be shelled. There are two places for shelling peas: the backyard and the back porch. Not the front porch. Peas are never shelled on the front porch.

Today Grandma wants to shell on the back porch. But before we start, she decides I must be washed and dressed. Mama is out of the bathroom, and Grandma and I stand before the high pedestal sink. I can barely see myself in the mirror, but she is standing behind me. I am told to wash my face and brush my teeth. While I do this, she brushes my brown hair to get the tangles out, then twists and turns it expertly into a ponytail. I ask for pigtails today, but no, she says I must have a ponytail. She is in a hurry to shell the peas. The brushing and twisting and turning make it difficult to spit into the basin. When the washing is over, I go into my closet and choose pink pedal pushers and a sleeveless shirt. We are ready to shell peas.

Peas must be shelled in a certain way. Clemmy and Grandma sit on the glider, each with a pile of peas in a large bowl in her lap. They are long pods, speckled white and purple. The two of them begin to shell, pinching off the ends, pulling off the threads, and using their thumbs to push out the peas. They discard the hulls on a piece of newspaper put down between them. The *Jackson Daily News*. I begin to badger Grandma to read the smudged headline to me. "You read it, Treesa," she says without looking up. I turn this way and that and finally say, "Grandma, you know I can't read." She stops and laughs, a sound like ruffled feathers. "Treesa, you're so tall, sometimes I forget."

The peas are finished, and Clemmy gathers everything up and goes into the kitchen, where she and Grandma cook the meal. Debbie comes in through the back door, sweaty and brown. She says she has to go right back out after dinner because she and the Parker boys are going to build a fort next door in the vacant lot. I can't come, she says, because I am a baby. I say I don't care, because after dinner the men are coming to tear the roof off, and I want to watch.

Peas, pork chops, gravy, buttered rice, sweet potatoes, sliced tomatoes, sweet tea. Grandma's favorites. Grendaddy and Daddy come home from the grocery store, complaining about the heat. Clemmy draws the shades in the breakfast room, and it turns dark until Grendaddy cuts on the electric light. We sit down to eat. Mama shuffles in, still dressed in her housecoat. Grandma calls into the kitchen and asks Clemmy to switch on the attic fan. I can hear the motor start and then the soft purring. The window shades begin to move back and forth with the breeze. I don't want to eat the pork chops, so Grandma fixes me a tomato sandwich with mayonnaise, salt, and pepper.

After dinner, Clemmy and Grandma clear the dishes, and Grendaddy and I go into the wide center hall, which doubles as the TV room. Grendaddy sits in his recliner, smokes a cigar, and turns on *The Loretta Young Show*. I sit next to him, and he pulls penny candy out of his pockets for me. I imagine that Miss Young is my mother, since both are tall and pretty with dark, wavy hair. Whenever I miss Mama, I can watch her on TV.

I become more and more sleepy, lulled by the hum of the fan, the darkness of the room, and the familiar smell of Grendaddy's cigar. I hear distant sounds. Clemmy and Grandma washing dishes in the kitchen. My parents' voices from their bedroom, soft at first, then louder. Mama is saying, "The baby, the baby," and then I hear the muffled gurgling sounds. I know this is when she puts her head into the pillow. I have stood in their doorway and watched.

Then the blue phone on top of the television rings. Grandma comes in from the kitchen to answer it. "Roofers will be here shortly," she says. Grendaddy nods, turns off his show, puts out his cigar. He and Daddy leave to go back downtown to the store.

Clemmy gives me a bag of wooden clothespins and an ink pen and tells me to draw faces on them. Later she brings in a cardboard box and scissors, and she, Debbie, and I sit on the hall floor and make a house for the clothespin men. Gayden Parker appears on the front porch and yells for Debbie to come outside to build the fort. I am not invited.

I want to go to Mama and ask her if I am a baby, if I am making her cry, but I am afraid she will tell me to go away. Just then the roofers appear at the front screen door. Grandma speaks to them while I stand by her side. They are getting the ladders out and going up on the roof even though Grandma says it is too late today. They are going up on the roof at the hottest part of the day. But they want to get started.

Soon they begin throwing the old roof off the house and into the garden. Roof is flying everywhere, and Grandma is getting more and more riled up. "I'm goin' to have a tizzy fit," she says. Soon Mama, Clemmy, and I are in a tizzy, too, as we stand inside and watch the roof rain down into the yard. Grandma is upset about the purple larkspur that grows in a big patch near her garden shed. It has just come into bloom, and we can see the shingles hitting the stalks and bending them this way and that.

By now it is late afternoon, and we all think we have had just about enough of these roofers. Then one reappears at the screen door and shouts that they are done for the day but will be back in the morning. It is also time for Clemmy to leave, and Grandma and I walk outside with her to see what they have done to the house. I must be careful not to step on a nail, they say. The old roof is in the flowerbeds, and Grandma is so upset about her poor larkspur. "It is ruined," she says. The ground is streaked with electric-blue smudges.

I watch Clemmy walk through the rickety back gate and disappear down Thirteenth Street toward her house, two blocks away. The sun is already low in the sky, and the locusts are singing their song, *wee-oh-wee-oh*. Two blocks east, the Little League players are warming up before their game. *Go Dynaflows! You can do it, you can do it!*

Then it is nearly dark. Everyone is home. Grandma fixes me a mayonnaise sandwich, and I ask to eat it out on the back steps. Soon it is time for a bath and bed. Grandma puts Debbie and me in the tub and leaves to finish clearing the supper table. She tells Debbie to wash the dirt beads off her neck and to wash my hair and says she will be back in a jiffy to rinse us off. Debbie pours the shampoo on and begins to make a ponytail that sticks straight up in the middle of my head. Suds drip down into my eyes, and they begin to burn. Grandma reappears, rinses us off, and helps put us in our pajamas. I want to wear the blue baby dolls.

We kneel at the side of our bed and say the prayers Father Hunter taught us. He is a kind man and often comes to the house to speak to Mama and Daddy. After we climb into bed, with the light off, I must say good night to everyone or I cannot fall asleep. Mama and Daddy are in their bedroom, Grandma and Grendaddy in the center hall watching TV. I call out, "Good night, Mama, good night, Daddy, good night Debbie, good night, Grandma, good night, Grendaddy," and each person calls back good night to me.

Finally I am ready to sleep, except I remember that I haven't sprinkled the holy water on my pillow. I tell Debbie I have to turn the light on again to get the holy water, but she begins to yell at me. I am afraid to go to sleep without the holy water, so I turn the light on anyway. I get it from the dresser and put a few drops on the pillow where my head will be. I ask Debbie if she wants some, tell her it will keep the devil away during the night. Even though she is mad at me, she can't argue with this, and I let the drops sprinkle her face and pillow. When we are settled down, Grandma comes in one more time and turns off the light. I look at the dark shapes made by the heavy old furniture and listen to the sound of the big trucks out on the highway.

No sooner am I asleep than I feel water on my face. At first

I think Debbie is playing a trick on me with the holy water. But the old house is quiet, everyone still asleep. Now there is a trickle of water, and I feel the bed is damp. I sit up and say as loud as I can to the dark house, "It's tee-tee-in'!" Mama comes into our bedroom and turns on the light. I see a stream of water flowing from the ceiling. I hear the rain outside coming down in buckets, as Clemmy likes to say. Soon everyone is setting up buckets and pans inside our room. We are all in a tizzy again about the roof.

Then Mama bends over and holds her stomach. She says to Daddy, "Sol June, the baby, the baby." He screams at her, "Florence, what do you mean, the baby? Is it time for the baby?" She is holding her stomach and looking at her feet. Big, wet drops fall down her cheeks. She waddles back to their bedroom, clutching her belly. Daddy follows her. Debbie and I are standing by our bed, watching. Grandma and Grendaddy, too. There is water everywhere, on the bed, on the floor, on us. There is nothing to do but wait.

Mama and Daddy go outside, crank up the purple Chevrolet, and start for the hospital. I pray this isn't like last time, when Mama went to the hospital and came back without the babies. They would have been blind, she told me, because they were born premature. One lived one day, one lived three. They named them Ed and Fred. Now they are in the cemetery next to Grendaddy's parents, George and Rosa, who came over from the Old Country. But Mama doesn't like to visit them because they don't have headstones yet.

We all wait, though I am not sure for what. Toward morning the rain ends, and we hear Daddy's car pull into the garage. He opens the squeaky gate and comes up the back steps. He looks tired, even more stooped over than Grendaddy. The screen door bangs, and we see him walk through the porch, past the glider, to where we stand in the kitchen. He looks at Grandma and Grendaddy, then at me and Debbie. He wags a finger. "Well," he says, and I can't imagine what he will say next. "Well, your brother, Solomon Thomas Nicholas III, was born today." It was July 2, 1957.

Two

After my brother was born, everything began to change: my sense of place and time, my sense of happiness. Also, we began to run out of room in the fine old bungalow that we thought of not as my grandparents' but simply as Grandma's. When my parents brought my brother home from the hospital, Mama put Sol Boy in a slatted crib next to their double bed, so five of us were now sleeping in Grandma's two back bedrooms. There was a black-painted door between our rooms, which my parents would leave open so they could keep watch over Debbie and me. But I used to lie in bed when they thought I was asleep and listen to them talk. That was how I came to find out that Mama wanted to move from Grandma's. I strained to hear what Daddy had to say, but it was Mama who raised her voice.

"Sol June, I've lived here for seven years. Seven long years. I want you to buy me a house of my own. We're puttin' Grandma out. You know I don't like to put nobody out." But Daddy didn't answer her.

Soon after, my parents invited Father Hunter to visit so he could bless my brother. Mama showed him to a chair in the dark center hall—not Grendaddy's recliner, but a straight-backed chair next to the doorway of my and Debbie's bedroom. Then she went to get the baby. Grandma stepped in from the kitchen to say good morning, but she did not call him Father. She attended the First Baptist Church and didn't believe in our religion. She said we were heathens.

Then Daddy arrived and shook Father Hunter's hand. He took a seat in a cane chair, pulling it right alongside the priest's. Even though Father Hunter sat in the shadows, I could see him smiling. He had an elongated face, and when he smiled he reminded me of the comedian Daddy liked, Stan Laurel. Father Hunter nodded me toward him, but I remained across from him, leaning against the wall next to the dining room.

We continued sitting in the darkened hall, listening to the clattering of the attic fan. Finally, Mama came back with the baby and placed him on Father's lap, on top of his long, black cassock. Then she bent down and unwrapped the baby's snug blanket so he could examine him. I took a step forward so I could look at him, too. He was fat, with his legs pulled up like the roly-polies on the sidewalk in front of Grandma's house. On the baby's stomach, a knotted, angry scab. I leaned over to smell it. It smelled rich and dark, like upturned earth.

"No!" Mama yelled. "It's the cord."

I moved back toward the wall again. *What cord?* I wanted to ask.

But Father Hunter was saying, "This is a healthy baby." I knew he meant, *Not like the twins.*

Daddy said, "Father, please bless him."

Then Father Hunter raised his smooth hand and made the sign of the cross over my brother.

Mama said, "Thank you, thank you." She wasn't raised a Catholic but a Baptist—not a First Baptist, but a Primitive Baptist, from Midway, out in the county. She converted when she married Daddy.

Mama took the baby from Father Hunter's lap, and she and

Daddy disappeared into their bedroom. I was alone with Father Hunter; he signaled me closer. I took a step and smiled at him, but he drew back. When Mama and Daddy returned, he exclaimed, "This child has dimples! Two of them, one on either side of her mouth."

Dimples? This was the first I'd heard of them. I looked from him to my parents. They were staring at me.

Father Hunter repeated, "Dimples."

After he left, Mama went to the front porch and called Debbie, who was next door in the vacant lot with the Parker boys. They had finished making their fort, deep in a hollow, with branches and scraps of tin for a roof. They spent all day there every day. Sometimes they even ate there, raw hot dogs that Debbie took over in the package. But today she had to come home for dinner. We all sat at the mahogany table in the dining room, and for the first time Daddy told the story: Father Hunter became the discoverer of my dimples.

Grandma had laid out Grendaddy's Old Country food, which his mother, Rosa, had taught her how to make. This was not Grandma's food, fried pork chops and chicken and slabs of thick ham, steak and gravy. This was Grendaddy's, served on Sundays and special occasions. Grandma had even prepared his favorite dish, cubbie. She liked to say that she didn't go out for those weird-sounding names Grendaddy used, so kibbe she called cubbie. Tabouli salad was sap soup and imjadara, jolly-jolly-jing-jing-jing. Grandma claimed that cubbie made her break out in a rash, so whenever she formed the chopped meat and cubbie grits into balls for frying, she wore long, yellow rubber gloves. She curled her lips so that the upper one went to the left and the lower one to the right. These were her camel lips, and she'd taught me how to make them. She wanted me on her side in the Cubbie War, but I liked cubbie and all of Grendaddy's Old Country food.

Grandma was born in Holmes County, out the dirt road past Eden. Her parents named her Vashti, after the Persian queen. The name, she said, meant "beautiful," and the first time Grendaddy saw her, as she was standing next to the drink box in the grocery, he decided she was the prettiest girl he'd ever seen. Her family, the Pettuses, owned 240 acres, but Grandma described it as worthless hills and hollers, where they eked out a living growing cotton on what bottomland they could clear. She bragged that her family hailed from Georgia, the state beyond Alabama. All Grendaddy could say about his parents was that they came from someplace "way over yonder." He believed Syria, but Daddy insisted "over the hill, in Lebanon." Since we were not sure where this place was, we called it the Old Country. The townspeople referred to us as the Arabs. There were other Arabs in Yazoo City, and they had their own shops on West Broadway—Hassin's Department Store, Weber's Shop-Rite Grocery, the Marylena Shoppe, Alias Cash Grocery. Next to our grocery store was Great-Uncle Fred and Aunt Natalie's Army-Navy and Great-Uncle Sam's Bon Ton Café.

Grendaddy liked to tell how right after the turn of the century, he and his parents, George and Rosa, had sailed to Ellis Island in steerage from the Old Country. His papa couldn't speak much English, and whenever Grendaddy talked about him, his own slight foreign accent got stronger. Papa had a pack, and he traveled the Mississippi River selling notions, things that people couldn't get back then. Zippers. Thread. Buttons. Finally, they got to Vicksburg and then settled in Yazoo City.

But still Papa peddled. Mostly he walked—sometimes to Benton, sometimes to Midway, sometimes south to Valley.

He might be gone a week, working every house along the way. Grendaddy said Papa knew the value of money, and he saved enough to open the store on West Broadway. I tried to imagine that far-back time when notions were so hard to come by. Now Grendaddy sold them from the narrow shelves behind the cash register. When he took over his papa's store in 1938, he renamed it the "U Save Nicholas Grocery." According to Grandma, "Grendaddy gave away too much on credit to the Nigras." When the store reopened after the bankruptcy, he called it the Nicholas Cash Gro. But Grandma still complained that Grendaddy gave away too much on credit to the Nigras.

Daddy loved the Nicholas Cash Gro. He loved the fire-engine-red drink box with *Coca-Cola* written on its side in white letters. He loved the peanut parcher and the overhead fan in the shape of a baby airplane. He loved to sift through the cash register to find coins for his collection, which he kept in Aunt 'Cile's castoff suitcase. But after my brother was born, Daddy couldn't work at the store any longer. He had to make more money, so he'd started helping Great-Uncle Dan, another of Grendaddy's brothers, at the Yazoo Motor Co., which Daddy called the Place. Uncle Dan sold cars—Buicks, Pontiacs, and Oldsmobiles. Daddy loved cars, too. He was good with numbers, and he would keep Uncle Dan's books.

Now in the afternoons, instead of Daddy returning to the store with Grendaddy, Grandma went with him. I did, too, so she could look after me, while Debbie roamed the neighborhood with the Parker boys. But before we could leave, Grandma had to ready herself at her bedroom vanity. She and Grendaddy slept in the romantic front bedroom with the rose-patterned wallpaper, in a bed made of bird's-eye maple. Besides the vanity, there was a tall bureau, where Grandma kept her costume jewelry, which she bought at the Marylena Shoppe. She would sit on a low chair with a velvet cushion and examine herself in the vanity mirror while I stood next to her and watched. Grandma had blue eyes, the only one in our family to have them. She applied a great quantity of mineral oil to her face with cotton balls. She did it slowly, the way she did everything. She brushed her thick brown hair and sprayed it stiff with Aqua Net and put on a print shirtwaist dress and pumps. Then we'd squeeze into Grendaddy's white Opel. The car's tiny fan, clipped to the dashboard, would rotate as he drove us the two miles to West Broadway.

In downtown Yazoo City, tucked behind the five blocks of Main Street, there were alleyways scattered with gravel, just wide enough for a car to pass. Grendaddy always approached the grocery through the alley off Mound. He parked the Opel behind the two-story redbrick building, right next to the railroad tracks. The storefront had a large plate glass window patched with masking tape, which shook when the freight trains went by. Inside it was long and narrow and dim toward the back, because my grandparents said they were trying to save on the electric. There was a blackened concrete floor.

The metal and wooden shelves were to the right, and these held the bags of bread and packages of honey buns and the little fruit pies and the canned goods that Grandma said the Nigras favored—potted meat, sardines, tuna fish, and Campbell's soups. The drink box and the ice cream freezer were over against the right wall. To the left was a long counter. On top of this counter were the peanut parcher and the glass jars with cookies and hard candies and the cash register. Grendaddy had patched the countertop with bubble gum and brown shoe polish, which Grandma called just another one of his messes. Sometimes in the faint light of the grocery, behind her back, he called her the Old Battle-Axe. But I believed they loved each other because they slept in the bird's-eye maple bed in the front bedroom with the romantic rose-patterned wallpaper.

We would sit on tall metal stools behind the counter. I would drink a Chocolate Soldier while Grendaddy chewed a cigar and stared out the window toward the Rose Oil, where Mama's twin, Brother, pumped gas. Grandma did the crossword puzzle and word jumble in the *Jackson Daily News*. After a while, she might attack the floor with her broom and wave a feather duster over the merchandise. We didn't have many customers, and I would feel my grandparents' excitement whenever one happened inside. Once or twice a week, Hambone hobbled across the railroad tracks on his peg leg, tall, and round and black as a truck tire. He made his way to the shelves and came to the counter with a few small cans. Grendaddy always talked to Hambone in a friendly voice while entering his purchases in the ledger, and Hambone made his *X*. But when Hambone left, Grandma complained that she didn't like waiting on a Nigra's monthly check before she got paid.

Over the store was the Nicholas Hotel. The door was to the right of the grocery, past the pay phone, up a set of narrow, rickety stairs. I was not allowed up there. Not even Grandma was allowed up there, because Grendaddy's roomers were men. Most came and went, but Snake, Johnny King, Goober, and Mr. Quakemire were regulars. One day, Snake drank too much whiskey and set his bed on fire. The next day, after getting out of jail, he returned to the hotel and drank another bottle of whiskey with Mr. King. Grendaddy had to phone the chief of police, Ard Russell, who came to the grocery store and complained to Grendaddy about his drunken roomers.

But Grandma maintained that Mr. Bill Hackett was from a good family in Vicksburg. Mr. Bill often leaned out his window above West Broadway, dressed in a sleeveless undershirt. I would stand on the sidewalk, hanging onto the parking meter, looking up at him. Mr. Bill would come downstairs when he saw me, but first he'd put on a shirt. He had blue eyes, and he lowered his face very close to mine. Sometimes he asked me how old I was; sometimes he gave me a dime. Other than Grandma's house with its garden, there was no place I liked as much as the Nicholas Cash Gro. and Hotel.

One day, Daddy came from the Place to pick me up at five o'clock, bringing a packet of photographs. They were from the day Sol Boy was born, black-and-whites about the size of Daddy's palm. Most were of my brother, but there were also some of me dressed in my cotton nightgown and Grandma's black heels. In one, I am pulling the nightgown out in front to keep it from catching as I walk. My legs are long, and my hair is stringy and dark brown. I am standing next to the iris bed under the pecan tree, smiling at Grandma, who is crouching down among the tall leaves. Her long-handled lopper is nearby on the ground. She is smiling at me.

When we got home that day, Daddy went straight to his closet and put the packet of photographs with all the others in the brown camera bag. Over the years, when I would pull out these snapshots, they would remind me that once, when we'd lived with my grandparents, I'd been so happy.

Three

January 1959, a month before I turned five, Mama had another baby, a beautiful girl with downy black hair. Mama wanted to call her simply Lisa, but Daddy insisted she have a saint's name like the rest of us. He had named me after St. Teresa of Ávila, the patron saint of headache sufferers, whose symbols were a heart, an arrow, and a book. He had even given me for a middle name the Spanish town where she was born. But for once Mama persevered, and Father Hunter christened the baby Lisa, though Daddy tacked on Maria. She was called Lisa Maria, the two names sounding like one.

When my parents brought her home from the hospital, they placed a white-skirted bassinet next to their bed and slid my brother's slatted crib over against the windows that faced onto the back porch. Daddy took a photo of his growing family and put it in the camera bag. Ever since Sol Boy's birth, Mama had been insisting that we couldn't go on living in two bedrooms, and now I lay in bed and heard her begging Daddy again for a house of her own. Then, in the living room, in front of the gas fireplace, Mama and Grendaddy had an argument, something about us children. Not long after, Daddy said we'd be moving out.

Those mornings we got up early. The baby had the colic, and nobody could sleep anyway. Mama tended to her and even

found time to help Grandma in the kitchen. When she stood at the sink washing dishes, Sol Boy would pull himself up by the hem of her dress to bite the back of her knees. Mama's legs would buckle, her kneecaps knocking against the cabinet door. But she didn't scold him, she laughed—a quiet laugh, not like Grandma's cackle. Mama laughed because she was excited: She was finally going to have a house of her own.

When Mama was growing up in the Delta, her family, the Hoods, sharecropped and had never had a house of their own. "We was nomads," Mama would say, renting one-room shacks where the rain sounded like drumming on the tin roof. Then when Mama was five, her daddy, John Wesley, died, she said from the Hood heart. Even though it was August, Grandma Hood managed to transport his body the fifty miles from Arcola to Midway in a wagon pulled by mules. They buried him there in the hills, in the little churchyard at Midway Primitive Baptist, just to the left beyond the big curve.

After that, Grandma Hood moved her ten children from the Delta to the hills around Midway, where they still rented one-room shacks and sharecropped. To make an extra ten cents a day, they worked for their Uncle Will, who Mama said was like a giant, the way he stood straight up in the noonday sun and had them hoe his peanuts. But still she felt she was taking charity from Uncle Will. Mama often said, "I don't like to take nothin' from nobody." Even though she'd lived in Grandma's house for nine years, she'd never felt at home. And she believed that Grandma looked down on her because she'd been a sharecropper.

One cold morning, the six of us piled into the Chevrolet. Mama held Lisa Maria in her lap, while Debbie, Sol Boy, and I took up the small back seat. Daddy had decided to take us riding, out toward Carter, where we'd rarely been. "We got us a bright sunshiny day!" he exclaimed as he turned the ignition.

Until now, I hadn't paid much attention to Daddy except when he performed tricks for us. When he put his hands together and blew through his thumbs to make a sound like a dove's call. Or when he drew Fifis, little dogs with smiley faces and curlicue tails, on the backs of our hands. Or his best trick, when he covered his left thumb with four fingers, waved both hands in the air, then pulled his thumb off, so that only a stump remained. But since he'd decided that we had to move, I couldn't help but notice Daddy. His big, watery brown eyes, his hooked nose and ample forehead. His fleshy lips and his crooked teeth. I couldn't help but notice Daddy and his exaggerated features, because he was always working them, since he was so worked up over moving.

That sunny morning, he drove us downtown, past Grendaddy's store, over the railroad tracks and the Yazoo River Bridge. I could see the river below like a muddy snake, the trees smeared along the bank, and the brown cotton fields beyond. Then Daddy made a right turn onto Carter Road, and we stopped. The stalks of the cotton plants were sticking straight up out of the hard winter dirt. We waited in the car because it was too cold to get out. But what were we waiting for?

Finally, another car pulled up in front of ours. A man got out, and so did Daddy. Daddy took a large piece of blue paper from an envelope, flattened it on the Chevrolet's hood, and pointed toward the withered cotton. The two began talking fast, and Daddy did some figuring on the back of the envelope. Then he started to talk louder and wave his arms in the air like cartwheels. Back in the car, he jabbed the blue pages at Mama.

I leaned over into the front seat. "Are we movin' to Carter?"

"You ask too many questions, young'un," Mama snapped.

Daddy sped back to Grandma's. "I can't afford to build us no house," he said, poking out his lips.

Soon after, my grandparents suggested that we move next door to Aunt Pauline and Uncle J.T., one house away from theirs. Years ago they'd bought this large corner lot, and they offered to give it to us. They also suggested that Daddy buy an older home and move it there. Now every evening, when he came in from the Place, we would crowd around the metal table in Grandma's kitchen, our knees touching, while he described the prospects he'd seen that day. One evening he told us about three older houses for sale across from the Main Street School. Then the next night he came in, leaned on Grandma's kitchen doorway, and grinned, his cheeks pushed up like Alvin the Chipmunk's. He'd found just the house for us, he announced; in fact, he'd already bought it. "What do you think of them apples?" he wanted to know. He danced a little jig around the kitchen, singing, "Didididididididididi." Then he fished out the elderberry wine, which Clemmy had given us for Christmas and which Grandma kept in a Mason jar in the back of the refrigerator, and helped himself to a celebratory swig.

The next day, Daddy took us to see the house. We got up early, even earlier than usual. It was sunny but cold, with a glittering of frost on the grass, so I put on my new checkered car coat with the oblong wooden buttons. As we walked across the back porch, down the steps, and past the gate, I felt happy to be in my new car coat. Mama was also happy, because she was finally getting a house of her own.

We climbed into the Chevrolet, and Daddy drove the two miles to the Main Street School. He made the left at Ricks Library and another left onto Washington Street and pulled up in front of the three houses. He parked, ignoring the passing traffic, and we got out and stood on the sidewalk. Just as he'd said, the houses were old. The two on the left were large and painted fresh white, with floor-to-ceiling windows and a wide front porch like Grandma's. But the one on the right was a duplex, long and narrow. It had two stoops and two front doors, and next to each door was a short window. The duplex didn't have a foundation but sat propped on concrete blocks. It was supposed to be white but looked more peeled than painted. We knew without his even having to tell us: Daddy had bought the duplex.

Even Mama's family didn't live in a duplex. After the war, Mama and Aunt 'Cile and Uncle Brother had pooled their money to buy a small house on Dunn Avenue and had brought Grandma Hood from the hills to live with them. Their house wasn't as nice as Grandma's, but it was not a duplex. Even I knew that only poor people lived in duplexes, people whose children ran around barefoot and runny nosed. The only thing beneath a duplex was a shack, where the colored people lived. Everybody knew this—everybody but Daddy.

That morning Mama had on her long black coat, which she reserved for Sunday Mass. Usually she held her head up high and her shoulders back. We may not have much money, she would tell us, but we could have good posture. I could see Mama's shoulders sloping and sense her disappointment, the way I sensed my grandparents' excitement whenever a customer happened inside their grocery.

But Daddy wanted to show off the duplex. He herded us to the front door on the right side, and we shuffled through the living room, hallway, bedroom, dining room, and kitchen. There was one bathroom, the walls and cabinets painted light pink, with a sink and tub so tiny they reminded me of one of Grandma's knickknacks. The narrow rooms in the duplex flowed like boxcars on a freight train, with the kitchen hitched at the back like the caboose. It smelled sour, like the Public Health Department, where we went to get our shots. There was a wooden cabinet with a gummy linoleum countertop, a sink with the porcelain worn off, and two dripping faucets. Above were three tiny scratched-up metal cabinets.

Mama hadn't said anything, and Daddy steered us back to the front door. He wanted us to see the left side of the duplex, but these rooms were even more run-down. The wallpaper in this living room was dirty and peeling, the floor lined with termite tunnels. The dining room ceiling had billowy dark circles like black clouds. This bathroom, instead of pink, was painted stark white.

We went outside again and stood on the sidewalk in front of the three houses. I looked at the two houses Daddy hadn't bought. I looked at the duplex. Daddy was waiting for Mama to say something. Finally she asked, "Sol June, just how do you plan on us livin' in a duplex?"

"Damn, Florence," he shot back, "I'll rip out the dividin' wall. We're goin' to live in the duplex like it was one house. Can't you see the potential?" He shouted, "Damn!" again—two, three times, fast.

Then Daddy rushed us back into the car. But as he drove toward Grandma's, he hung his head and promised Mama that he would fix up the house. Not just rip out the dividing wall. Fix up the house. It was the first time we heard those words from him, and Mama seemed to accept them.

But first, the duplex had to be moved. "That'll be easy," Daddy said. "Easy as *P-I-E*." He would hire a few workers to lift it off its concrete blocks, place it on a truck, and drive it to our lot. So on yet another bright sunshiny day, Daddy parked the Chevrolet near the Main Street School, and again we stood on the sidewalk in front of the duplex. Soon the workers arrived with their flatbed truck. At first, Debbie and I watched them, but they took so long that we ran across the street to play around the Confederate monument. Debbie was in second grade at St. Clara's Academy, where Sister Albert Louise said she was the smartest student, so she could read the monument's strange inscription. *As at Thermopylae, the greater glory was to the vanquished.*

At last, we noticed the duplex loaded on the truck, in the middle of Washington Street. We ran closer and watched the unwieldy truck trying to make the tight turn onto Canal, but there was a commotion—the duplex was stuck, its roof tangled in the overhead wires. People were yelling. Then a police car came, and the gleaming fire truck. Nobody seemed to know what to do, including Daddy. The electricity had to be cut off to the whole downtown so the workers could climb up on the roof and saw off a corner. *Easy as P-I-E,* I thought. Finally, they were able to snake the duplex the thirteen blocks down Calhoun Avenue and deposit it on our lot.

That evening, back at Grandma's, we ate supper at the kitchen table, as always. But no one talked. When we finished, Mama got up and turned on the radio. She went to stand at the sink, her back to us, and started washing the dishes. One by one, she put them into the drainer to her left. Above the drainer, attached to the cabinet, was a little lamp that shed a warm yellow light. Then we heard the story of our house-moving broadcast on Nanette Embry's radio program, *The Talk of the Town.* Mama sat at the table again and put her head in her hands. Daddy had bought us this awful house, a duplex—and now a public embarrassment.

A week later, I was waiting on Grandma's front porch next to the glider. I could see my breath. Light so bright I had to squint. Again I had on my checkered car coat with the oblong wooden buttons. Debbie and Mama waited beside me, Mama holding Lisa Maria in her arms. Sol Boy was in the front yard, playing on the swing set. The pickup truck should arrive any minute.

We were moving.

I didn't know what it meant to move, but I was excited, because everyone was excited. Grendaddy and Grandma came out on the porch to be with us, standing back next to the clapboards. Then I saw the pickup making its way around Goose Egg Park, down Grand Avenue. It belonged to Aunt Pauline's husband, J.T., who'd lent it to Daddy for the day. When Daddy got to Grandma's, he made a U-turn and backed up the curving walkway. He began loading our few belongings: cardboard boxes filled with clothes, a cane chair that Grandma and Grendaddy were giving us. The last thing Daddy did was to take down the swing set.

Mama, Lisa Maria, and Sol Boy got into the cab, but Debbie and I begged to ride in the back. Daddy told us to crouch down, and he banged the tailgate shut. As we jolted down the walkway and off the curb, I turned to wave at Grandma. It was my first ride in a pickup, and I wanted her to notice me. She waved back, but not with her usual pumping up and down of hands and arms.

Seconds later, Daddy parked the pickup in the street in front of the duplex. He was supposed to be fixing it up before we moved in, but he hadn't painted the outside. He also hadn't repaired the roof or laid a foundation. We followed Daddy over some rough stones set into the grass. He hadn't removed the extra front door, either, and we stood behind him on the left-hand stoop. This was the entrance we were to use, he informed us. As he unlocked the door, he exclaimed, "Home again, home again, jiggedy-jig!"

We walked into the boxy living room. Daddy had bought a green leatherette wing chair and placed it against one wall. Next to it, a red plastic couch, the seat cracked, the cotton stuffing coming out. He'd bought a tall metal stand and a TV and set them in the corner. But he hadn't hung new wallpaper or replaced the termite-eaten floor.

Daddy motioned us into the hallway to illustrate how he'd removed the dividing wall. But he'd only knocked out its center, and the torn-up ends still stuck out of the walls. Next he wanted to show us our bedrooms. There could have been four in the duplex, but Daddy had turned one into storage space. He called this the Junk Room, and he'd already hung half a dozen long, pink garment bags in it, because there were only two closets. He'd decided that Mama and Lisa Maria would share the bedroom on the right side of the duplex, and he and Sol Boy would share the one on the left. He'd bought my brother a narrow wooden bed and placed it next to his double one, but to get to the dining table you had to pass through their room, snaking your way between the beds. As for Debbie and me, we would sleep in what used to be the other living room. But since Daddy hadn't removed the old entryway, our bedroom still had a front door in it. He locked this door and pocketed the key.

Finally, Daddy explained how we were to use the duplex's two bathrooms, which were located across the hall from each other. He said the Pink Bathroom was for the girls, the White Bathroom for the boys. The girls must never use the boys' bathroom. It went without saying that the boys would never want to use the girls'.

I spent my first night in our new bedroom arguing with Debbie. We stood next to the lamp, she turning it off and I turning it on, over and over. Her big brown eyes shone with all her fury, because she was stuck with me again in the duplex. When Mama tired of hearing us fight, she strode in and switched the lamp off once and for all. I climbed into bed and said my good nights. "Good night, Mama, good night, Daddy, good night, Debbie, good night, Sol Boy." It was strange not to be saying good night to Grandma and Grendaddy.

Daddy had put my bed under the window next to the former front door, and I lay awake watching the strange shape made by the overhang. I straightened the brown scapular I wore beneath my footed pajamas, and I prayed to the Virgin Mary that if I should die tonight, she might save me from eternal fire. But still I couldn't sleep. I watched the light go from dark blue to pearl gray. I remembered the prayers Father Hunter had taught me, and I added another: I prayed that Grandma would come for me, to any one of the duplex's many doors.

I would start a campaign to get back to Grandma's house. This would become my obsession, what I would live my days for. I hadn't known what it meant to move, but now I understood. It meant to long for something I used to have.

Four

In the duplex, there were no sunbeams to catch, no transom over the front door, the windows too stingy to let in much light. It was February when we moved, and the wind whipped under the brittle, termite-eaten floorboards. Daddy hadn't replaced the outdated gas space heaters, with their open flames that looked like the Cheshire cat's grin; he would let us light only the ones in the living room and bathrooms, and then only during the day, because he was afraid we might asphyxiate. At night he would leave the water faucets dripping to keep the pipes from freezing, but one by one they froze anyway. We had to wait until the weather warmed up before we could bathe, but we couldn't wait on the weather to eat. To get the kitchen drainpipe flowing again, one morning Daddy finally marched outside with a hammer and knocked a hole in it.

There were only three trees on our lot—a chinaberry and two hard-to-climb hackberries—so when spring came, Daddy planted two sycamore saplings and named them for Sol Boy and Lisa Maria. He planted an exotic gingko for Debbie and for me, a stumpy bush. Daddy not only collected coins from Grendaddy's cash register but also began to hoard almost anything he came across. "These'll come in handy someday when I need to fix somethin'," he would say, fingering rusty screws or sprung rubber bands. To house his childhood toys, like his

"Poosh-M-Up Big 5" pinball game and all his other "junk," as Mama called it, behind the duplex Daddy built himself a one-room shed, which he painted red and started calling the Little House. Now we owned both a duplex and a shack.

When summer came, Daddy knocked another hole in the duplex, a large one in the ceiling where he installed a noisy attic fan. Then he did some decorating. Over the refrigerator he positioned his green-and-orange Dr. Pepper clock (*Drink Dr. Pepper, Good for Life*), which was always slow. On top of the television he placed the mahogany Sessions clock, which had been a wedding gift from Grandma. But Daddy couldn't be bothered winding it, so it stood firm at 11:55. For the dining room, he bought a graphite-colored Formica table and plastic chairs in a tiger-stripe design and for the living room, a plain pine coffee table. This fast became a prop for more of Daddy's junk—dog-eared *Popular Mechanics*, broken transistor radios, bags of Christmas bows, and one of his proudest possessions, the cigarette box whittled by Grendaddy's sister's husband, Mr. Weebe. There was even a miniature coffee grinder. On the walls, on top of the exposed cheesecloth and lath, Daddy tacked up his Sacred Heart of Jesus prints. Into their frames he stuck dried fronds, the relics of Palm Sundays past. Finally, over the dining room table he hung a plastic sign, *God Bless Our Home*.

Mama retaliated by covering the cracked seat of the red plastic couch with a pink cotton bedspread. She maintained that Sol Boy and I wriggled it off to annoy her, but we couldn't help ourselves, the way Sol Boy also couldn't stop himself from picking off what was left of the living room wallpaper. But Mama had been a sharecropper, and she knew the meaning of perseverance. As soon as we'd messed up the bedspread, she would appear, bending over the couch, smoothing out the furrows and pushing the fabric deep between the cushions.

Now that she finally had a house of her own, Mama was going to take care of it, even if it was awful. Cleaning became her obsession, as if soap and water might fix what was wrong with the duplex. But unlike Grandma, Mama didn't touch every plank of the floor when she swept; she just ran the broom over the visible parts, then dragged the mop in hasty circles. Next she would move into the bathrooms, where she swabbed out the toilets with Pine-Sol and a long-handled brush that she left lying beside them, ready for the next day's scrubbing.

Mama didn't have help, the way Grandma had Clemmy, so while she was cleaning she was also cooking our dinner and washing our clothes in the Maytag, hanging them on the clothesline and then folding them when her favorite soap opera, *The Edge of Night*, came on at three-thirty. Unless you counted the time she spent hunched over Great-Grandma Mugga's foot-powered Singer, sewing our clothes until her calves ached, this was the longest Mama sat during the day. After a makeshift supper, she would gulp a BC headache powder and take to her bed, where she lay very still with the lights out.

Now and again Mama might ask, "Sol June, when you goin' to fix up the house?" But he'd just glare at her with hooded eyes. Or if he did answer, he would say, "Florence, I don't have the money." But that was just an excuse, and we all knew it. Daddy was handy; after all, he'd built the Little House, and with his tools and his spare parts, there was plenty he could have done to fix up the duplex if he'd wanted. The truth was, Daddy liked the duplex just the way it was.

Besides, fixing up the house wouldn't really have solved anything. Fixed up, it would still have been filled with shabby furniture and decorated with Daddy's Sacred Heart of Jesus prints. Fixed up, it would still have been filled with Daddy. He paced the duplex's tiny rooms in his heavy shoes. He took possession of the one good place to sit, the green leatherette wing chair, and picked which TV programs we watched, cranking the volume up high. He sang along with *Sing Along with Mitch*—not the lyrics, just his favorite nonsense syllables, "Didididididididididi." He cackled over *The Jackie Gleason Show* and carried on during *The Red Skelton Hour*, especially over the character Clem Kadiddlehopper. Clem unleashed the clown in Daddy. He crossed his eyes and jutted out his lips while clipping his long yellow toenails, letting the trimmings fly around the room and calling out, "Duck! Here comes anothern!" We couldn't even escape from him when we were in our beds. It was debatable which was louder, the whistle of the freight train at the crossing two blocks away or Daddy's snoring.

Mama had thought she was getting a house of her own, but really it was Daddy who got himself a house. He made more rules for us to live by, and one of these was *No visitors*. He said visitors threw him out of whack. If a neighbor dropped by with extra summer squash, the squash was accepted, but the neighbor was thanked on the front stoop. Mama's relatives were especially unwelcome, but Daddy's brother and sister didn't visit, either, though they lived in the same block. Since I was ashamed of the duplex, this rule, at least, was fine by me.

Grandma and Grendaddy were the exception. Once a week, after dinner on Sunday, they walked the length of Thirteenth Street carrying cane chairs on top of their heads so they would have a place to sit. But it wasn't the same as when we'd all lived together. We sat like strangers, with Grandma and Daddy the only talkers. "The clouds look like they've been scratched up by hens," she might say. "Dadgum weather," he would answer.

The weather was an affront, a source of much discussion, because their livelihood in the grocery store depended on the cotton crop. They would inevitably move on to state politics, an even greater affront. Grandma complained bitterly about the "Nigras agitatin'." Daddy complained about the colored people, too, but he called them niggers. All the while, I would see Grandma taking in our furnishings out of the corner of her blue eyes. I knew that she, with her imitation oil paintings, didn't approve of Daddy's Sacred Heart of Jesus pictures; I'd heard her say many times that Papism was un-American. She even seemed miffed that Daddy didn't keep the Sessions clock wound properly.

My grandparents' visits soon tapered off. I begged Mama to let me visit them and most of all to let me spend the night there. Occasionally she'd let me, and there was nothing more exciting than watching her pack me an overnight case with a toothbrush and a pair of baby doll pajamas. But usually I visited Grandma only in the mornings. Mama was taking care of us now, and there was no reason for me to go to the store in the afternoons. When we'd lived at Grandma's, I hadn't had much awareness of time. But inside the duplex, time stretched out. I blamed Daddy. It was Daddy who'd given me this sense of time as misery.

It was a morning during the summer after we'd moved, warm but with a coolness still around the edges. I was on my way to visit Grandma, skipping the length of Thirteenth Street from Calhoun to Grand, past Aunt Pauline's ranch with its new brick den, past the Carters' two-car garage. I reached Grandma's gate, lifted the string latch, and let myself into her backyard. On my left was the fanciful larkspur patch; on my right, the watermelon-pink crape myrtles with their flower-heavy heads.

I climbed the three steps to the screened porch and called out, "Grand-ma!" and she answered, "Woo-oo!" Then she appeared from the kitchen to unfasten the hook.

We strolled out into her yard. Next to the wooden garage was the tilting garden shed, with a plank door and no windows. Once Debbie had nailed a cardboard Girl Scout insignia on the door to designate it as a clubhouse, but club activities had been limited to creeping along the narrow passage between the shed and garage, enjoying the dank smells and the spongy moss underfoot. The garden shed was Grandma's province. We were told to stay out of it, because it was full of forbidden metal objects.

That morning, Grandma and I lingered near the wire fence where her property bordered Aunt Pauline's, in front of the cedar of Lebanon. The trunk grew straight, of a piece and thick, and the leaves hung like green icicles. We inched underneath to a damp spot, out of the way of the building heat, and began to examine the small, hard, blue berries.

Then I noticed Debbie running toward us through Aunt Pauline's yard, struggling with Lisa Maria on her hip. She stopped at the fence and screamed, "Grandma, Mama said come to the house!"

Grandma grabbed my arm, and we rushed out the gate and into the street. She took the baby from Debbie, and we ran toward the duplex. We went first to the back door, but no one was in the kitchen. Then we raced through all the duplex's rooms, one after another. When we got to the living room, we stopped in the doorway.

Mama had thrown open the door and dragged the cane chair in front of it. Her back was to us. She was bent over Sol Boy, and I could see his little shoes jutting out from her lap. He was screaming and writhing, Mama weeping and dabbing at something. From across the room I could see blood on the floor. Even Grandma didn't move. As soon as Mama noticed us she shouted, "Bring me more toilet paper!"

Grandma ripped the roll off the holder in the White Bathroom and rushed it to her. There was bloody toilet paper all over them. Grandma ran and got another roll. But there was no time to ask Mama what had happened, because the Chevrolet was coming toward us down Calhoun Avenue. Mama hurried to climb inside with Sol Boy, and Daddy sped off to King's Daughters Hospital.

They were gone a long time. Grandma got the bottle of Pine-Sol and a brush and tried to scour the blood off the chair and floor. She prepared dinner for us. I kept picturing Sol Boy's right index finger, dangling by a thread of flesh. Debbie said she had been cutting the grass using Daddy's rusty push mower when Sol put his fat baby fingers around the blades. She'd told him to remove them, but he wouldn't. It took only one turn, not even.

When they finally arrived home, Sol had a bulbous white bandage around his severed finger. It was awfully quiet in the duplex. We sat at the dining table to eat, while Sol Boy went outside with his new plastic rocket launcher. He played in the side yard beneath the dining room window, where Daddy could watch him. That afternoon, Daddy never did go back to the Place. For a long time he stayed at the table, then went out and carted the push mower to the dump.

After supper, while Mama was standing at the sink washing the dishes, we heard Nanette Embry broadcasting the news about Sol's accident. Mama strode to the radio on top of the refrigerator, reached up with her soapy hand, and cut it off.

No one ever said the accident was Debbie's fault. No one ever said it was Mama's, either. She'd been inside cleaning, same as every other day. It was another thing I blamed Daddy for, buying us the duplex in the first place, and isolating us in it, without Grandma and Grendaddy to help take care of us. I blamed Daddy, because all his rules, about which doors and bathrooms we were supposed to use, which heaters we were to light and when, weren't enough to keep us safe. Even pulling my brother's little bed right next to his, Daddy couldn't protect Sol Boy.

Five

Daddy was standing in front of the television, legs wide apart. He was wearing white canvas slip-ons from the Army-Navy, khakis held up by a leather belt, and a white short-sleeved shirt. It was eight o'clock in the morning. He pointed his index finger at the three of us. We were dressed for play, because there was still some summer left before Debbie went back to St. Clara's and I entered kindergarten. "Be careful!" he ordered. Then he bounded down the front steps, slid into the Chevrolet, and drove to his glass-enclosed office next to the Place's busy repair shop, which smelled of grease and sounded of clanging car parts.

Lately we heard these words often from Daddy. Sol Boy's wound had healed, and he seemed unfazed by what had happened to him, though now when he played with his G.I. Joes I noticed he liked to bury them in the mud or hang them by their necks from the clothesline. Still, Daddy made more rules for us. No more roaming the neighborhood for Debbie, no more spending all day in the fort in the vacant lot with the Parker boys. He didn't even like me walking by myself the hundred steps down Thirteenth Street to Grandma's house. He told us to stay in our yard, where there would be no more climbing the chinaberry tree. No more riding horses made from its branches, either, because it wasn't ladylike. I wanted to remind

Daddy that Sol's accident had happened in our yard, between our house and Aunt Pauline's, but I couldn't, because the accident became another thing we didn't talk about, like the death of the twins.

Even inside the house, we had to be more careful. No more hiding in the pink garment bags in the Junk Room, because we might suffocate. Without much else to do, we moped, picked at one another, and picked at the wallpaper. Again I felt time like misery. But despite these new rules, one evening my parents left the four of us alone in the living room, where Debbie and I were roughhousing on the couch, worrying the pink bedspread into a ball. Daddy had placed an old-fashioned fan with rotating metal blades under the TV stand, and Lisa Maria began crawling toward it. Just as she was about to stick her finger in the blades, Sol Boy managed to pull her back by her diaper.

Every day, Daddy would come home from the Place for dinner, timing his arrival with the noon whistle. He would go straight to the dining table, and Mama would summon us, shouting, "Dunnertime! Y'all come on!" My seat was in the middle, beside her. She held Lisa Maria in her lap, next to the swinging door to the kitchen. Debbie sat across from Mama and me. Daddy was at the head of the table, with Sol Boy awarded the other end.

Before we could eat, we had to recite the Catholic grace. "Bless us, O Lord, and these Thy gifts which we are about to receive . . ." Daddy drowned us out, and we followed along, heads bowed, hands folded. Mama set the platters and bowls closest to Daddy, so he could serve himself first. Though Grandma had taught her how to prepare the Old Country dishes, she also made them only on special occasions. Most days Mama cooked the food she'd been brought up on, an unappealing assortment of gizzards and livers, backs, necks, and bitter greens.

Another one of Daddy's new rules was *You must eat a good dinner*. No more snacking on raw hot dogs, no more mayonnaise sandwiches like we used to eat at Grandma's. But I didn't even like how Mama's food smelled and how after every meal she would leave it on top of the stove, so the odors permeated the duplex. She had gotten this habit from Grandma Hood, as if the two of them still didn't know what it meant to have a refrigerator.

No one talked during these obligatory dinners, but Daddy filled the silence with his noises. He sang his favorite nonsense syllables, slurped his iced tea, let his cutlery clap onto the Formica tabletop, and smacked his lips. He gulped down black-eyed peas, crooning, "Mmm, potlikker."

One day at the table, Mama ordered me to stop stomping my feet.

"It isn't me," I answered back. "It's Sol Boy."

Mama hissed, "It can't be Sol Boy, 'cause his feet don't touch the ground."

I wanted to shout, *It is too Sol Boy! He's kicking the table leg!* But I was afraid of attracting Daddy's attention. A moment passed, and I thought I'd gotten away with it, when Daddy hollered, "Te-re-sa," drawing my name out to its full three syllables, "eat your food!"

He'd stopped eating. His eyes bulged. Sol Boy and Debbie ran from the table, and Mama took Lisa Maria into the kitchen. Daddy stomped in after her. From my place I saw him rummaging in the little metal cabinets above the sink and heard him rattling forks and knives in the plastic keeper. When he returned, he was holding a jar of peanut butter, a packet of saltines, and a table knife.

He jammed the knife in the jar, scraping at the glass sides. "It's a fact, Te-re-sa," he said, "you have to eat."

He thrust a cracker at me. He had smeared peanut butter on one side and put another on top. I took it from him, half-heartedly put it in my mouth. A double-sided peanut butter cracker is dry and oily at the same time. I was chewing, but I couldn't get it down. The lump grew in my mouth, and the longer I chewed, the angrier Daddy seemed to become. I was willful. I was disobedient. Worst of all, I was skinny. This was an insult to Daddy, a slur against him as provider. "You have to eat," he said again. "It just don't add up." He, who was always taking two and three helpings of everything Mama put in front of him, just didn't understand how a person couldn't eat. I watched him making more peanut butter crackers, lining them up on the edge of the table, where they sat like false promises.

I was furious at Daddy for forcing me to eat, at Mama for going along with him. Later, I sneaked off to her bedroom and opened her mauve velvet jewelry box, which contained her tiny imitation gold watch, her 1944 class ring from Benton High, and her aquamarine birthstone, a present from Daddy from when they were courting. Usually, turning the square stone in the light, I imagined the clear, blue water of the public swimming pool where we occasionally spent summer afternoons. But now I threw the ring as hard as I could on the wooden floor. When I picked it up, I saw that the setting was loose. I returned the ring to the box, never telling anybody what I'd done.

I felt as if we were becoming Daddy's prisoners in the duplex. We hardly went anyplace, but after Sunday Mass he might drive us to the farm implement store on Highway 49, where we pressed our noses to the window and marveled at the little red tractor, its shiny unreachable perfection. Every now and then, when the weather was "just right," we'd go to Brame Park for a watermelon cutting. The only time we ever left Yazoo City was

to visit the Jackson Zoo. There, Daddy busied himself taking pictures of the monkeys. He posed us in front of the monkey house, bashful children, summer browned, gazing into the eye of his camera. The monkeys were black-and-white blurs swinging from the ropes of their little monkey castle. For every photo of us that he put in the brown camera bag, there were five of the monkeys. Whenever we returned from one of these excursions, we lined up on the front stoop behind Daddy. He was still the only one with a key, and as he inserted it into the lock, he would call out his favorite catchphrase, "Home again, home again, jiggedy-jig!"

Since moving into the duplex, I'd learned there were two sides to Daddy's personality. Sometimes he was Cartoon Daddy, who did tricks for us with his hands, took us to admire the little red tractor, and snapped pictures of the monkeys in the zoo. Cartoon Daddy was silly, la-la-ing and deedle-dum-ing like Foghorn Leghorn, the good-ole-boy rooster who stuttered, "Ah say, ah say, ah say." Cartoon Daddy looked like Fred Flintstone, the big-nosed, big-footed caveman who yelled, "Yabba-dabba-doo!" But sometimes Cartoon Daddy turned fierce, like one of the afternoon thunderstorms that crisscrossed the Delta. And he shifted back and forth between Cartoon Daddy and Angry Daddy without warning.

I began spending more time in my bedroom. I wallowed in bed and daydreamed, and I played with my Betsy McCall doll, a birthday present from Grandma. I realized I was lucky to share a room with Debbie, not to have to sleep with my parents like Sol Boy and Lisa Maria. Debbie and I were becoming outsiders together. She'd always been an escape artist, and now she found a new place to hide, a forbidden place where nobody could touch us—under the duplex.

Since the duplex sat on concrete blocks, there were many entrances to choose from. Debbie decided that we would enter from the east, where there were fewer pipes to bang our heads on. We crawled on our bellies, using our elbows and knees to drag ourselves forward. I had a close-up view of the dirt, fine and gray and cool, not at all like the clotted gumbo in the backyard. The underside of the duplex, with its brown recluse and black widow spiders, was a thrilling place. There, everything was different. We could hear what went on above the floorboards, but the sounds were distant, Daddy's booming voice and his footsteps muted, the TV at normal volume. It was like doing a handstand, looking at the world upside down. Under the duplex, we ate raw hot dogs straight from the package.

From here on, all I thought about was escape. I even started sleepwalking. At first, Daddy would wake up and follow me. Sometimes when he roused me, I'd be sitting on the low bench in the hall, sometimes on the toilet seat in the Pink Bathroom (never the White Bathroom). Sometimes I'd be standing before the front door, fumbling with the lock. I knew where I was trying to go, and so did Daddy. Before long, he installed a second, harder-to-reach lock. Nightly, I was bolted into the duplex.

Six

The fall after we moved into the duplex, I was enrolled in Gussie White's kindergarten, which was held in an airy corner room on the first floor of St. Clara's convent. We called Gussie simply by her first name, without the prerequisite "Miz," perhaps because she picked some of us up each morning in her big black Buick. The class quickly split into cliques. There were the popular girls—Nell, Donna, Ginger, Pam, and Susan—with their peaches-and-cream complexions and Old South manners, and then there were the rest of us. The popular girls had lawyers and cotton farmers for daddies, and they lived on Grand Avenue and in the new subdivision, Bella Vista. When the popular girls cried, they covered their faces and wept into their palms like little ladies. They didn't get their vaccinations at the Public Health Department. I fell in with the other ethnic girls, Mary and Georgette. Mary was Italian, Georgette Arab. Their daddies were also in retail.

Gussie's curriculum consisted of three activities, coloring, recess, and napping, and by far the most stressful of these was coloring. Daddy's tyranny extended all the way to the long tables where we sat in the little chairs. It was he who decided on my coloring book, and he'd bought me one that featured his favorite, Porky Pig. But Porky was naked from the waist down, and though I drew on a variety of Crayolas for his jacket, being a realist I would use only my flesh crayon on his bottom. That fall, with Daddy supplying me one Porky Pig after another, I began wearing down this crayon at an alarming rate. Even worse, while the popular girls were coloring princesses and fairies, they could see that I was saddled with a half-naked pig.

After class, I often caught a ride home with Mary and her five siblings, and one day I whispered to her in the backseat that I'd resolved to toss my newest Porky Pig coloring book under the duplex. I would tell Daddy that I'd finished another one and this time beg him for something new. To my surprise, the ruse worked, and Daddy bought me a replacement, Bugs Bunny. But I began to suffer from a different and more terrible anxiety, which I was reminded of every time Mary would ask me if Daddy had found the old one yet.

Late one gentle afternoon in the spring, I was lolling on my bed with the windows thrown open. Daddy was cutting the grass with his new gas-powered mower, which he kept chained to the water meter next to the duplex's back doors. The lazy drone of the lawnmower was getting closer to my bedroom when suddenly the motor went dead. Then I heard Daddy shout for Mama, and I peered out the window to see her running toward him with the baby and Sol Boy.

Daddy stuck his big oval face next to the rusted screen. "Te-re-sa, get out here!"

I took the longest route possible, sauntering the length of the duplex, down the back steps, and around to where he was standing in a big patch of clover. Daddy was waving my Porky Pig coloring book.

As soon as he saw me, he yelled, "You lied to me, Te-re-sa! You told me you needed a new colorin' book when you didn't." He pointed to a low concrete pillar supporting the duplex. "I found this right here. You ain't colored half the pages."

But I had thrown the coloring book far under the duplex, through the opening that Debbie and I used. I could only figure that a gust of wind must have picked up the flimsy paperback and wedged it next to the pillar. I looked at Daddy. He was angry all right, but there was something else. He thumbed to a half-colored Porky. "How could you just throw him under the house?" he asked in a plaintive voice.

But right then, I couldn't explain to Daddy all about kindergarten. How I didn't fit in, and how having to color the pig only made it worse. I stared at the yellowed pages, splayed open and splattered by dirt and rain, and Porky, poor Porky, exposed.

"Carry him back to class and finish colorin' him," Daddy said. Then he shoved the book at me and started to jerk on the lawnmower's cord.

By now I knew Daddy's pattern. Something would set him off, he'd yell and threaten to "beat the stew out of us," then stomp out. When he'd return hours later, he'd give us the Silent Treatment, slamming dishes on the table, cussing under his breath, and not speaking to us for days. I'd expected that behavior from him if he ever found the coloring book, but I hadn't imagined he would be more concerned about the pig than about me.

But for the first time I stood up for myself. "I've already worn out my flesh crayon," I said.

"So?" he asked. "Use another color on him. You still got your green, don't you?"

He'd missed the point entirely. Daddy was always bringing up facts. "It's a fact, Te-re-sa, you have to eat!" he often yelled at the dinner table. Now I searched for the one fact that I thought he might understand. "You know Porky Pig doesn't wear pants. How can I color his booty green?"

From behind Mama's skirt, I heard Sol Boy snicker. But Daddy stopped fiddling with the lawnmower and stared at me.

He blinked several times. "I see what you mean," he finally admitted. I didn't know why he hadn't already noticed. If there was one thing Daddy hated more than lying, more than wastefulness, it was nakedness, even in a pig. He strode straight to the garbage can in the backyard and dropped Porky inside.

Afterward, I decided to ask Grandma to explain Daddy. Since starting kindergarten, I saw her less often than before, and she spent more time with my cousin, Aunt Pauline's daughter. I was afraid that she was becoming Grandma's favorite. But still I went to visit Grandma Sunday mornings after Mass.

One Sunday we were alone in her kitchen, at the metal table. She had on her long, yellow rubber gloves, up to her elbows in a stainless steel bowl of chopped cubbie meat.

"Grandma," I began, "why is Daddy the way he is?"

She stopped kneading the meat and gazed at me over the top of her glasses. "Your daddy can't hear out of his right ear," she said, as if that explained everything.

It did explain the TV's volume and why he talked so loud, but I didn't see the connection between Daddy's hearing and his behavior. I must have scrunched up my face at her, because she bowed her head, like one of the parishioners in the back pews of St. Mary's before they confessed to Father Hunter.

"And your daddy saw a special doctor once in Jackson, a psychiatrist."

I realized that Grandma had revealed an appalling secret, though I didn't know what it meant. But I concluded that there must be something awfully wrong with Daddy. Why else would he have gone all the way to Jackson just to see a doctor?

In the fall of 1960, I moved across the alley from Gussie's kindergarten to St. Clara's elementary school. At St. Clara's, I still didn't fit in with the popular girls, but I found another group to aspire to, the Sisters of Charity. After they taught me to read, they suggested books for me, eventually including some by Dr. Tom Dooley, a handsome missionary whose death at the age of thirty-four only added to his appeal. I began to read all the time, partly because it was something I could do it while lying on my bed, away from Daddy.

That Christmas, the sisters chose me to play the Virgin Mary in the school's pageant, dressing me in a white robe and luscious blue satin veil, and further isolating me from my classmates. One Saturday, they invited Debbie and me to have brunch with them in the convent, where they served us scrambled eggs off china plates and discussed our vocations. Afterward, we got to tour their tiny chapel and were even allowed to tiptoe the polished wooden stairs to the edge of their private quarters. I became fascinated with the nuns, down to their undergarments. While Grandma perused the display cases at the Marylena Shoppe and added to her costume jewelry collection, I would cajole the Thomas sisters into showing me duplicates of the nuns' bras and girdles. Then on a sunlit morning, while kneeling and waiting for eight o'clock Mass, as dazzling colors streamed through the round stained-glass window over St. Mary's altar, I vowed to become one of them.

But then things started happening, things that I didn't understand. One evening we were watching television in the living room, crowded on the red plastic couch as usual, when there was a knock on the front door. I peeked out the side window to see two strange men on the duplex's stoop, dressed in suits and carrying briefcases. We didn't know anybody with a briefcase. Daddy opened the door but only partway, and I heard the men introduce themselves and ask Daddy what he thought about the public school situation in Yazoo City. Daddy replied that he didn't care to discuss the public school situation with them or with anybody. That his children went to St. Clara's, and that as far as he knew, everybody was satisfied with the schools as they were. Then Daddy slammed the door and telephoned the chief of police. He came out to the house and also stood on the stoop, asking Daddy questions.

"What did the men look like? What did they want?" Chief Russell demanded. "What make car did they drive? What state was their tag from?"

But Daddy said he hadn't noticed. I wondered if he was in trouble for talking to these strangers, but Chief Russell thanked him and left.

Another day, another incident. Mama picked us up in the Chevrolet after school and drove us to Grandma Hood's for our weekly visit. Daddy never accompanied us, because another one of his rules was *No visiting*. I hated visiting Grandma Hood, too, and once told Mama that as we were getting ready to go and she was brushing my hair. "She doesn't have any teeth," I added.

Mama popped my head with the plastic hairbrush. "Well, she has some, but she don't want to wear them."

Grandma Hood was squishy fat, not hard fat. She wore stained housedresses like tents and occupied a green Naugahyde chair in her underfurnished living room. Whenever I tried to run by her, she would grab me, pinch me, and clamp her lips on my arm to blow fart sounds. She called me her "nigger gran'child." Once, on the way home from one of these visits, my feelings hurt, I asked Mama why.

"She's just teasin' you," Mama explained, "because you have an olive complexion."

It was true that I turned very dark during the summer. But at that moment, I realized that my skin wasn't like my Scotch-Irish Hood relatives'; mine had a greenish-yellow cast, inherited from the Nicholases. Later, in the duplex, in the privacy of our kitchen, I confirmed this ghastly fact by holding a bottle of olives next to my forearm.

On that afternoon at Grandma Hood's, I was surprised to see not only Grandma Hood parked in front of the television but also Uncle Brother and Aunt 'Cile. Though the black-and-white picture was fuzzy, and though I lurked a safe distance behind, I could make out a colored man and soldiers and Governor Ross Barnett.

Mama was quiet, but the others were agitated. "Nigger," Grandma Hood repeated. She was talking about James Meredith, who was attempting to enter the University of Mississippi. "He has some gall! Nobody in our family has ever been to no college. How is it that a nigger could?"

But secretly, I took the colored man's side. I knew how I felt when Grandma Hood called me her "nigger gran'child." And I thought, *Why shouldn't he go to Ole Miss?* But I didn't say anything.

Yet another morning, Daddy drove us to St. Clara's, where we encountered a small crowd. He left the Chevrolet in front of the vacant house where we held our Brownie meetings and played Red Rover on the sloping lawn, and we rushed toward the others, standing in a semicircle near the gymnasium. They were staring at three charred wooden crosses stuck into the ground. I wondered, *Why would anybody want to burn crosses in front of our gym?* I heard the grownups whispering that it couldn't have been the Klan, because they had been run out of town years ago. But who was the Klan, and why had they been run out? Nobody, not even the Sisters of Charity, would explain to me.

The last thing that I didn't understand had to do with Daddy. We got new next-door neighbors, Helton and Jimmy, boys about my age. They were Protestants, which made them exotic, and I started spending time with them. Helton and I would climb the mimosa tree in his front yard, and he'd beg me to let him look down my underpants. I'd refuse, and still he'd beg. One afternoon, while up in the tree, I did allow him to put a tiny toy car in my pants.

I made him swear not to tell, but Helton couldn't keep a secret. A few days later, while I was soaking in the tub in the Pink Bathroom, staring out the window toward the pecan trees in Grandma's front yard, Mama burst in and told me what she'd heard from Helton's mother. She was going to have to tell Daddy, she said. I pleaded with her not to, and finally she agreed.

Even though Helton had betrayed me, we remained friends, and one day after school I did the unthinkable and invited him and Jimmy over to watch TV. Mama was ironing in the Junk Room, at the back of the house. I was nervous about having guests, and when Helton said he was hungry, I decided to fix him a tuna sandwich. I sneaked the can from the kitchen, along with the can opener, and went into the White Bathroom. As I was working over the sink, struggling to open the can, I cut my thumb on the lid.

The pain was startling, sharp and deep, the cut tracing along the first joint and curving inward, like the letter C. I dabbed at it with toilet tissue, but it wouldn't stop bleeding. There was blood in the sink and on the floor. But I kept on dabbing, because I didn't want Mama to find out. Finally, the bleeding slowed a little, and I wrapped my thumb in a wad of tissue. I went back to the living room and pretended that nothing had happened. But Helton ran to tell Mama.

When she saw me, she grabbed my hand and ripped off the makeshift bandage. "What have you done to yourself?"

She yelled for Helton and Jimmy to bring more tissue. But just as Mama got the bleeding stanched, Daddy came in from the Place. He ignored Helton and Jimmy, and after Mama told him what had happened, he dragged me by my hair into the White Bathroom. He shut the door against Mama. She pounded on it and shouted at him to let her in, but he wedged his leg against it.

He was moving fast. He stripped off my pants and pushed me over the edge of the bathtub. I struggled, but he pinned me with a hand on my shoulder. I could see his hand, and the smooth white porcelain of the tub. With his other hand he unbuckled his leather belt, and I heard the whisking sound of it being pulled through his pant loops. Then he began to whip me.

Mama finally managed to push the door open and pull him off me. But then he got his hands into my hair and yanked me up as hard as he could. Mama kept shouting at him to let me go, and at last he dropped me on the floor and left.

It was the first time that Daddy had beaten me, and I didn't understand what I'd done to deserve it. Was it because I'd disobeyed his rules and invited visitors inside? Or because I'd dared to enter the White Bathroom? What if I'd gone into the Pink Bathroom to open the can of tuna? Or had Daddy beaten me because I'd cut myself? But when Sol Boy had cut his finger, he hadn't gotten whipped—he'd gotten a new rocket launcher.

At supper that night, Daddy smacked his lips and sang his nonsense syllables, the same as always. But for me, that beating was the end of Cartoon Daddy. Afterward I hated his touch, even the sight of his hands. I knew his hands, the only part of his body I really knew. Square fingers, well proportioned. Should he accidentally brush his hand against my hair or lay his palm on my shoulder, I felt repulsed. I understood the power of his hands over me. At the dinner table, in the living room, he would wag his fingers at me, slice the air with rigid palms like great, flat cleavers, and slam the table with closed fists. He was always right, hands down; there was the never the leeway, with him, of *on the other hand*. Finally, I understood that I was in his hands.

Seven

One Sunday after ten-thirty Mass, Grendaddy and I were by ourselves in the grocery, the light through the plate glass window soft, milky. He was behind the cash register, while I was on the other side of the counter facing him. He opened the register and began counting the bills. I watched him, biding my time. These days, Grendaddy seemed shorter and rounder, his hair more grizzled, his complexion more sallow. He seemed more alone. At Mass today, as usual he'd tiptoed up the center aisle and sat with us in our pew, in his regular seat beside Debbie. As usual, he hadn't said the prayers or sung the hymns or taken Communion. Not participating, I told myself, was just another way that Grendaddy was different.

He finished counting and returned the bills to their metal slots. Then with great slowness, he reached inside the register and removed four quarters, the weekly allowance I was to parcel out to my siblings. My glance wavered to the crowded shelves behind him, to the notions and aftershaves, the loose-leaf tobaccos and rolling papers, the chewing tobaccos and the gums and headache powders. If I were going to ask him, it had to be now.

I'd stopped associating with Helton and Jimmy, but I had

a new friend, Patty. She and her family had recently moved to town and were suspect for no other reason than that they came from Alabama. Patty had brought with her some strange notions, which I'd decided to ask Grendaddy to explain. After that incident with the toy car, I couldn't ask Mama, and Grandma was too preoccupied over the colored people threatening a boycott of the white stores.

I'd been looking forward to this time alone with Grendaddy, but I didn't know how to begin. I couldn't tell him that Patty and I had taken to spying on her older brother, Buddy, trying to catch a glimpse of him as he came out of the shower. Neither could I tell him what Patty had said about how babies were made, a procedure said to involve just the thing we were trying to get a glimpse of. Instead, I'd decided to ask Grendaddy to clarify a phrase I'd heard Patty bandying in the schoolyard.

"Grendaddy, what are the birds and the bees?"

His expression hardly changed, but I knew I'd made a mistake. I hadn't thought it possible to feel disapproval from Grendaddy, who was so gentle and patient, but I felt him pull back from me.

"Sugar, I don't know nothin' about that," he said, slamming the register with a *zing!* Then he shuffled the few feet to the peanut parcher and began scooping the roasted nuts into short brown bags, twisting two little ears on each one. I asked him if I could help, but he shook his head. A little while later, we climbed into the Opel, and he drove us to our block. We didn't talk, but that was nothing unusual. I expected he'd forgotten all about it, and I did, too.

So I was taken aback when, the following Sunday after Mass, Daddy waylaid me in the living room. I was flopped on the couch reading the funny papers, the television blaring Sunday preaching from the First Baptist Church. Daddy came in from the store and stopped in front of me, holding a bag of groceries in one arm.

"I want to talk to you right now!"

I jumped up, and newspaper slid to the floor. We faced each other in front of the television, and Daddy put his mouth next to my ear. "Who did you hear it from?"

I shook my head, trying not to let his lips touch my hair.

"Don't you act dumb. Grendaddy told me what you asked him."

I was surprised that Grendaddy had told Daddy, but I wasn't surprised by Daddy's reaction, not after what had happened last summer. I'd been walking home from the public swimming pool two blocks away, dressed in a one-piece bathing suit and wrapped in a towel. A car of teenage boys stopped and asked how old I was. When I told them twelve, they said I was tall for my age, then laughed and drove away. I was a little scared but also flattered, and as soon as I got home I told Mama, who went to find Daddy. This time, Chief Russell came to the house to ask me questions. We stood in the front yard, with the big police chief in his uniform and me still in my bathing suit.

"How many of them was there? What make car did they drive? Was they niggers or whites? What happened exactly?" But I couldn't tell him, because nothing had happened.

Now in the living room, Daddy was waiting for my answer. But I wasn't going to tell him anything, either. I didn't care what he did to me, because Grendaddy had betrayed me.

"Don't you ever ask anybody that question again. Especially not your grendaddy," Daddy said. Then he stomped into the kitchen, where I heard him slam the grocery bag on the counter.

A half hour later, seated at the dinner table, Daddy still

brooded, smacking his lips distractedly. Afterward, I went outside and whistled for my black cat, Boogie Boo, a present from Great-Aunt Janice. I kissed down his ears, first one, then the other. Through the open door, I glimpsed Daddy staring at me. Then he stepped the two feet into the kitchen, and I heard him shouting to Mama that he had himself a weirdo on his hands, a weirdo that no man would ever want to marry. We were, he said, dog people.

Those days, it seemed our town moved like a body, with Chief Russell its mouth and hands, interrogating citizens, typing reports. The Klan may have been run out of town years ago, but another group had taken its place, the White Citizens' Council. Our own doctor had served as its head, and they met Fridays at Great-Uncle Dan and Aunt Marie's Danrie's Restaurant on Main Street. Daddy kept Citizens' Council literature on the coffee table in the living room. "Read these here facts," he would urge me. I was the one he was most keen to convince. Lisa Maria and Sol Boy were too young; Debbie, a senior in high school, too beyond his influence. But the pamphlets, printed in patriotic red and blue ink on stark-white paper, repulsed me; there was so much anger on those pages that I was reminded of Daddy himself.

There had always been two of everything in town. The colored people had their own barber and beauty shops and their own restaurants, with names like the Busy Bee Café and the Dew Drop Inn. At the movie theater, they had their own seats, in the balcony. At the doctor's office, their own waiting room: Over the doorway we used had long hung a sign, *Colored Entrance, One Door East*. They had their own hospital, the Afro-American Sons and Daughters, their own churches, and even their own section in Glenwood Cemetery. And they attended their own schools. Not just public—there was also a colored Catholic school, St. Francis, up the hill from St. Mary's.

But from his pulpit, Father Hunter had started preaching that there should be only one Catholic church and one Catholic school. Daddy became so angry that he refused even to say the name of the priest who had once been our only welcome visitor. Not long after, the bishop in Jackson made Father Hunter a monsignor, and later he was assigned to another parish. We started to get the Irish missionaries, who preached less about race relations and more about damnation brought on by miniskirts, bootlegging, and Gulf Coast gambling. I became angry, too, when one Irish priest informed us that our sins could even provoke Gulf Coast hurricanes—so angry that I gave up the idea of becoming a nun.

As we were about to enter the eighth grade, the popular girls left St. Clara's for the public school. Only thirteen students remained in my class, and only we three olive-complexioned girls: Georgette, Mary, and me. Then just before our graduation, we learned that St. Clara's high school would be closing for lack of students and that we'd also have to transfer to the public school. As I was leaving, Sister Joanne recommended one last book for me, *To Kill a Mockingbird*.

At Yazoo High, I loved the long, dark corridors, which smelled of sweat and cleaning products and formaldehyde from the second-floor biology lab. I loved the lockers and the bigger classes, with as many as thirty students. Those of us from St. Clara's were considered outsiders, "transfers," but I made friends with some Protestant kids. Johnny sat in front of me during Mr. Moore's general science class, and we passed notes back and forth. I thought he was the cutest boy I'd ever seen, with an upturned nose and brown hair longer than anybody else's.

Then during fall of sophomore year, we heard that the following semester the colored students from N. D. Taylor would be integrating Yazoo High. I was excited by the prospect. Catholic and Arab, too tall and skinny and olive-complexioned, I'd never fit in, either. My own grandmother had called me "nigger." From his pulpit, Reverend Yates, the First Baptist minister, had spoken in favor of integration, along with some other preachers and town leaders. But the question was, come January, how many whites would remain in the public school? Johnny's family was Baptist, and he planned to stay. But the popular girls, who'd added to their number and started calling themselves the Big Ten, would be going to Manchester, the new private academy.

Daddy had already decided where we would go to school. By now, Debbie had graduated from Yazoo High and attended Ole Miss on scholarship. Lisa Maria could continue in St. Clara's elementary, but Sol Boy would go to Manchester. Daddy was taking him out of the Catholic school because he'd discovered that one of the nuns, dissatisfied with my brother's penmanship, had been beating his severed finger with a ruler. Daddy wanted me to go to Manchester, too. He swore he'd find the money somehow.

It was another Sunday morning after Mass, and he and I were in the living room again, standing in front of the television. Sol Boy and Lisa Maria were seated side by side on the couch, while Mama was in the kitchen, frying chicken. I chose this moment to tell Daddy that I planned to continue in the public school, partly because I believed it was the right thing to do, and partly because Johnny would be there.

He said, "Te-re-sa, you have to go to Manchester."

I shook my head.

He took a step toward me. He raised and lowered his arms.

He pointed his index finger. Then he started. "Nobody has the right to force my kids to go to school with anybody they don't want to, especially nigs. Those outlaw nigger lovers comin' into Mississippi teachin' about how rotten politicians are in Mississippi because they hate nigs. You can't tell me that is right, now can you, Te-re-sa?"

He paused, and I tried to answer. "Well, but I—"

"And if you think it's right, then you, dear daughter," he smirked, "then you, dear daughter, stink as much as those nigger lovers stink."

Then he turned and stomped into the kitchen. I looked at Sol Boy and Lisa Maria. They were sitting up straight, their hands at their sides. "That hypocrite," I whispered. It was all I could think of to say. They didn't answer, but I could tell they felt sorry for me.

In the kitchen, Daddy was cussing. "Damn, damn, damn," I heard him yell over the sound of chicken popping in the hot grease. Then he stomped back to take his position in front of the television. "And another thing, all those nigger lovers want to do is take everythin' away from the white people, just everythin' away from the white people, everythin' they work for under the hot sun, under the name of Our Lord Jesus Christ"—he bowed his head—"and give it to the damn nigger."

"Daddy—"

"Who don't know how to do anythin' because they are so ignorant. No, sir. Nobody is goin' to come in here and teach my kids politics. What the hell does a kid have to know about politics for? Listen, Te-re-sa, I'm just givin' you the facts, the true honest-to-God facts, and if you don't believe them, then you're just as stinky as they are and playin' with fire, too, and if they aren't true, then I'll just turn into a nig myself. Now, what do you have to say about them facts?"

"I don't believe them," I said.

"Shit, what did I ever do to deserve you? Don't I pay two dollars every Sunday in the collection plate, and don't I follow Jesus Christ, and don't I go to church?"

Once again he stomped into the kitchen. This time I heard him shouting to Mama that not only was I weirdo, I was a nigger lover.

Sol Boy and Lisa Maria crept off to their beds, and I was alone in the living room. I knew that soon Daddy would leave the house and that when he returned, he'd give me the Silent Treatment. This time it would last for days, maybe as long as a week. When I sat at the table or passed him in the hall, I would be invisible to him. But toward the others, he'd chirp and carry on as if nothing had happened.

I thought about his words, *Shit, what did I ever do to deserve you?* I took them into myself, where they became a part of me. They hurt even more than being called a weirdo, even more than being called a nigger lover.

Playing with fire. That's what Daddy would have called it, if he'd known. Called my attending voter registration drives at St. Francis, where Johnny and I met Julian Bond and John Lewis. Called my support of the black boycott, which was destroying my grandparents' pretense of a livelihood from the grocery. (Grandma and I didn't fight about the boycott, because I rarely saw her anymore.) Called my correspondence with Sister Joanne, who now lived in Fayette, Mississippi, where she had joined the NAACP and was campaigning for Charles Evers in his bid for governor. Called my interviewing Mayor Evers for the student newspaper, the *Yazooan*. But Daddy didn't know any of this, because I kept everything secret from him. I spent all my free time at school, staying on after classes to write the newspaper, pouring out all the opinions I was not allowed to express at home. And I made sure that he never saw a copy.

I kept secret that senior year my best black friend, Denise, put my name forward as a candidate for class secretary. Denise wore cat-eye glasses and straightened her stiff, thick hair to flip up like Laura Petrie's in *The Dick Van Dyke Show*. We exchanged notes in homeroom about her unrequited love for a popular black boy, Johnny B, and we talked on the telephone in the late afternoons while I sat on top of the Maytag. If I was still talking to Denise when Daddy came home from the Place, he would slam the refrigerator door as he put away the groceries.

On the day ballots were to be cast for class officers, we assembled in the high school auditorium, and the principal announced that we would have to stand to cast our votes. The blacks had a slight majority, and though there was some mixed voting, the black candidates won the positions of president and vice president. When it came time to vote for secretary, my name was called, and every black student stood up to vote for me. But not one white student, not even Johnny.

Later in homeroom, Denise passed me a note that said, "We the Black People Thank You." I thought, *Thank me for what?* I refolded the note and looked around; every black student in the class was looking at me, Denise with something like pride in her shiny dark eyes. She was sitting next to Johnny B. Afterward I never spoke about the election, not to Denise or to any of my white friends. I also kept secret from Daddy that someone had started smashing eggs on the windshield of the Rambler station wagon that I drove to school.

I certainly kept secret from him that a handsome black boy named Marcus, who sat next to me in afternoon study hall, loved me. I didn't love him, though I did let him try on my junior ring, and once, just once, hold my hand. And I kept secret that despite everything, I was still in love with Johnny. I wrote him in a letter that I felt trapped, never good enough, and that more than anything, I longed to get away from Daddy and his damn duplex and the entire state of Mississippi.

To escape, Johnny and I went riding. We would climb into his family's blue Ford LTD, and I'd feel anticipation mingling with other sensations: the smell of the warm plastic seat covers, the sight of Johnny's square, capable hands on the steering wheel, the sound of the hottest songs playing on the radio, which owing to the backwardness of the place, we might hear months or even years after they'd been issued. The very first time we went riding, I heard "Cherish," and the dreamy lyrics of the Association seemed to describe my dilemma. But no matter how much I might wish it, I couldn't mold Johnny into someone who cherished me. Johnny didn't love me back, although when we were freshman he'd written under the Y-Teen photo of our annual, "Let's get married someday."

Johnny and I went riding, but we didn't just drag Grand Avenue, we drew circles from the end of South Main to Twentieth Street and made loops on Highway 49; we ventured out into the county. Most often this meant the Delta, land so flat that land met sky, a wide dome sitting atop fields unrelieved in sameness except for the occasional stand of distant trees. This terrain was part of us, and we absorbed its lonely expanses and deep sadnesses. It was during these rides that we plotted how to get out of Mississippi.

I'd decided to become a writer, Johnny an architect. We pored over college catalogs in Ricks Library, encouraged by two new adult friends, architect Jack DeCell and his wife, Betty. We'd met them one day when I stood on Johnny's shoulders to peer into their antebellum house. "Would y'all like to come inside?" Betty had asked, as our eyes met through the kitchen window. She'd gone to Duke but recommended that I apply to Swarthmore College. "I once dated a boy from there that I liked," she said, and on that tenuous basis I applied. Johnny would go to Yale, Jack's alma mater. We were the only two in our class who submitted applications to colleges out of state.

But I found out Daddy was also keeping secrets from me. We faced off one afternoon in the grocery store, standing in the half-light in front of the drink box. Daddy informed me that he'd already accepted a place for me at Louisiana State, my safety school. I informed him that I was going to Swarthmore, where I'd been offered a scholarship. He refused to notify LSU of my decision and left it up to me to explain to them.

The day I left for Swarthmore, I got up early and wrote Mama a note, which I put on top of the television for her to find later, asking her not to be sad that I was going. We hugged good-bye, and I felt guilty for abandoning her in the duplex with Daddy. I'd already said good-bye to Grandma; she promised to write often, and I knew that she would, lengthy letters in her neat hand. Despite every bewildering thing that had happened, I was still her Treesa. For graduation, she had given me a tiny silver pendant from the Marylena Shoppe with my initials engraved on it. I was wearing it the morning Daddy and I climbed into our most functional vehicle, the Pontiac.

As he took me to the home of the girl who was giving me a ride up north, Daddy drove slowly even for him, the car creeping along the gutter, stirring up the early fallen leaves. He stopped outside Alice's house, not bothering to turn off the motor. Our farewell consisted of his placing his heavy right hand on my shoulder. "Good-bye, daughter," he said. I felt the pain of that hand's heaviness, the weighty emotion that lay buried between us. And I silently begged, counting the seconds his hand rested upon me, that he remove it.

Part II

"You Don't Know Your Daddy"

Eight

Mama called.

It was a blinding January morning, the kind that happens rarely in New York, when the slow gray clouds of a winter storm finally lift and the sun comes out startling strong, composing the day into hard blue skies and white-capped lawns.

Even before her stroke, Mama would always wait for me to phone her, ever since I'd left Yazoo City twenty-two years earlier. I dutifully telephoned weekly, when I would talk to Mama and Daddy for ten minutes or so, long enough to find out that nothing much had changed with them, at least not for the better. Daddy also didn't call much, though he had earlier this month.

The morning Mama called, we had just returned home after our Saturday errands and were fumbling with the keys at the back door when the sound of the phone ringing broke through the glass panes like jangling waves. Gerry pushed into the narrow vestibule leading to the kitchen, with its glass and oak cabinets, and set a sack of groceries on the tiled counter. As he reached over and answered the beige wall phone, I headed back to the car to get more groceries. But when I returned seconds later, I heard Gerry saying, "Mama? Mama?" into the receiver.

He turned to me with a worried look. "I'm pretty sure it's your mother, but all she said was your name."

"Mama, is that you?" I asked when he handed me the telephone. Then I recognized the familiar sound of my mother's stammer. "I'm going to my bedroom," I told her, giving the phone back to Gerry. "Take this while I run upstairs." I needed quiet to concentrate on my mother's faltering speech.

I quickly crossed the small butler's pantry with its tiny, brass-fauceted sink, moved through the dining and living rooms, blurs of color and texture, antique furniture and hooked rugs. I rushed up the stairs and sat down on my brass bed, its Mississippi-made quilt with blue, yellow, and red squares so dissimilar to the more formal furnishings in the rest of the house.

"Mama," I said into the handset, "I'm here." Still there was only silence. I could see her hunched in her La-Z-Boy, that ratty beige chair where she always sat, dwarfed by the run-down furniture Daddy had jammed into the living room of the duplex. Though he'd hung a vintage 1950 black wall phone in the hall and one circa 1960 in the kitchen, Mama kept a slim Touch-Tone under the recliner, with important numbers keyed into the memory, and would fish it up onto her lap when she absolutely had to make a call. I suspected—no, I knew—that something awful must have happened.

There was nothing for me to do but wait. The curvaceous receiver of my 1950s-style phone, raw from years of use, felt rough in my hand; its pyramidal body, cast of black metal, had a rotary dial with a Belzoni, Mississippi, number written in fading blue pen on a dirty white circle still pasted on the center. Daddy collected these old black telephones. That had been the reason for his call earlier this month—to tell me he'd just found this one, and it was on the way. The phone had arrived a week ago.

With it, Daddy had enclosed a rusted metal clipboard that

fit over one side of the cradle, so you could fill it with notepaper and take down messages when people called. It said *Andries Welding Supply, Jackson, Mississippi* at the top, but you could hardly read it because most of the letters had rubbed off. He had included a note, written on a yellow index card, that said in his surprisingly precise handwriting: "This little clipboard was lying on my desk at the Yazoo Motor Co. for forty years, and I wanted you to have it, Teresa." Of course I'd known that this piece of junk had lain on Daddy's desk for forty years, because when we were children he'd made a point of showing it to us, turning it over slowly in his hand as if it were molded of precious metal.

I was surprised that Daddy had wanted me to have it. But at Christmas, when I was home for my annual visit, we'd fought, and I realized he was trying to make up to me in the only way he knew, first by calling, then by sending me the worn telephone and this favorite keepsake.

Finally Mama managed to say, "Treesa."

"Mama, Mama, what is it?" I heard my voice echoing along the vacant line.

She could not be rushed, ever since two years ago when she'd suffered the stroke. It had occurred on the day that Brother underwent an angioplasty at St. Dominic's in Jackson. She and Daddy were waiting at the hospital with Brother's wife, Willie Belle. As they left the parking lot after the procedure, Mama passed out in the front seat of the Oldsmobile, her head lolling forward like a giant rag doll.

Many weeks afterward, when Mama finally began to speak again, she sounded like a Dadaist poet. Her doctors were "elephants," a group of doctors a "herd of elephants." She repeated, as if this explained everything, "I had the weight of the whole world on my shoulders, and I dared not knock it off, but y'all knocked it off." After she came home from the hospital, her use of odd metaphors continued. Now when she spoke, it was a little like starting up an old engine.

"Mama, what is it?" I asked again, smoothing the top of the quilt. I listened closely. My parents lived alone, but in the background I could make out men with deep voices and strong southern accents. In particular I thought I heard Sol's father-in-law, who had a thick, slow way of talking. But why would James be there? He rarely came to the house anymore.

By now Gerry had joined me upstairs, pausing in the doorway of the bedroom. We'd been married seventeen years, and we were close in the way that childless couples could be. We even shared the same profession, book publishing.

"What's the matter?" he asked.

I held up my hand to stop him from talking. But Mama was only burbling consonants. Then she came out with a complete sentence: "I wouldn't have gone to the beauty shop."

"Mama, what do you mean, you wouldn't have gone to the beauty shop?"

But she only replied, "What will they think at the Jitney Jungle?"

Words began to trickle from her like molasses from a sticky bottle. "I thought he was just sleepin' late, I thought he was just sleepin' late. I wouldn't have gone to the beauty shop, I wouldn't have gone to the beauty shop. What will they think at the Jitney Jungle, what will they think at the Jitney Jungle?"

She followed this with such a long hiatus that I was afraid she was done talking for good. In the background, more voices, the sound of a door slamming.

Then Mama blurted out: "He's dead."

I knew she meant Daddy. Daddy was the only "he" left in our family since Sol had died of leukemia five years before.

"Daddy's dead," I repeated, and saw the expression drop on Gerry's long, sweet face.

"They just took him away, they just took him away in the am-bu-lance." Mama sang this last little song of keening, and I heard again the banging of the front screen door. Life gone, body gone, and all so quickly.

Solomon Thomas Nicholas Jr. Dead at sixty-eight, on January 29, 1994.

"I'm coming, Mama," I said into the quiet telephone. "I'm coming home tonight."

In the first few seconds after Mama's phone call, Gerry and I looked at each other. Inside, quiet filled the house and outside expanded until it seemed not like silence but noise. Then from the backyard came the racket of a crow cawing in the barren branches of the sassafras, reminding me of a time when we were little and an owl had taken up residence in one of Grandma's pecan trees. Each night we'd heard its mournful cry begin at dusk. My mother, full of country superstitions, had listened closely, repeating, "I don't like no hoot owl." To hear an owl meant death was coming, most likely to somebody close.

So Daddy was dead. I waited for that fall-to-the-floor, wailing grief to come upon me, so instinctive, so primitive it needs no explanation; that kind of grief had descended after I'd received the news that Sol had died. When Daddy called to tell me that cold October evening that my brother was gone, I sank to my knees on the blue carpet in front of our television. No, I certainly didn't feel that for Daddy.

Then Gerry sat next to me, and I obliged by burying my face in his neck. "What happened?" he asked.

I raised my head and reached around to smooth out the quilt that I'd squirmed into a bunch and began to piece together the story as best I could. Mama had thought that Daddy was sleeping late, and as usual she'd gone to have her hair "pressed." Every Saturday morning for thirty years, she'd visited Miz Pie's beauty salon next to the post office on Main Street. She would sit in the waiting room, where the air was sticky with the sweet smell of shampoos and hairsprays, and when her turn was called, she would disappear behind louvered doors. She would emerge an hour later, her short hair pasted into a tidy half circle around her head.

After getting her hair done, she'd stopped by the Jitney, probably for a carton of milk. I knew it would be to buy something absolutely necessary, because grocery shopping was Daddy's domain. Since the Nicholas Cash Gro. had closed twelve years ago, bargain hunting in the Jitney Jungle, Piggly Wiggly, and Sunflower had become his pastime. All the cashiers knew him, and the lady who'd waited on Mama that morning would have been surprised to see her and would undoubtedly have asked about Daddy. "Home sleepin'," Mama would have replied in her spare way, and now she worried what the cashier would think when she found out what had really happened.

It would have been about eleven o'clock by the time Mama returned to the duplex. She probably stood in the living room and peered into his bedroom, only fifteen feet down the dark hallway. He slept with his door open—had to, because none of the duplex's doors closed properly—and Mama could see right in. Sometimes he slept late, but eleven was unusual, so she must have decided to tiptoe to the threshold. No one except Mama ever went into Daddy's bedroom, and she entered only to fix his covers every morning, pulling up the nubby white bedspread, creating a neat zone in his cluttered sanctuary. His bed took up most of the space in the small room, and all around it lay Daddy's junk, a jumble of metal, plastic, fabric, color, and pattern spread out on the floor, crowded on the tops of his blanket box and bureaus.

As she stood at the entryway of his bedroom, she would have called his name. When he didn't answer, she must have moved closer to the bed. Maybe she even poked him with a finger. I could see her standing next to him, the strong east light filtering through the tiny holes in the window shades, with the realization coming over her.

"I have to call Debbie and Lisa," I told Gerry. Why Mama had decided to phone me I didn't know. Lisa was her favorite; Debbie, a doctor. Either, I thought, would have been a more logical choice. When I finally got my sisters on the phone—Lisa in southern Mississippi and Debbie in South Carolina—they didn't cry, either.

"I can't get there until tomorrow," Debbie said. "But I'm worried about Mama." For years, we'd all worried about Mama, not just since her stroke; she was an insulin-dependent diabetic who also suffered from hypertension and a thyroid condition. Besides, she seemed not to know how to live in the world, and I was sure that she wouldn't be able to handle the funeral arrangements, much less pay for them. It was for Mama that I was determined to get home by the end of the day.

I had to make more phone calls—to the airline for tickets and to my boss at the publisher where I worked to tell him that I wouldn't be coming in for the next week. "Let me do that for you," Gerry suggested, but I shook my head. My boss, Ed, was sympathetic; he had recently lost his father, who had lain in a Texas hospital for nearly a month, and he told me to take as much time as I needed.

Gerry was stretched out on the quilt with his feet crossed, listening to my conversations, watching. I knew he wanted me to stop and react, but I couldn't. I rushed to the mahogany dresser and counted out underwear for a week, then ran to my closet, began riffling through my clothing, settled on a gray silk-and-linen pantsuit. *These are the clothes that I will wear to Daddy's funeral,* I thought. Only then did I feel like crying, but I hung on to the arms of my suit and stifled the impulse.

But I couldn't stop myself from remembering. I stood at the closet door, recalling the last time I'd seen Daddy. How appropriate that we'd argued. Two days after Christmas, on his sixty-eighth birthday, the four of us—Mama, Daddy, Gerry, and I—decided to go riding in the hills where Mama had grown up, to visit the cemetery at Midway Primitive Baptist Church. She got Daddy to take her there as often as he would so she could visit her parents' graves.

Daddy had wanted Erin, Sol's only child, to come with us. She was now eight years old and since Sol's death had practically grown up in the house as my parents' fifth child. I expressed my doubts.

We were standing in the living room in front of the TV, our old battleground. "You don't want to play with Erin," Daddy accused me.

"Play with" Erin? We were on our way to a cemetery. I looked at Daddy in astonishment. He and I were both six feet tall, so we stood eye to eye; I could see how his oversized glasses magnified his large brown eyes. But it was his nose, thick and hooked, that made him look foreign, as it did most of the men in Daddy's Lebanese-Syrian family. He generally wore a hat inside the house, a tractor cap in summer and in winter a red watch cap. That day he looked like an angry Arab Santa.

Now he was working his mouth, yelling, "You don't love Erin, Te-re-sa!"

From the dining room doorway, Gerry looked on in horror. Mama had retreated to her bedroom. Just as in the old days, I stood by, mute with anger, unable to meet his verbal assault, while he informed me of how I felt. How could I counter his insane thinking? I wanted to snatch the ridiculous cap off his head.

Ultimately, I gave in. But when we stopped to pick her up, Erin wasn't home, so only the four of us drove to the cemetery after all. It was balmy for December, and the midafternoon sun streamed through the dry woods that grew close along the road. Daddy drove slowly, maddeningly slowly, looking to the left and right, never straight ahead. He was brooding over our fight, as was I.

He veered onto Chew Forks Road. Mama pointed out her aunt Lula's house, its yard full of junked cars, but we didn't stop to visit. Finally we came to the big curve, and Daddy turned onto the gravel road, past the little yellow-brick church and into the cemetery. He parked close to the headstone shared by Mama's parents.

Nettie Gilmore Hood, Jan. 7, 1898–March 20, 1975
John Wesley Hood, Sept. 28, 1885–August 27, 1929

Behind these simple words lay the story of their hard lives and that of my mother, who preferred to sit in the car to remember. I didn't know how she remembered, whether it was with sadness, hurt, anger, or nostalgia. I suspected she felt all of these, but I only knew that for her, to remember was important.

While Mama sat in the backseat, Gerry and I got out to stretch our legs. I wanted to walk up the little hill to the two old pecan trees beyond the graves to hunt for the sweet brown nuts, and in a conciliatory gesture, I leaned into the driver's window and asked Daddy to join us. But he only shook his head.

Standing beneath those trees, I watched him get out of the car. On that warm December day, he was wearing a pair of cut-off shorts, and I saw his bald, white legs jerk as he moved toward Nettie's and John Wesley's graves. Though I hadn't known it then, something was wrong with Daddy: He couldn't even walk a short distance. But I hadn't recognized the sign, because when he'd refused me, I hadn't been able to see through my anger. I hadn't been able to forgive him, not for our fight over Erin, not for any of our fights. We'd driven in silence back to Yazoo City, and the next day Gerry and I had left.

Now, barely a month later, I was going home for Daddy's funeral.

Nine

I was standing at the living room window, watching for the car that would take us to the airport. I had called Mama twice while we were getting ready to leave. The first time she hadn't been able to say anything except, "Y'all are comin' today, ain't you?" The second time, James had answered; so that *had* been his voice I'd heard in the background. Sol and his father-in-law had worked side by side in the maintenance department at Mississippi Chemical Corporation. Gray-haired yet still muscled at sixty, James had done manual labor all his life, and he had not only the calloused hands to prove it but the confidence of someone who knew how to do things, whether it be fitting pipes or fixing a washing machine. I asked him how he came to be at my parents' house, and he explained that after Mama found Daddy, she'd fallen into her La-Z-Boy to call the ambulance, but she'd punched the wrong memory button and gotten him instead. He promised me he would stay with Mama until her relatives arrived.

A black sedan finally pulled up, and the driver got out. I knew this man; he'd often picked us up, and as he helped us into the backseat with our two small bags, I felt the urge to explain what had happened, why we were making this sudden journey to Mississippi. For the first time, I heard myself use the past tense while talking about Daddy.

I could feel Gerry watching me, and I knew he worried about my ability to cope with this latest news from home. The string of family misfortunes had started six years ago, when Sol was diagnosed with leukemia. A year later, shortly after his death, had come Grandma's fall, her diagnosis of Parkinson's, and her admittance to the nursing home; then had come Mama's stroke. Debbie had been in a near-fatal accident when her truck skidded off an icy road in South Carolina; Lisa had almost died while giving birth to her daughter, Elizabeth, when she'd developed a blood clot deep in her abdomen. Now Gerry reached over to take my hand, but I didn't need to be consoled over Daddy. This wasn't going to be hard, burying my father, not at all.

I looked out the sedan's side window as we started off and took a last glimpse at our pretty yellow house with its green shutters and welcoming front porch, the red-ribboned Christmas wreath still hanging on the door. The driver offered his condolences while maneuvering through the village's back roads, past the yawning country club at the end of our street. A few weekend athletes were cross-country skiing on the new snow, violating the exclusive club's private property.

Nearly everything about Bronxville was faultless, its well-kept homes with their manicured quarter-acre plots, its nationally recognized school system, and its main street, with old-fashioned lamps and shops such as House of Botticelli, which had attired village brides for generations. Usually I was comforted by its perfection, but other times I wondered what we were doing in this conservative suburb, where every second car seemed to be a Mercedes, its driver attired in green golf pants. We didn't have children to send to the pricey public school, we didn't belong to the country club, and we didn't vote Republican.

I also wondered what I was doing on the 7:01 commuter train to Manhattan every morning. Instead of becoming a writer, I'd gone to work for a publishing company. Fifteen years ago, my job had been about producing books; now it was about budgets and pretax profit. I was a newly made vice president, and I'd expected that this promotion, which I had wanted for so long, would make me happy. But it hadn't. I'd comforted myself by buying a delicately painted Georgian armchair from Sotheby's. The house was perfectly cared for by our housekeeper, Bernice, and while we were at work fourteen hours a day, it sat as silent as a museum.

We reached the highway, and when I saw the sad, gray industrial buildings of the Bronx, I turned away from the window. Still, I didn't want to be leaving New York for Yazoo City. Even my hometown's name was ominous, the word said to mean "waters of the dead," or "river of death," or sometimes just "death," because its unruly namesake river, a tributary of the Mississippi, used to flood each spring. The five thriving blocks of its downtown had once nestled into a bend of the Yazoo, where cotton had been shipped to New Orleans, but to prevent flooding this branch of the river had been cut off from its source and grown stagnant. Main Street had still bustled with commerce when I was a teenager, but now its fine, two-story buildings were also stagnant and crumbling.

The airport's unloading area was deserted on this Saturday afternoon. When I shook the driver's meaty hand, I felt I was saying good-bye to the city itself, to efficient anonymous faces with unknown lives, to the background noise of sirens and honking horns, to the bus's vacuum hissing as it kneeled to pick up its passengers, to the corner stores (*We Have Good Cigars*) and placards advertising psychic readers. As we checked in for our flight, I hunched over the stainless steel counter, watching the bare conveyor belt circle until I noticed familiar patterns in the black rubber. Finally, we boarded the plane and took our seats.

In Atlanta, we changed to a thirty-seat prop jet for the short flight to Jackson. At first it looked as though we were going to be the only passengers, but then a basketball team from Hattiesburg entered, each player bending from the waist to make his way down the low aisle. Then we were airborne, barreling through the dark space beyond the tiny windows. Inside, Gerry read by the yellow cabin lights while I sat watching the perky white stewardess, conveniently diminutive and possessed of an accent thick as Karo Syrup, passing out crackers, peanuts, Cokes, and Breath Savers to the black athletes.

We arrived late. The airport was empty except for the basketball players, and Gerry and I hurried through the jarringly lighted corridors to the car rental agency. The trip had taken all afternoon and nearly all evening, but we still had the thirty-six-mile drive north on Highway 49 to Yazoo City. While Gerry drove, I stared out the window. There is no place darker or lonelier on a January night than Highway 49. The black sky, full of pointed stars, seemed to bear down on us, and we seldom met another car. Before I left Mississippi, this highway had been a treacherous back road, a surprisingly hilly gateway to the Delta, but now it was four smoothed-out lanes. The two roads still ran side by side in places, and I could see the chewed-up asphalt on Old Highway 49, with the kudzu vines, browned by winter frost, covering everything, even the telephone poles, and coming right up to the pavement's edge.

In Pocahontas, beside the railroad tracks, we passed Big D's Barbecue: *Good Enough to Stop a Train,* its neon sign beamed to no one but us. Down the road in Flora were an explosion of mobile homes, a half-built shopping center, the unrelenting fluorescent lights of fast-food joints, their proprietors long gone home. Past these, darkness reclaimed the highway, but I could make out the swirling waters of the Big Black River in the shine of our headlights. To anyone driving this way in winter, my aunt Willie Belle, who works for the Yazoo County sheriff's department, advises with the authority of her station, "Get slap dab in the middle of the road, point the car straight ahead, and don't brake on them bridges," because they slick up, just like the signs say. Many a wreck has occurred because the driver lost his nerve, slowed down, and wound up in the Big Black.

It was past eleven o'clock when Gerry caught the traffic light at Four Points, the main intersection outside Yazoo City. A giant new Kmart, looking like a flattened tin can, spread over the countryside, surrounded by its vast, dark parking lot. When the light changed, instead of turning left down Broadway the way Daddy used to, Gerry continued on Highway 49. This portion of the road was named after Jerry Clower, an employee at Mississippi Chemical who later made it big as a comedian at the Grand Ole Opry. We passed a store that sold western wear, a sign that advertised paycheck advances, and close to Fifteenth Street, a McDonald's, Taco Bell, Subway, and Pizza Hut. I felt myself slipping into a familiar gloominess.

Gerry made a left at the light, crossed the railroad tracks, then turned left again at the Shell station onto Grand Avenue. He slowed down when we came to the Nicholas family block. On the corner of Grand and Thirteenth was my grandparents' elegant old house, with its white paint peeling and its porches sagging. Grendaddy had died in 1976, but Grandma had lived here by herself another dozen years, until she'd had to go into the Martha Coker Convalescent Home. The house had sat deserted ever since. Her formerly fine garden was nearly barren; even the trees had suffered, the linden cleft by a lightning strike. Only the stately pecan trees remained.

We turned onto Thirteenth Street. Aunt Pauline still lived next door in her tidy ranch, but since she'd become a widow, she'd installed metal bars on the windows and doors. Across the street, Uncle Moe and Aunt Helen still lived in their cottage with latticework trellises. Just beyond, on the corner of Calhoun and Thirteenth, was the makeshift duplex that we called home.

What I saw surprised me: Cars parked everywhere, up and down the street. Mama's relatives had anticipated our arrival. They'd left space for us to pull up into the yard, between Daddy's Oldsmobile and Sol's GMC pickup, which Daddy hadn't been able to part with after my brother's death.

Since I'd left, Daddy had reconfigured the duplex again, making a living room out of his and Sol's old bedroom and adding a front porch, which he'd used to store more junk: a burned-out TV, a wobbly table from Great-Uncle Sam's Bon Ton Café, two broken-down chairs, a big wooden spool that once held telephone cable, a child's metal garden chair painted red with white arms, Erin's tricycle. I paused on the porch before the screen door, then entered.

Inside, a blast of heavy, hot air from the gas space heater in the corner, a blur of people in the tight room. These were Mama's family, with country faces full of sun-hardened wrinkles, come from as far away as Tchula, in Holmes County. Crowded onto the dirty green and white velour love seat and the dining room chairs, they were sitting bolt upright, out of habit and respect for the dead. At first I couldn't find Mama in the confusion, then I saw her: She wasn't in her recliner but was slumped on the soiled brown corduroy couch. This behemoth, which

Daddy had bought twenty years ago at Unclaimed Freight, took up an entire wall. A tan pillow with a butterfly appliqué and frilly white edges was propped in a corner; nestled next to it was a homemade Raggedy Ann doll with bright yellow hair and black embroidery for a smile.

Somebody made space for us, and I sat on one side of Mama, Gerry on the other. She lifted her head and said clearly, "I'm so glad y'all are here. I don't know how to do nothin'. He did ever'thang." And that was it. She was perfectly dry-eyed. I didn't know what to say or do, so I stroked her forearm, felt it fine and dry like parchment, saw it full of the brown speckles of age.

Mama's relatives had waited with her all day. "I made your daddy's bed up with clean sheets," said efficient, wizened Aunt Bet. She had found a way to prop closed the cantankerous door to his room so we wouldn't be reminded of what had happened in there.

I turned toward the take-charge aunt, Willie Belle. "When's the funeral?" I asked.

She seemed surprised by my question. "We hadn't done anythin' about that," she sniffed. Then she stood up; then everybody stood up. Now that we'd arrived, they could leave. I said good-bye to them without moving from Mama's side. Nodded my head, shook a few hands. Some reached down and hugged my neck. This was our prerogative, the right of grief, to sit still.

When we were alone, Mama said, "We'll visit Buster in the morning." Buster was the owner of Stricklin-King Funeral Home and had buried Sol. Tomorrow we would go together, mother and daughter, to arrange Daddy's funeral.

Ten

After the relatives left, we remained on the corduroy couch in uneasy intimacy, with Mama slumped between Gerry and me. I thought I needed to say something about Daddy's death, but I couldn't think of what; the phrases that came to mind—*I'm sorry,* and *Everything is going to be all right*—didn't seem worth much. Two or three times, Mama repeated in a pitiful tone, "He did ever'thang. I don't know how to do nothin'." When I began to feel an immense awkwardness seeping out of me, so great that I wondered if Mama and Gerry could sense it, too, I suggested we go to bed.

I led my mother by the elbow the few feet into her bedroom, where she sat down heavily at the dresser before her portable makeup mirror. She flicked the switch, and the mirror's many squat bulbs lit up her face and hair. Though her skin was unlined even at sixty-nine years of age, her short hair was white as a cotton boll. She removed her glasses and began to brush her hair slowly, while I lay across the quilt on her bed and watched.

The strong fluorescent lights cast a blue glow, revealing the dozens of old photographs Mama had tacked to the wall. I hadn't known her to be sentimental, yet she'd surrounded herself with these photos, among them Debbie's 1972 graduation picture from Ole Miss, snapshots of Gerry and me during our honeymoon trip to Europe in 1977, a computer-generated portrait of Lisa Maria made when she was in high school, and Erin's and Elizabeth's studio baby pictures. But most prominently displayed were photos of Sol, including one with his young wife, Cindy, taken at a party when he must have just gotten back from a hunting trip, still dressed in a camouflage shirt and cap. Since his death, none of us mentioned my brother except Mama, who in her stroke-phased, forgetful way, might let slip his name during Christmas dinner, just to say how she'd made his favorite dessert, lemon meringue pie, before she remembered the family's unspoken pact never to bring him up again.

Mama continued brushing her hair methodically while I looked around her bedroom. Somehow—it couldn't have been easy—she'd convinced Daddy to put up dark paneling and white ceiling tiles. This was the only room in the duplex with decent furniture, a mahogany-stained dresser and matching bed and bureau. But there was also a scarred cedar chest for storing quilts and a rocking chair with the springs spilling out. Mama's bedroom had been her haven, not only from the rest of the duplex but also from Daddy.

She put down her hairbrush and turned toward me. "What brand of tuna do you buy, Treesa? Do you buy it in oil or water?"

I wanted to laugh, but she looked so grave that I couldn't. "I don't know. Gerry buys it. We'll ask him tomorrow."

This seemed to satisfy her, and she picked up a jar of cold cream, turning her back to me, so that once more I saw the reflection of her thin face in the makeup mirror. "Don't know how to balance no checkbook," she said to herself, "and can't write no check, neither." Since the stroke, she was ashamed of her handwriting, her letters grown spider-legged, nearly impossible to decipher.

She caught my glance in the mirror. "First thang I can remember was my daddy dyin' when I was five." For once, she seemed to have no problem finding her voice. "He got up one mornin' and was havin' some pains. So he took a big dose of soda water and leaned against the hen house." August 27, 1929—I was aware of the date of John Wesley's death, having seen it many times on his tombstone in the Midway Primitive Baptist churchyard. I'd heard Mama say how he'd died of the Hood heart. But I'd never heard her describe her daddy's death in any of its details.

"He slid down the hen house and died. Mama could yell the loudest of anybody, and she yelled for Uncle Will to come." But it was too late to help John Wesley, who was just forty-three. "I remember the church service. I went to sleep on a bench, and my aunts thought that was just terrible. But I was only five years old," she protested. After all these years, the hurt still clung to her like a set of worn-out clothes.

Because she'd had to work the fields, Mama was twenty before she finished high school. She had to raise a red and white calf to pay for her graduation; they sold it for sixty-five dollars, and she spent part of the money on her class ring, which now lay in the bottom of the mauve velvet box atop her bureau. Afterward, she moved from Benton to Bentonia to Greenville to Holly Bluff to Canton, working in meat-processing plants and lumberyards, until finally she came to Yazoo City and became an operator at Southern Bell Telephone and Telegraph. There she met Daddy, who made a lot of calls just to hear her voice.

They courted, but slowly. Oftentimes they went riding in Grendaddy's borrowed Buick, enjoying the fragrant night air. They visited a roadhouse near Wolf Lake called the Quonset Hut, played bingo at church suppers. One day Sol June called the switchboard and asked if he could pick her up right after work, and Mama thought from his voice that he was agitated about something. At five o'clock, he was waiting for her in the Buick, parked outside the drafty telephone building on Jefferson Street. For once, he suggested they have supper in a restaurant, the Rotisserie, a popular Jackson eatery that featured an orchestra every weekend night and was known for a garlicky salad dressing called Kumback Sauce. Before he started the car, Sol June fumbled in his suit coat pocket and brought out a round box, the small diamond he had purchased at Miron's on Main Street. They stayed engaged for two years, because Daddy rarely did anything in a hurry. They finally married on May 21, 1950.

Now I had another photograph in mind, one that Mama didn't display with the others. She kept it in a tattered album buried in a dresser drawer, but I'd often pulled it out and studied it. The photo is black and white, beautiful and rich in contrast. She and Daddy have paused on St. Mary's stone steps, and Mama's wedding dress with the lacy bodice billows against the dark door. Later, she would let this dress decay in a cardboard box in the hall cabinet; once a year, I would be allowed to try it on, until the delicate lace hung in yellow shreds. But on the day of their wedding, all is still bright and fresh. They look so young and happy.

Mama was watching me in the mirror. "Treesa," she asked, "why does ever'body I love die?"

I remained quiet, because I was afraid that if I answered I might let out a sob. It was true that Mama had seen a lot of people pass from her life. She had buried not only her daddy but also her mama and all but two of her nine siblings, Brother and Ada Belle. Gone were Annie and Johnny, Wilmer, Otis,

J.W., Ethel, and 'Cile, many of them felled by the Hood heart. It totted up a lot of loss for one lifetime, not even including the twins, Sol, and now Daddy.

"I guess I've lived a lonely life," Mama said.

"Let's go to sleep," was all I could finally think of to say. I got up from the bed, leaving her slump-shouldered, poised to begin the ritual of removing her makeup.

When I walked into the hallway, I saw Gerry still sitting on the corduroy couch, staring into space. "We have to make up the bed in the Toy Room," I said and continued walking toward the Pink Bathroom. He dutifully followed. I opened the pink cabinet and took some sheets off the pink shelves. "Here, we'll use these."

The Toy Room had been one of the duplex's two living rooms, an eight-by-twelve box without a closet but still with one of the original front doors. Daddy had nailed up sheetrock over the wooden lath, though he'd never painted it; the joint tape had unfurled from the seams, making the room look as if it were decorated with flypaper. Besides the double bed, the only furniture was a child-sized oak desk and two tiny chairs. Daddy had turned this into the Toy Room after Sol died and he began keeping Erin while Cindy worked part-time at Murphy's Florist. He'd hung onto all our old toys and games, and the bed served as a repository for my dolls: Betsy McCall; Barbie and Ken; Chatty Cathy and the Tiny Chatty Twins, dressed in matching blue and white baby outfits; my bride doll; and my favorite, Shrinking Violet, a misshapen little girl who batted spiky black eyelashes and told you how shy she was when you pulled her string. There were also two black Barbie cases, dresses, shoes, hats, and a plastic orange convertible.

Daddy had called the Toy Room "the laughing place," and when he and Erin played there together, sitting at the knee-high desk in the tiny chairs, having watermelon parties and drinking make-believe tea, there was much laughter, his like cackling, hers like tiny peals. But I couldn't think of the Toy Room as a laughing place. When it had been my bedroom, while I was in high school, I'd tacked up a blue and white Martin Luther King poster over the sealed-off front door, and the room had become another of our battlegrounds.

Now I raked my dolls onto the floor. Gerry and I made up the bed, covering the sagging mattress with many layers of quilts, because when we exhaled, we could see our breath. I got into bed and huddled in one place while Gerry snuggled beneath the quilts until only his brown hair showed. I'd always worried what he thought of the duplex; I'd kept him away from here until five months after we married, when we visited for our first Christmas. He had grown up in New York State in a suburban home with three bedrooms, a living room with a picture window, a breakfast nook, a kitchen with copper-colored appliances, a basement complete with a pool table and bar. He'd had central heat and air-conditioning.

Soon he was asleep, adapting as usual. I lay awake under the heavy covers, my head on the icy pillowcase. There was the repetitive *ca-thunk, ca-thunk, ca-thunk* of car tires hitting the pavement seams on Calhoun Avenue and the recurrent, cheerless call of the freight trains as they lumbered through the crossing two blocks away. A few times I heard Mama coughing in her bed up the hall. But I must have dozed toward dawn, because I woke several times with nervous starts, stepping into deep holes, falling from cliffs. And whenever I awoke, I wouldn't be able to remember where I was right away or what had happened, until I sat up and shook off the sleep. I felt the narrow room start to close in on me, crowded with old playthings and bitter memories. And for the first time I started to think, *How do we bury Daddy?* What did it mean to put someone like him behind you? And what would become of Mama, who didn't even know how to buy canned tuna?

Eleven

I woke up when the light turned gray in the Toy Room. This was Sunday, the quietest day, the through trains halted elsewhere, maybe out West, and the car traffic, the little that there was, deliberate in its mission: By eleven o'clock, the Baptists would assemble on Grand Avenue for another day of worship. Downtown, the black street sweepers would also be out, cleaning up the broken whiskey bottles from Saturday night.

I examined my bedraggled dolls, heaped on the floor where I'd brushed them aside the night before. They had once meant everything to me: wished for out of Sears, Roebuck catalogs, eagerly unwrapped on Christmas mornings, played with often but carefully. After Erin's hard use, the bride's yellow hair was matted, her wedding bodice ripped, her eyes hooded in old age. Though Shrinking Violet's purple dress was intact, her long eyelashes were stuck together. I still knew their expressions by heart, but this morning my dolls seemed to stare at me incriminatingly, as if to ask, *Where have you been all these years? We've been here.*

Gerry was still asleep, his body rolled toward the center of the spongy mattress. I swung my feet outside the quilted cocoon, touched the chilly wooden floor, rough with termite tunnels, and hurried to the Pink Bathroom. The small white heater was warming the room nicely, proof that Mama had gotten up long before. The fixtures were all undersized, a bathroom for little people. I was used to drawing up my knees when I bathed in the tiny tub and stooping to wash my face in the miniature sink. As I mixed water from the hot and cold taps in the basin, I examined myself in the jagged shard of mirror that had hung above it for thirty-five years. I had the Nicholas looks, prominent nose, a tendency to sallowness, almond-shaped eyes. My eyes were not Grandma's, round and blue, or my mother's, neat and black; these were Daddy's eyes, large, messy brown, full of light and feeling. In them I thought I could see all the way back to the Old Country, to Daddy's grandparents, George and Rosa.

I washed my face and went looking for Mama. But she wasn't in the La-Z-Boy, where I'd expected her to be; she was rooting around inside Daddy's clothes closet, which due to the duplex's slapdash layout was located off the living room.

"Mama, what are you doing in there?" Daddy's crammed walk-in closet was a place she rarely entered, least of all because you had to push the love seat out of the way to open the door. I saw her stooped over, rummaging through his shirts, light-colored short-sleeves, heavy flannel plaids. She emerged with an armful of clothing, which she began stuffing into a black plastic garbage bag.

"What's that?" I asked, sliding the love seat back into position. She sank into her chair, just a few feet away from the closet door.

"Daddy's buryin' clothes. We got to take 'em to Buster." Then I remembered that Daddy had been removed from the house in his pajamas. I hadn't realized that death came down to these ordinary details; when Sol died, I'd arrived home after he'd already been placed in his coffin, dressed in a white shirt and dark suit as if he were headed for a prom.

"What are we burying him in?" I asked Mama. As far as I knew, Daddy didn't have any decent clothes. Since he'd retired five years before, he'd worn canvas slip-ons, along with an open-necked shirt and cutoffs, except during the coldest winter days, when he'd worn khakis instead of the shorts.

"The suit he wore to Sol's funeral," she said. I'd forgotten about Daddy's one suit, which he'd bought many years ago. Mama pulled a corner of it from the bag so I could get a glimpse: light gray polyester, not too different in color from the one I planned to wear myself. "I thought this pale blue dress shirt would go nice, and this here." She held up a wide copper tie with small polka dots from the 1970s.

I watched my mother. She was out of breath from even this little activity, and I was sure she hadn't slept. "Should we visit the funeral home before you go to Mass, or after?" I asked. I'd stopped going to church the moment I'd gotten away from Daddy.

Mama shook her head. "Naw, I'm not goin'. As soon as y'all git ready, we'll leave." This would be the first Sunday I'd known Mama to miss Mass, other than for childbirth or illness. "Buster'll be expectin' us," she said.

After I got dressed, we sat in the living room to wait for Gerry. I felt sure that Mama would be tongue-tied and indecisive in the funeral home, and I wanted him with me to help make the arrangements. By ten o'clock, the three of us were walking through Stricklin-King's double front doors and into Buster's office, a softly lighted room with an expansive wooden desk and a tufted leather couch and wing chairs. He appeared right away, nodding, handshaking, a large man with large furniture. He gestured Mama into a chair opposite his desk and situated himself behind it. Gerry and I sat on the edge of the cold green sofa.

Buster began to talk. He told us that he was sorry about Sol June, delivering practiced sentences that nonetheless sounded genuine. Mama was straight-backed and grim-faced, at her least talkative, but I listened appreciatively, grateful that his commentary covered up the awkwardness of grief. When Buster finished, no one said anything, and in the uncomfortable quiet I had a quick picture of Daddy lying somewhere inside the funeral home. Where exactly was he? On a cold steel table? Was he still dressed in his pajamas?

Then Mama jammed the garbage bag containing Daddy's clothes toward Buster. He rested the package on top of his desk, knowing its contents, repeating a scene played out multiple times each week. He leaned toward my mother and spoke quietly. "When do you want the service, Miz Florence?"

She turned to me, and I started to calculate. Sol had died on a Thursday, and we'd held visitations for three days, then buried him the following Monday. It had seemed to go on forever. I was vacillating between Monday and Tuesday for Daddy's funeral when Mama shifted back toward Buster, her ill-fitting beige car coat swishing against the hard leather.

"Tomorrow," she said. "I want a short visitation for Daddy here in the home startin' tomorrow at eleven, followed by a Mass at St. Mary's."

And that was that. Buster picked up a fancy pen from his desk set and made a note. "Miz Florence, there's the question of the casket. Shall we go take a look at them?"

He went to her, raised her by the elbow, and escorted her toward the back of his office, while Gerry and I tagged behind. Next door, caskets were stacked like bunk beds three and four high, in different materials, hardwood, steel, copper, and in a variety of colors, bronze, silver, metallic blue.

Mama halted in the doorway, waving her hand. "Just use the

same style coffin we used for Sol Boy," she blurted out. Then she fled back to Buster's office, where she dropped into the leather armchair again.

Gerry and I retook our seats on the sofa, and Buster repositioned himself at his desk. He picked up his pen, and I dreaded what was about to come next, because I knew Mama didn't have the money to bury Daddy and she wouldn't want to take any help from me. Would Buster bring up the subject, or was I supposed to?

But instead Buster asked, "Miz Florence, what about the coffin liner?" and began explaining the pros and cons of the one that came with the particular model Mama had just ordered. Would it do?

"Naw, naw, naw," Mama only said, and made for the door. As far as she was concerned, the whole business was over. Gerry and I stayed behind just long enough to shake hands with Buster and ran to catch up with her. She was already in the parking lot, standing beside the car, waiting for us.

Gerry looked at me uncertainly before starting the motor, but I stared out my window at the church across the street. This tan brick building had once been a Sunflower grocery, then a bowling alley; to convert it to St. Matthew Church of God in Christ, they'd just added a tall concrete entryway with the proportions of a Cracker Jack box. I turned in my seat and looked at Mama. We'd never gotten around to discussing expenses with Buster, but there wasn't much to arranging a funeral here, and Mama had done it.

"Isn't there something I can do?" I asked her. "Like arrange a plot for Daddy?"

I knew that, like the rest of the family, Daddy would lie in Glenwood, which stretched from the swampy canal to the hills above the town. The original graveyard was thick with cedars of

Lebanon, cypresses, and broadleaf magnolias and over the years had become so crowded that a newer area had to be opened up on the steep hill beyond. From there you could see for miles, past the rusting Yazoo River Bridge to the diaphanous light of the Delta. In addition to being segregated by race, with the blacks occupying a parcel behind a low fence, the cemetery was also organized by religion—Protestants, Jews, and Catholics. My great-grandparents George and Rosa and the twins, Ed and Fred, had plots in the Catholic section near the main road, while Grendaddy and Sol were closer to the woods. I assumed Daddy would be with the Catholics, but where?

Mama shook her head. "We got a place for Daddy next to Sol Boy, so don't need to do nothin' about that. But there's somethin' else we got to do. We got to go see Miz Nick." This was the name she'd always called her mother-in-law—not Vashti and certainly not Mama, which she'd reserved for her own mother.

We didn't talk as we rode the two blocks to Martha Coker. Gerry parked the car in front of the low yellow-brick building, and he and I walked the few steps to the front door. Mama lagged behind at the curb, smoothing the wrinkles from her lap. In the five years Grandma had been in the nursing home, I could count on five fingers the times that Mama had visited her. It seemed cold to me that no one had told Grandma yesterday that her elder son had died.

But the truth was, I'd also tried to forget about Grandma, because I couldn't bear seeing what her life had become even before she'd entered the nursing home. One afternoon not long after Sol died, I'd gone to her house for a visit. I'd found her barefoot, in a food-stained cotton housecoat. The as-yet-undiagnosed Parkinson's was already taking its toll, and she was barely able to shuffle the length of the back porch to undo the hook on the screen door. At last, after we'd situated ourselves in the wide center hall where she always sat, she admitted something was worrying her. She had a hangnail. Would I clip it? I took her shaking hand, the joints like hard knots, and snipped it away. Then I asked her if she wanted me to cut all her nails. She nodded, too proud to ask. Not long after that, Grandma fell and lay in the hallway for twenty hours until Daddy found her. She'd broken her hip and after leaving the hospital had been admitted to the nursing home.

As we entered, I saw her sitting in a row of elderly women off to the right, each in a wheelchair, lined up like birds on a telephone wire. The few men sat to the left, against the wall, and beyond them was the bare courtyard, gray in the soft winter light. We approached Grandma. She looked up at Gerry and me through owl-shaped glasses, and I noticed that her round, blue eyes were surprisingly vacant, like Little Orphan Annie's in the comic strip. She was ninety years old, but her light brown hair had just a touch of white around the temples. She wore a flowered duster and pink bedroom slippers with tiny pink satin bows.

I laid my hand on her thin shoulder, and a medicinal odor wafted up from her, as if she'd been scrubbed with strong disinfectant. She began to tremble. I reached down to take her right hand, tried to smooth it out where it was balled up, and noticed the back veiled with veins. Her nails were newly manicured.

It occurred to me she might not recognize me. "Who am I?" I had to shout, because she refused to wear a hearing aid. Her expressionless eyes roamed my face, and I repeated my question. Then an exaggerated look, perhaps frustration, came over her, moving across her features the way a lazy cloud ambles across a blank Delta sky.

"I know who you are," she finally answered in a drawn-out voice, as though she were flirting. If she'd had control over her muscles, she might have scrunched up her nose, another stock gesture of old.

"Then who am I?"

She studied me; everything about her was now so slow. "Why, you're Treesa! You brat, you!" She laughed her big, belly-rolling laugh, and I felt relieved that she was her usual self.

"How are you, Grandma?"

She appeared to be thinking hard. "There's nothin' wrong with me," she said unhurriedly. I nodded and smiled, relieved again, until she spat out, "Except that I'm stupid!"

I was taken aback, because in the past Grandma would never have spoken of herself like this. She lowered her voice threateningly. "Don't sell my house," she warned. "I'm goin' back there and never comin' out again." She wagged a finger. "Don't you sell my house."

By now Mama had joined us. "Hey, Miz Nick," she said. She inclined her head toward the lady on Grandma's left and whispered to me, "That's Miz Worley, Dr. Worley's wife."

I nodded to the lady, and so did Gerry, but I looked at Mama questioningly.

"Miz Worley was Daddy's seventh-grade teacher," she explained.

Then the lady sitting on the other side of Mrs. Worley called out, "Oh, is that Miz Worley?"

Mama nodded.

"Why, I used to play cards with Miz Worley!" she exclaimed, peering at the woman sitting not three feet from her.

During this exchange, Grandma had trained her big eyes on each of the speakers. The parts of her body seemed to work independently, so that first her eyes moved, then her head. She pointed to the lady in question, pronouncing with great authority, "Why, that's not Miz Worley. That's Miz Lafitte, kin to the pirates from Louisiana!"

And then I knew: We weren't going to tell Grandma that Daddy had died. To tell her, we would have to shout; even if she heard, she might not understand; and if she understood, she probably wouldn't remember. Would she even notice that Daddy had stopped coming to visit? Mama was standing by placidly, smiling down at Grandma. I realized Mama had already known all of this, which was why she hadn't come to the nursing home yesterday. She'd suggested we call on Grandma out of duty, even though the news couldn't be divulged.

Grandma squinted at me. "Y'all goin' to eat with me at my table?" It was customary for relatives to join residents for meals. Through the swinging doors to the right of the nurses' station, I saw the staff setting places in the dining hall.

"Not today," I replied. "Maybe some other time. We have to go." Gerry looked bewildered; he didn't yet understand that we weren't going to tell Grandma.

"Y'all not goin', are you?" she asked.

"Yes'um. We have to."

Her shaking intensified, and she begged, "Take me home with you, Treesa. I want to go home."

I looked away. "Nome, I can't, but I'll come back to see you again before I go, I promise."

She stared into the distance. She'd already retreated to someplace else.

I went out into the chill January air, but I couldn't get her plea out of my mind, *Take me home with you. I want to go home.* We climbed back into the car for the silent trip to the duplex, only six blocks away.

Twelve

It was well after noon, past time for dinner, but nobody had an appetite. Mama lowered the shades and drew the pink polyester curtains across the living room windows. She settled herself in the La-Z-Boy and clicked the remote, and the greenish light of the television flickered in the dark room. She stared at the Zenith, which Daddy had bought twenty years ago, after lightning struck the antenna and blew out the last set. An addicted viewer of reruns, of *Leave It to Beaver* and *The Andy Griffith Show,* she was especially fond of *Bonanza* and *Gunsmoke,* which played at this time every day.

Gerry stretched out on the longer of the two couches, but I stood next to the heater. "Mama, what can I do?" I asked. I was still looking for some way to help.

"Ain't nothin' that needs doin'," she said. Then she added, "Well, I guess you could order some flowers for him. But just them ones for the coffin."

From her begrudging tone, I supposed she was worrying about money. I walked to the black wall phone in the kitchen and called Murphy's, where my sister-in-law worked. But I'd forgotten that this was Sunday, and Betty, the owner, answered instead. I gave my name and explained that my father's funeral was planned for the next day.

"Mama wants an arrangement for the coffin," I said.

"Would that be a spray or a cross?" Betty inquired respectfully.

I hesitated. "I don't know."

"Probably a spray. Does she wish to honor an aspect of his personality in the design? Such as a hobby?"

Daddy's principal pastime had been collecting junk. "I don't think so," I answered.

"I have roses, gladiolas, and lilies. Do you know what your mother likes?"

"How about you just put together something nice for us." I read her my credit card number, charging the flowers for Daddy's coffin as easily as I might have a new pair of shoes.

Then I sat on the love seat in the living room. "I got Daddy a spray."

"Well, I guess that's all right."

"You don't have to worry about it. I paid."

Mama nodded. She hadn't taken her eyes off the western.

Now there really was nothing more to do. After *Gunsmoke*, there was a timid knock on the front door, but it was still too early for Debbie and Lisa to arrive. I jumped up and peered out the door's fan-shaped window. A round-waisted older lady was standing on the porch next to the burned-out TV. With her hooked nose, Mrs. Weber was immediately identifiable as a member of our Arab community. I opened the screen door a crack, and she pushed a foil-covered plate toward me.

"It's kibbe," she said.

I took the dish from her and reluctantly invited her in. She walked the few steps to where Mama reclined in the La-Z-Boy, extended her hand, and spoke her condolences.

Mama didn't look up from the television, but she did mutter, "Thank you."

I offered Mrs. Weber a seat but was relieved when she said

she couldn't stay. After all these years, I was still ashamed of the duplex. Not only did I worry what people thought of it, I worried what they thought of us for living in it. But that Sunday afternoon, there was no stopping the visitors. Though Mama's relatives had sat with her all day yesterday, they came again, bringing funeral food: Aunt Willie Belle, a ham and egg pie; Aunt Helen, a broccoli Cheez Whiz casserole; Aunt Pauline, spaghetti with Ro-Tel tomatoes. We received two platters of shaved meats from Patenotte's Grocery, and from my cousin Linda at Horseshoe Lake, a girdlebuster, a three-layer cake concocted with Cool Whip, cream cheese, and chocolate and vanilla pudding mixes. I didn't put any of the dishes in the refrigerator but left them sitting on the stove in their shiny tinfoil newness.

Then in the late afternoon, Debbie arrived, followed by Lisa with her husband, Joel, and their daughter, Elizabeth. We squeezed together on the couch and love seat in the tiny living room, with Mama still in her La-Z-Boy. She glanced at my sisters shyly and seemed to perk up with them in the house, for once even turned the sound off on the TV. It was the first time we'd all been together since Sol died, five years earlier.

Debbie was the shortest of the three of us and looked the most like Daddy, with the hooked Nicholas nose. She was a pediatric anesthesiologist at a Shriners hospital, and she'd spiked her short hair and dyed it purple since the last time I'd seen her, claiming it gave her better rapport with her young patients. Lisa also had an olive complexion and dark eyes, but her more regular features were like a rearranged, perfected version of ours. Like me, she'd gone to Swarthmore on a scholarship, but then she'd lived in Seattle and Montreal while Joel finished his Ph.D. They'd only recently moved back to Mississippi, where he worked at the Stennis Space Center and she was a freelance editor for New York publishers.

I told them of the plans for the funeral. Debbie said, "It's a good thing it's tomorrow, because I have to leave on Wednesday."

"So do we," Lisa said.

I felt a pang of jealousy, because Gerry and I would be staying the entire week.

Then Lisa asked, "Where are we all going to sleep?" Sleeping space had always been an issue among us, thanks to Daddy's odd reconfiguration of the duplex. Now the only free bed was his.

"The sheets on it are clean," Mama pointed out.

"I'm not sleeping in it," Lisa declared.

"Me, neither," said five-year-old Elizabeth.

Debbie appeared to be mulling it over. Since we'd be there the longest, I was determined that Gerry and I would continue sleeping in the relative luxury of the Toy Room, but I didn't say anything because I didn't want to provoke a disagreement.

Mama sighed. "I reckon I'll just sit up in my chair all night. Y'all can have my bed."

Then Joel spoke up. "I'll sleep in Daddy's bed," he said evenly.

But we still needed space for three more people. Finally Debbie, always practical, pointed to the corduroy couch and asked, "Does this thing open out?"

Mama nodded.

"I'll sleep here," she suggested. "Mama, you can join me."

"It's fine with me," Mama said. "I'm not goin' to sleep none anyway."

It was settled. Lisa and Elizabeth would have Mama's queen

bed, and I couldn't help but think, the best mattress. We sank into quiet. By now we'd been together for nearly an hour, and no one had mentioned Daddy. I knew my sisters had had their own difficult relationship with our father. Lisa's best friend in high school was a black girl, also named Elizabeth, and that had driven Daddy crazy. Debbie had escaped fights about race with him because she was already at Ole Miss, but I figured Daddy must be a large part of the reason she never came home at all.

Debbie began to quiz Mama about Daddy, probing in her clinical way.

"What did he do the night before he died?" she asked.

Mama stared back. "Watched TV."

"Did he give any sign that anything was wrong?"

"Naw."

"Was he in any pain?"

"Naw, naw."

"Just tell me what happened, Mama."

"I don't know," she snapped. "He just up and died, is all."

Then Mama adjusted the TV's volume and fixed her eyes on the WLBT nightly news. Debbie crossed her arms and legs and seemed to regret having volunteered to sleep with her on a three-inch-thick cellophane-covered mattress.

Finally, Lisa got up and started to prepare supper for Elizabeth. Soon Gerry, Joel, and I joined them at the dining room table. I removed the foil tops from the casseroles while Joel unraveled the elaborate plastic wrapping from one of the Patenotte meat platters and made himself a ham and cheese sandwich. Gerry began to strip the plastic off the other.

"Hey, that's not fair," Joel protested. "We've already got one open."

"He doesn't eat ham and cheese, Joel," I shot back. "The other one has turkey."

It was as if there wasn't much holding us together, and the slightest provocation could set us to squabbling like duplex children. From the dining room, I could see Mama's profile, and I had a vision from thirty years before: It is three-thirty any weekday afternoon, and she's watching *The Edge of Night*, shutting us out, trying to get a half hour of peace. We are sitting at the dining room table, doing homework and scrapping.

No, I didn't know how to comfort Mama; I only knew the stifling effect the duplex was having on me, an old feeling that had gotten more vivid with my sisters' arrival. I sensed my brother's absence like a column of dead air, but no one mentioned him, either. Then I piled my plate high as Christmas with my favorite, cubbie. By eight-thirty, we'd all collapsed into our assigned beds.

Thirteen

I slept even worse that night in the Toy Room than I had the night before. At dawn, with Gerry resting peacefully beside me, I watched the sunlight seeping through the sides of the window shades. I was remembering a photo taken on another sparkling day, this one in late October. Daddy is standing outside on the sidewalk under the giant American flag he'd hung from the front porch. He's dressed in cutoff shorts and a baseball cap, ready to play with Erin, who is sitting next to him on her tricycle. She has a wide grin that reveals her pointed baby teeth, and she's holding a bouquet of orange and black balloons.

The photograph, taken exactly one year after we'd buried Sol, had been reprinted on the front page of the *Yazoo Herald*. Daddy had preserved it in clear plastic, thumbtacking it to the living room wall. "I love my granddaddy very much," Erin is quoted in the caption. Behind her, beyond the shadowed trunk of the Sol Boy sycamore tree, is Sol's white, battered pickup, parked on Calhoun Avenue, as if he were present on the anniversary of his burial. But behind this ordinary moment or any moment of snatched happiness remained the fact that he was gone.

I could hear the traffic noises growing louder on Calhoun as people headed off to their jobs this Monday morning. Then

Gerry stirred and warned, "There'll be a crush in the Pink Bathroom. You'd better get up." I heard him shuffle into the White Bathroom, but anxious as I was to get the day over with, I stayed in bed awhile longer.

When I finally got up, I found Mama and Debbie already dressed and waiting in the living room. My sister looked especially dour. She'd put on a brown suit with an A-line skirt and tailored jacket, a conservative contrast to her purple hair. Mama wore a navy blazer and dark brown skirt. She'd applied her standard beige foundation and powder, without blush or eye shadow, and the makeup only drew attention to the creases around her mouth. I knew she must be tired. Yet she tapped her matte black pumps on the floor as she rocked in the La-Z-Boy.

I asked them how they'd slept.

Debbie replied, "Awfully. Even sleeping in spare hospital beds couldn't have prepared me for a night on this couch with Mama."

Mama's only response was to make a little noise, an exhalation that sounded like "Huh," which she did without taking her eyes from the TV.

Then Joel strolled into the living room. At least he appeared rested. After Lisa and Elizabeth finished in the Pink Bathroom, I washed and put on the gray pantsuit that I'd packed, along with a navy cashmere sweater. Reaching up to raise the window shade an inch, I could just see the top of Grandma's pecan trees half a block away, and I thought of her lying in bed in the nursing home.

Back in the living room, everybody just sat staring at the television, waiting for Mama to turn it off, signaling that it was time to go. Then I heard footsteps outside, followed by a rap at the door.

I looked over at Mama. As if on cue, she clicked off the TV.

"Are you expecting someone?" I asked.

"Just git it," she said.

I peered out to see Cindy and Erin standing on the porch. When I opened the door, my sister-in-law moved forward to kiss me on the cheek, and we retreated inside from the cold. Cindy waved at Erin, trying to coax her in, but she shook her head.

"I'm goin' to sit in my swing," she declared, her red and blue checked skirt swishing as she bounded down the steps.

Cindy walked over to Mama and extended her hand. I figured that Mama must have asked them to come so we could all drive to the funeral home together, but now that they were here, Mama still didn't seem disposed to leave. Debbie and Lisa made space for Cindy on the couch, and as she slipped between them, I saw how thin she'd become. She looked wasted, much older than her thirty years.

They had married when Sol was twenty-six and Cindy just nineteen. Since his death, I'd often felt tongue-tied in her presence, in awe of what she'd coped with, young widowhood and finding a way to raise a toddler alone. She'd gotten the part-time job making deliveries for Murphy's to supplement their Social Security and, when she was finally able to sell Sol's trailer, had scraped together enough money to buy the slab house next door to her parents.

I checked my watch: ten-forty-five. The visitation was at eleven. "Mama, shouldn't we go?"

"Naw, naw, naw, I want Cindy to tell y'all somethin' right now, because later on they'll be a lot of folks in the house," she said.

"It's about Erin," Cindy started.

I sat down on the arm of the couch. But before Cindy could say anything else, Erin began to scream. I pushed the pink curtains aside and lifted the window shade, expecting to see her sprawled on the ground, but she was winding herself around and around in her swing, brown hair flying, dragging her dress shoes in the dirt. At eight, her legs were now too long for the swing, which Daddy had hung from a low branch of the Sol Boy sycamore tree.

I dropped the shade. "What's the matter with her?"

Not since Sol's funeral had I seen Cindy so upset. "First it was just little things," she said. "Erin had some trouble concentratin', and her grades suffered. But Sol and me, we weren't never good students like y'all."

She took out a cigarette, and as she lit it I noticed that her hands were red and peeling. "I've been over to Jackson a few times to take her to see some doctors. They all say somethin' different. One said she might have ADD—you know, attention deficit disorder. He started givin' her Ritalin, but I don't think it helped her none. Listen to her. Now somethin' else seems to be happenin'. They think she might be havin' little seizures. She goes blank and stares into space." Then Cindy turned and looked at Debbie. "What do you think?"

Now I knew why Mama had invited Cindy to the house, so she might have the benefit of my sister's medical advice. But Debbie only folded her hands in front of her and said, "I don't have the answer for you, except I think you need to find another doctor."

Cindy stabbed out her cigarette in the chipped crystal ashtray that Mama kept on the table for her. Outside, it was quiet. My sister-in-law's words gave me a sense of foreboding that

I hadn't felt since I'd heard the news of Sol's diagnosis with leukemia. We sat a few minutes longer, then I said, "Let's go." It was just eleven o'clock.

Mama stopped on the sidewalk. "I won't git in no funeral procession in no car of your daddy's. Far as I'm concerned, we ain't got no car fit to be seen in."

I looked at the '85 Oldsmobile, Sol's '81 GMC pickup, the '60 Pontiac, the '63 Chevy, and the '67 Buick parked on the grass in the front yard. Daddy had hung onto these junky cars even though none but the Olds and the pickup ran reliably. "Creatin' classics," he'd called it, waiting for the day when these wrecks would be old enough to qualify for the coveted "antique" tag.

We crammed into the two rental cars to attend his funeral. Gerry drove the Prizm with Cindy, Erin, Mama, and me, and Debbie the Taurus with Lisa, Joel, and Elizabeth. We set off down Calhoun, past modest frame houses, the black projects, and the run-down laundromat where Mama took her clothes to dry in winter. When we rode by Martha Coker, I had another fleeting image of Grandma, by now likely propped in her wheelchair near the nurses' station.

Gerry parked in the nearly empty lot across the street from the funeral home, and Lisa and I walked in together. A group of men with faces gnarled as tree roots were gathered to one side of the foyer, and several ambled forward to greet Mama. I heard her calling them by their names, Buddy George and Beanie and Vertie Lee, and figured they must be some of her many cousins from Midway. My sisters stood with Mama, but Gerry and I continued down the narrow hallway to Funeral Parlor A, following the black sign with the white press-on letters.

Gerry went in, but I stopped at the entrance to the windowless room and peered inside. Against the far wall, a tulip-shaped torchiere glowed soft orange; next to it was the casket, the soft gray one that Mama had picked out yesterday, with the spray of flowers I'd ordered mounded below the opening. A long sofa had been positioned against the left wall, with several rows of metal folding chairs set up opposite. But only a handful of people milled about, relatives from both sides of the family. Mama's wore work clothes, boots, and jeans; Daddy's, dusted-off suits. There were forgotten relatives, like his first cousin Powell, who had come all the way from Louisiana. For years, owing to the vagaries of local pronunciation, I'd thought his name was "Pal." I also saw Daddy's brother, Moe, and his sister, Pauline.

Then Pauline stepped forward and took my hand between hers. She spoke in a loud, deep voice, so like Daddy's. "How're you doin'? I know this must be a difficult time for y'all." But I wasn't ready for my aunt to draw me into that room yet.

Brother was leaning against the wall, and we hugged hello. As onetime manager of the Rose Oil station, he had wrinkled up hard from a lifetime of working in the sun. His face and the back of his neck were covered with intricate creases tracing the letter *X* in his gray skin. When Mama, flanked by my sisters, finally caught up to us, he gruffly called out, "Suster," her family nickname. She patted his hand, then went inside Parlor A and stood beside the coffin, head bowed and shoulders straight. As she greeted those who came forward to pay their respects, she wore a public look on her face that was unfamiliar to me.

I saw Erin enter with Cindy and heard her ask, "Where is it?" She followed her mother to the casket, took a quick look, and then retreated, clinging to Cindy and crying quiet, grownup tears. Then Great-Uncle Sam was by my side, dear Uncle Sam, the last surviving of Grendaddy's brothers, so gentle in the same way that Grendaddy had been. He reminded me of Grendaddy, with his round face and hooked nose, with his dark eyes and sallow complexion. I could smell his Old Spice, and it, too, reminded me of my grandfather and of the grocery store, the dusty shelves of aftershaves and shampoos and hair tonics.

"How are you, Uncle Sam?" I asked. He had to be in his eighties. Since he'd moved to Jackson to be near his children, he didn't often get to Yazoo City.

"I'm fine," he said. "How are you?" He spoke with a slight accent, so familiar and yet so foreign, and again I thought of Grendaddy.

"Did you see your daddy yet?"

I shook my head.

"Let's go up together."

Sam guided me by the elbow. At Sol's visitation, I'd stood in this room for three days, greeting his friends, talking, even laughing at times. It had seemed like a macabre cocktail party, with his coffin pushed up against that same wall. He had looked not at all like my brother but like a piece of stone, his features chiseled in pain. Buster and his mortician's skill hadn't been able to help Sol. And Daddy? How would death have treated him?

We made our way past the knots of people until Sam and I finally reached the edge of the casket. All I had to do was look down, but instead I scrutinized the gladiolas arranged on slender metal legs in the corner of the room. But Sam was studying Daddy. Then he chuckled, "If anybody would go to heaven, it would be your daddy, because he was a saint."

I stared at my great-uncle. The last thing, the very last thing that came to mind when I thought of Daddy was a saint. Sam was nodding toward the casket. *Look,* he seemed to be saying. And then I turned toward my father. Daddy seemed almost himself, only smaller, the once-tight-fitting gray suit draped generously on his shoulders.

For the rest of the visitation I stood next to the coffin, staring down at him, my uncle by my side. I wanted so badly to ask Sam to explain his comment. What did he know that I didn't? But Buster was whispering to Mama that it was time to leave for St. Mary's. I kissed Sam on the cheek, felt his short stubble, again aftershave and memory intermingling.

"I want to talk to you after the funeral," I said, and he bobbed his large head enthusiastically.

We filed out the back door of Stricklin-King, down a long red carpet, past yet more stands of gladiolas, and got into our idling rental cars, which the staff had moved to the head of the funeral procession. Buster motioned to Gerry, who drove us slowly around the corner of the building, where the polished hearse waited. We followed Daddy's coffin through a black neighborhood of run-down houses, over the railroad tracks to Canal Street, past the Confederate Monument and Main Street School, to St. Mary's. The police had closed off part of the street so the cortege could double-park.

Car doors slammed softly, low voices spoke brief remarks. We walked at a slow pace up the concrete steps, which had always been St. Mary's gathering place. The steps, their rounded treads, even the cracks, evoked more memory. Here Mama and Daddy had posed after their wedding ceremony. These steps had also seen Daddy's baptismal and Confirmation days. I glanced back to see the pallbearers unhurriedly unloading the coffin, the smooth steel shining in the bright sunshiny day.

St. Mary's was jammed with mourners. As we made our way down the long aisle, I dug my hands into my pantsuit pockets. Instead of stopping in our customary place, right aisle, eighth pew, Mama turned into a seat on the left, nearer to the front.

The pallbearers, faces red, shoulders straining beneath cheap suits, came bearing their heavy burden and placed it carefully before the altar. The flowers that I'd ordered were once more laid on top, but now the coffin remained closed.

Then the priest began to recite the familiar ritual of the Mass and to eulogize Daddy. Like many of St. Mary's recent pastors, this one was Irish. At first I tried to listen, but my mind drifted on his brogue. Again I thought of Sol. Like my sisters and me, he was a lapsed Catholic, though he'd returned to the church on his deathbed. During his eulogy, this same priest had used the metaphor of the prodigal son, but it had seemed a castigation of my brother's life rather than a celebration of his return to faith. Now I heard the priest praising Daddy, saying he'd been a good Catholic all his days. To the priest, Daddy had been a faithful servant and to Uncle Sam, a saint. I'd known my father as a man who, yes, attended Mass every Sunday, and during certain times of his life, every day; a man so devout he went on religious retreats. But I'd also known him as a bigot, a bully, a force to rebel against, somebody I'd organized my life against. My sisters, I suspected, felt the same. To my brother, Daddy had been a man too odd to serve as a role model, a southern male who'd never hunted anything but bargains. To Mama, he'd been a husband of forty-four years, but I noticed she wasn't crying at his funeral.

The priest finally finished his eulogy. We were supposed to stand, kneel, sit, and stand again, but I could hardly summon the energy. Then it was over, Daddy's funeral Mass, the last Mass he'd ever attend.

We filed out past the blur of mourners, and I walked slowly, following Mama, avoiding the eyes. But as I passed the last pew, I saw Johnny. He'd come back to Mississippi after college and gotten a job in a photography studio in Jackson. Though we'd kept in touch through letters and phone calls, I hadn't seen him much since we'd both left. Yet he'd been at Sol's funeral, and now Daddy's. Gerry continued out to the car, but I stopped and took my old friend's hand. Johnny's eyes and long, straight hair had once been nearly the same light brown color, but now his hair was marked with gray. His face still looked young, thin and smooth, so that he seemed out of synch with himself.

"Come back to the house after the cemetery," I whispered.

The funeral procession made its way to Glenwood. Through the branches of the cedars of Lebanon, the winter sun cast long yellow shadows, its halfhearted heat dissipating despite the early hour. We gathered at the grave site, beneath the tan Stricklin-King tent, but Mama stayed off by herself. The crowd had thinned, but I located Uncle Sam, then Johnny, standing next to an arrangement of red gladiolas. Once more the priest prayed, and I hoped this time he would be brief. I glanced off into the nearby woods, past the curtain of trees and up the hill, and heard the echo of a rifle, from the day we buried Sol. Some crazy friend of his had hidden in the thicket to send him off with a proper salute, and the retort had ricocheted through the hills, sharp, startling in the way it broke the silent air.

Then they lowered Daddy into the ground. I wanted to throw a fist of dirt on his coffin, a final knock, but instead I buried Daddy without a good-bye, and without forgiving him.

Fourteen

There's that moment after a funeral when nobody knows what to do. When the service was over, the mourners milled awkwardly, then drifted back to their cars. Only the family remained under the tent, lingering at the foot of Daddy's grave, with the heavy Mississippi earth heaped close at hand. Then my sisters walked away, and Gerry and I stayed behind with Mama. In the navy shadow of a cedar tree, I saw two black gravediggers, their dirt-encrusted shovels, so I took Mama by the arm and guided her to the car. We had one more ritual to go through, the gathering back at the house.

People had already started arriving by the time we got there, huddling in their parked cars against the increasing afternoon cold. Gerry pulled up in the yard, and we slowly made our way onto the front porch. We waited behind Mama while she rested the screen door against her side, opened her shiny black purse, and began searching through its contents. Out of the corner of my eye, I watched as my cousins Renadale and Linda stood next to the curb, staring at us with blond heads cocked, not knowing whether to advance. They had been raised in a modest frame house on a fifty-acre farm in Holmes County, where cotton grew in dusty rows right up to the screenless windows, but as soon as they could, they'd moved to double-wides. I knew my cousins couldn't understand the dilapidated duplex, the derelict cars in the yard, the broken-down chairs and tables and appliances on the front porch.

Then Mama exhaled, "Huh." She raked increasingly panicked fingers through her pocketbook, through half-spent lipsticks and crumpled tissues and the little clear pouches containing her plastic rain bonnet and crystal rosary. For the first time that day, Mama lost her good carriage, head and shoulders sinking. She dangled the disappointing bag. Daddy had always been the one with the key, and we were locked out.

"Mama, how can I help?" I knew she was torn between not wanting to let anybody into the awful house and not being able to. "What if I cut a screen?" As I'd lain in bed all those sleepless summer nights of childhood, I'd fantasized how easy this would be for an intruder. Now I imagined pulling the rusted wire away from the window frame, lifting the heavy wooden sash, and hoisting myself into my old bedroom.

"Naw, naw, naw. All them cords is broken. You couldn't git no window to stay up long enough to crawl through."

Behind me, I heard Lisa's low giggle, her typical reaction to any predicament. I turned and saw Joel and Elizabeth standing impatiently by her side, and Renadale and Linda picking their way through the yard.

Mama snapped her purse closed and sputtered, "The *ay-ennnn*, the *ay-ennnn*, look under the *ay-ennnn*."

"Grandmother, what's an *ay-ennnn*?" Elizabeth asked in her high girl's voice. Having lived in Mississippi for less than a year, she wasn't yet used to southern accents, much less to Mama's hill-country, stroke-affected speech.

Even I didn't know what she meant. As I watched the approaching cousins, I repeated my niece's question. "Yeah, Mama, what's an *ay-ennnn*?"

She shifted her weight from one leg to the other. "It's just an *ay-ennnn,* Treesa. Go look under it!" Then she pinched my forearm through my gray suit.

I rubbed my arm and howled, "Don't do that!" She'd learned this motivational technique from Grandma Hood, who had pinched sometimes to show affection and sometimes to castigate, but it was never clear which.

Mama stared at me. I hissed, "Where exactly is this *ay-ennnn?*"

Then Debbie stepped forward to take control, her typical reaction to any predicament. "I'm just going to break the damn door down!"

"Naw, naw, naw. Y'all listen to me." I could see Mama trying to collect her words, marshaling them forward. Finally she spit out: "The Little House. The key is under the *ay-ennnn* of the Little House!"

I bounded down the front steps toward the backyard. "I've got it!" I called over my shoulder. On the termite-eaten door of the red shack where he kept his overflow junk, Daddy had hung a wooden plaque, a crest emblazoned with the family's initial, a big, black *N*. Underneath he'd hidden a spare key. I grabbed it and ran back to the crowd gathered on the porch.

"Home again, home again, jiggedy-jig!" I exclaimed, presenting Mama the key.

"Behave," Mama said. She inserted the key into the wobbly doorknob. Debbie was right—with a good shove, we could have pushed our way past.

Mama walked over to the heater in the corner of the living room, bent down, and struck a match on the grate. Then she planted herself there, her back hunched like a question mark, while my sisters and I squeezed next to her. As the visitors filed in, stiff with cold and awkwardness, I surveyed them warily. How ironic that Daddy had wanted to keep people away but his death had brought them together under our roof. And there were even more Hoods than Nicholases: in addition to Linda and Renadale, Linda's husband, Alan; their brother, Zack, and sister, Ruth; Willie Belle and Brother and their two sons, Danny and Lee; Mama's sister, Ada Belle. Only Pauline and Moe were there from Daddy's family. I looked for Uncle Sam to ask him about his baffling comment in the funeral home, but even he hadn't come.

Renadale and Linda took charge and with practiced motions unloaded the heavy casseroles and sagging meat platters from the refrigerator. Soon a cacophony of smells filled the duplex as my cousins ferried the funeral food to the table, stripping off the tin foil and folding it into neat squares. The crowd snaked from the dining room to the living room and curled back in front of Mama's La-Z-Boy. Only the Nicholases were taking the Arab dishes: On Aunt Pauline's plate, a wedge of fried cubbie rested next to a dollop of bright-yellow potato salad. A few people sat at the dining room table; some perched on the grimy couches, balancing plates on knees. Mama still hugged the fire, though Brother had brought her a café chair from the dining room.

As I watched her, I started to worry—about her ability to take care of herself, about her safety living alone. My sisters would be leaving in two days, Gerry and I four days after that. Who would show her how to shop for food? Who would teach her how to write a check? Who would help her manage the little money she'd have coming in from Social Security? True, she lived next door to Aunt Pauline and across the street from Uncle Moe, but she'd never been close to Daddy's siblings.

Then I had an idea, something I could do for Mama right away. Alan, Linda's husband, was a carpenter. I walked over to the corduroy couch where he was eating a piece of the girdle-buster that his wife had dropped off yesterday.

"Do you happen to have your tools with you?" I asked.

"Why, yes," he drawled. "What do you need?"

"Would you mind putting a lock, a really sturdy lock, on Mama's front door? I mean, right now?"

"I might could," he answered, "but I don't have a lock with me. You'd have to buy one first."

My cousin Danny, who was sitting next to him, spoke up. "I'll go down to Gilbert's for you," he volunteered.

A half hour later, the buzz of Alan's electric drill was filling the living room and sawdust was accumulating on the floor, but nobody paid the proceedings any mind. A short time later, I was admiring the neat brass orb just above the old doorknob.

I bounced over to Mama, who still sat next to the heater. "I got you a deadbolt," I said.

"A what?"

"A deadbolt."

"What for?"

"To keep you safe," I explained.

"But I don't need no deadbolt."

Before I could answer her, someone pounded hard on my arm. It was the Irish priest. I looked down at his beaming Leprechaun face, his milky complexion. He wore a navy beret over thinning gray hair and stood gesticulating with little hands.

"What side of the family are you?" he shouted up at me, hitting me even harder with his fist.

"I'm a Nicholas!" I answered. "And stop hitting me!"

He turned to Mama to offer his condolences. When he moved away, she whispered to me, "He ain't got all his chairs pulled up to the table." I heard him working the room, repeating his question to Debbie, and saw my sister stare at him with big, hard eyes. I noted he hadn't dared hit her.

Then Mama stood up to introduce me to Charlene. "She

started cuttin' our grass last summer," Mama explained, "when your daddy got to havin' problems with his legs."

Charlene had a pasty complexion and white hair and wore blue polyester pants and a white shirt with red, purple, and blue flowers.

"Like my Wally World blouse?" she asked. "I'm so pale, if I don't wear some color, I wind up lookin' like a can of Crisco."

I nodded, unsure how to respond.

"I heard a lot 'bout you, baby girl," Charlene went on. She patted my hand with her plump palm.

"So you cut my parents' grass," I said.

"Yes, ma'am, this lawn and 'bout six more, and I run errands for half of Yazoo's widows. And I have leukemia," Charlene informed me. Mama appeared to be listening to Charlene with more interest than she had to the priest.

"Really," I commented.

"Yes, ma'am, but don't stop me none." I wondered what kind of leukemia Charlene could possibly have. When Sol had been sick with the disease, he'd spent the last months of his life lying on the couch in his trailer, too exhausted even to watch television.

"In remission. Been in remission now for nearly a year." She continued, "You remind me of my daughter-in-law, Erma. She's big, too. Bigger around than you, but not as tall. Don't know Erma, do you?"

"Nome," I said, trying to ease past her.

But she took my hand and held it. "Thought not. Erma's got her a problem with the pituitary. That's like the electric switch in the house, the one that controls all them other switches. Hers is messed up." Then Charlene announced in a voice loud enough for everybody to hear, "And that's how she comes to weigh 450 pounds!"

"Weigh what?" I blurted out.

She repeated the incredible statistic, and a few more heads turned. "And Erma's got her a problem with her sugar, too. Way, way up. Doctor said Erma's sugar was over 300. Miz Florence, yours ain't that bad, now is it?"

Mama shook her head emphatically.

"Didn't want to go to the doctor, but Daryl—that's my son—he made her go. He's overweight, too, but not as heavy as Erma. Nobody's heavy as Erma. You say you don't know her?"

"Nome, I don't." Charlene was no small woman herself, and she still held my hand.

"If you'd of met her, you'd of remembered her. When that girl got back from the doctor t'other afternoon, she sure got herself a problem." Charlene shook her head. "Well, sir," she began, though there was no man in our circle, "Erma is so tired when she gets back from the doctor, she wants to lie in the bed. She has two nighties, a shorty and a longy. She puts on the shorty and goes to lie down. But she's so tired she can't get herself up on the bed. So she puts a little step stool next to it and decides to walk up backwards and drop herself down. She and Daryl, they have a queen. Well, sir, she missed. Fell right slap dab on the floor, that girl did, and couldn't get up.

"Daryl called the preacher, and he come on over. Preacher and his wife. But they couldn't do nothin'. He suggested they call the Volunteer Fire Department, but they wouldn't come, Erma 'n 'em was so far out in the country. But they did say to Daryl, 'Whatever you do, don't pull her up by the arms. If you was to pull her up by her arms,' they said, 'it might pull 'em right out of the sockets.' They did say that much.

"Daryl and the preacher even called the star of the high school football team to come over, thinkin' he'd be strong enough to get Erma up, but he wasn't no help, neither. Finally,

’long’bout two A.M., Daryl persuaded some EMS volunteers to come to the house with a big ole board, and they rolled Erma on it, and got her sittin’ up in bed. Two A.M., imagine that, all those hours that girl spent on the floor.

“You sure do remind me of Erma,” Charlene concluded. “But you don’t have no problem with your pituitary. That’s the cause of it, the pi-tu-it-tary. That girl, she eats just like a bird, I swear she does.”

Finally, I was able to wrench my hand away. But before I could reach the door, Aunt Pauline blocked me in front of the television. Though we’d hardly spoken in years, now she seemed anxious to talk.

“Treesa, it’s about Mother,” she said, rolling her dark eyes.

I stared at her. *Mother?*

“We’ve run out of money for Mother.”

I realized she was talking about Grandma, but I’d never heard her called *Mother* before.

“Money for the nursin’ home,” she continued. “I was goin’ to talk to your daddy. But now . . . What are we goin’ to do?”

I tried to maneuver around her.

“What can we do?” she went on. “Borrow money? Sell somethin’? We ain’t got nothin’ we can sell.” She looked away from me as she said, “Except her house.”

Then I realized: My aunt had already decided that this was the thing we had to do. But sell Grandma’s house? The place she loved most and longed to return to? The place we all loved most?

“Your daddy wouldn’t ever let us sell. But now . . .” Her voice trailed off again, this time because I had left.

I pushed through the visitors, who were gesturing and laughing in the packed living room. I had to get away—from them and from the decrepit duplex.

From the doorway, I glanced back and saw Mama looking at me questioningly. I knew she was right: A deadbolt wasn't what she needed. I was just being selfish. What I'd wanted was a way to make my job easier, the job of leaving her again.

I slipped past Alan, who was sweeping up the last bits of sawdust. After the stifling living room, the cold air felt like a reprieve. I closed the door behind me.

Then I saw Johnny standing on the sidewalk. "Let's go riding," I said, taking his hand. "Just like we used to." I was practically running.

Johnny drove downtown and at the end of Main Street steered his Nissan Stanza up a steep rise. I recognized Bell Road, one of the loveliest and oldest in the county, the original way to Vicksburg. Long ago, bells had been placed along the narrow, winding path so that wagon drivers could signal one another and avoid backing up their mules. Over time, the roadbed had sunk below the loess walls, bluffs of fine, dry earth deposited by the wind, and leafless trees rose far above us. Yet in places the walls receded, and I could glimpse the Delta and the Yazoo River winding through barren fields. After so many absent years, I felt oddly comforted to see this again. How perceptive of Johnny to have brought me here, I thought, on the day of Daddy's funeral.

"In the spring," he was saying, "these walls are full of wild white hydrangeas."

"It's hard now to imagine hydrangeas in bloom," I said.

He looked over at me. "Spring comes early here. Don't you remember? By February, the daffodils and violets are out." He seemed about to add something but stopped.

We passed a few houses as we drove. One was beautiful, white and rambling, partly hidden behind the loess wall, but most were trailers and shacks, surrounded by abandoned cars, tractors, and rusty farm implements. Neither of us said anything. Talking had always come easily to us, but we'd also spent many hours in the quiet of each other's company. We continued a short way when Johnny abruptly braked.

Before us was a trail only wide enough to walk, bordered on either side with tree-filled gullies so deep you couldn't see the bottom. Johnny put the car in reverse, taking care not to slip a wheel into the ravine. When another car appeared, he maneuvered close to the bank to let it pass. As the driver crept by, he shot us a suspicious look, and I was reminded of how much like an outsider I could feel here.

Soon we were back on Main Street, where Johnny parked in the first block, near Miron's Jewelry. Though it was midafternoon on a workday, there were few people about. We got out to walk, peering into the empty storefronts—what had been Danrie's Restaurant, Ellis's Department Store, and Saxton's Hardware, which still had its name emblazoned on the second floor in giant cursive letters. Across Jefferson Street, a Christian bookshop occupied what used to be Ingram's Shoe Store, but I could make out the back-to-back chairs where Mr. Ingram had let us try on the Bass Weejuns he knew we could never afford. A few paces beyond, I looked for Kuhn's Five-and-Dime, where I'd pored through bins of penny-cheap merchandise with Grandma, but this too existed only as memory, of a time when a dime-store purchase and my grandmother's company seemed all I needed.

We continued down the curving street toward the Black and White Store. Though the coin-operated scale was gone from the checked tile entry, the pink neon sign was lit overhead; at least something remained from when Johnny and I were growing up here. We turned back toward the car, passing more vacant buildings, but I couldn't remember what they had been. I asked Johnny if he could recall, but he shook his head. I leaned against the street clock in front of Anderson's Jewelry.

Johnny touched my arm with his fingertips. "Are you okay?"

"Everything has changed," I said. "If Daddy were here, he'd be able to tell us what shops were where." Daddy had held onto his vivid and closely guarded memories, just as he'd held onto everything else he'd collected in his life. Now I'd lost what he'd known, and I was surprised that it seemed to matter so much.

We climbed back into the car. Turning west on Broadway, we passed the block that had housed the Nicholas family stores. The neon sign for Uncle Sam's Bon Ton Café hung rusted and forlorn above the abandoned restaurant. Grendaddy's Nicholas Cash Gro. had become a package liquor store, the expansive plate glass replaced with stingy new Plexiglas windows and steel bars. Only Uncle Fred and Aunt Natalie's Army-Navy remained, its dirty windows stacked with overalls and rubber boots and orange hunting caps. Momentarily, I saw these dilapidated structures as a stranger might, until once again they exerted the sad, sweet power of memory.

We reached the railroad tracks, passed the Woo Hor Grocery and Harris's hot tamale stand, then came to the black projects. I stared into the unwavering highway toward the Delta. Finally we came to the levee, and Johnny pulled the car off the road.

He turned to me and asked, "You're not going back, are you?"

Johnny was one of those people who could bring things into focus with just a few words. I remembered that after his father died, he had stayed to help his mother. And I thought of my own mother, in that house, and couldn't imagine her there alone. For so many years, the duplex had been too small for all of us;

now it seemed too big for her to manage by herself. I thought of Grandma in Martha Coker, reduced to living in housecoats and a wheelchair, in danger of losing her beloved bungalow. And I thought of Erin screaming in her swing, suffering from some as-yet-unknown disorder. Finally, I thought of Daddy in the cemetery. By now, the black gravediggers would have finished their task, and I could picture the raw earth mounded over his grave. I knew that in the spring, the Bermuda grass would grow quickly, until one day it met in the middle; I knew, because I'd seen it happen that way with Sol.

Still, I wanted to return to New York, where I could forget all this. But aside from Gerry, what was there for me except fourteen-hour workdays? It wouldn't be like when I was growing up here, I told myself. I had a plane ticket and could leave anytime I wanted.

Then Johnny repeated, "You're not going back, are you?"

I shook my head, and he smiled.

We sat watching the winter sky. Delicate strands of clouds patterned the eggshell blue, yet the lowering sun threw startling light, casting shadows through the bare trees and onto the stubbled fields. We continued in silence, and the shadows themselves began to remind me of what I thought I had forgotten.

Fifteen

When I arrived back at the house, the visitors had already departed. Mama was in her La-Z-Boy, still dressed in her funeral outfit, clutching one of Erin's baby dolls, a blond imp in a pink dress. My sisters, Gerry, and Joel had changed into jeans and were sprawled on the two couches, while Elizabeth sat on the floor absorbed in a game of solitaire. The television blared a commercial for Herrin-Gear Chevrolet.

Lisa asked after Johnny.

"He's okay," I answered a little guiltily. Gerry inched over to make room for me on the corduroy couch. "What have you been doing?" I asked Mama.

"What we been doin'? Just sittin'. What else is there to do around here?"

For two days we'd planned, arrived, arranged. We'd committed Daddy to the ground. We'd even hosted, in our embarrassed way, the after-the-funeral gathering. But we'd neither wept nor lighted candles in his memory. Sol had taught me that to mourn was to remember and to remember was to forget. After we'd buried Sol, I'd tried putting him out of my mind, but he'd kept coming back on the monthly anniversary of his death. Only when I was worn down by my attempt to stop thinking about him did I allow myself to remember, and with remembrance came, if not forgetting, at least some measure of acceptance. But on the night we buried Daddy, I went to bed without speaking of him. We all did.

Daddy spent his first night in Glenwood under the light of a fat, milky moon. He used to tell me whenever we spoke on the telephone, "Same moon shines on me, shines on you, Teresa." That night, while Gerry slept beside me, I lay awake watching the moonlight cast its shadows in the Toy Room. When sleep finally did come, dreams came, too, all the day's feelings bleeding together on mental celluloid. I am coming home by myself for a visit. Daddy has driven to the airport to get me, but Mama isn't with him. I feel uneasy about her absence, but I'm afraid to ask Daddy where she is. I take her place beside him in the Oldsmobile. The cloth lining of the car's roof, which long ago came undone, drapes around our heads like a peaked cap of brown velour. Daddy doesn't jabber as usual, and I feel a repulsive intimacy between us. He meanders through Jackson's back streets, then just outside the city limits slows down even more on a stretch of road sprinkled with black night joints, the Club Papa Doo and the New Moonlight Lounge. Cars whiz by us as we poke along toward Highway 49. Daddy peers out his window at a cemetery with flat headstones and a treeless landscape. He says, "We have it much better in Glenwood than they do over here." To punctuate his satisfaction, he turns to stare at me.

I woke up, blinking back his big vivid face, then stumbled out of the cold bedroom into the overheated living room. Gerry, Joel, and Elizabeth were loafing on the couches in their pajamas, watching the *Today* show. But Debbie, Lisa, and Mama were clustered in the wobbly café chairs at one end of the dining room table. They were dressed, with even Mama wearing blue jeans, which she put on whenever she cleaned. The three of them were reading from a mountain of papers on the pink cotton tablecloth.

I claimed the oak desk chair at Daddy's end of the table, sitting gingerly so its unpredictable metal rollers didn't scoot out from under me. I'd never understood why he'd insisted on keeping an office chair in the dining room. As in the other rooms, the wallpaper was peeled to the lath and the ceiling was spotted with black stains from the leaky roof. In the corner behind the gas heater, a faded, octopus-shaped blotch defaced the wall, where one summer evening thirty years ago, a carton of chocolate milk had flown out of my hand.

When I looked more closely at the mountain of papers, I realized that it was Daddy's mail, which my sisters had sorted for further examination. Most of the envelopes were business size, but there were larger ones, too, along with other things he'd saved—sheaves of church bulletins from St. Mary's, piles of yellowed *Yazoo Heralds,* stacks of previous years' income tax returns. Mama was poring over a letter using Daddy's handheld magnifying glass, which made her black eyes appear enormous.

"What are you looking for?" I asked.

Without glancing up she answered, "What we lookin' for?"

I was familiar with the pattern. I'd ask Mama a question, and she'd repeat it; I'd repeat the question, and only then would she respond. It was something she'd started doing after the stroke to give herself more time to think of a reply. So I tried my question again, but this time Mama didn't answer at all.

Lisa laughed, "We're looking for Daddy's fortune."

"No, seriously," I said.

"We're going through his old mail," Debbie explained, slicing envelope tops with a metal letter opener. "Mama says Daddy had a bank account, and we have to find the checkbook or a statement. We have to show Mama how to write a check. It's nearly the first of the month, and her bills will be coming due."

"Don't know how to write no check," Mama mumbled. "Y'all know, when it comes to money, I stumble around like a blind dog in a meat house."

She'd never paid a bill in her married life. Mama was a financial nonentity, anonymous to banks, utilities, credit card companies, even the post office. She didn't receive mail of her own, and she'd never been in the habit of reading Daddy's. But she insisted that Daddy had a checking account, though she didn't know in which of Yazoo's two banks it might reside. Nor could she say how much money might be in it. She didn't even know how much they'd lived on each month, only that Daddy's Social Security check was "a paltry sum."

Debbie added, "Get some coffee and help."

So the dismantling of Daddy's estate had begun. I shuffled into the kitchen and poured a cup of Maxwell House from the aluminum percolator that Mama kept warming on the stove's pilot light. Then I resumed my position at the table, sipping the lukewarm liquid.

Lisa looked at me wearily. "We haven't come across anything so far." I wasn't surprised. I wouldn't have put it past my father to have paid all his bills in cash, and I didn't expect he'd left Mama with a dime other than the Roosevelts and Mercurys in his coin collection.

"We're going to have to chip in to help Mama," she went on. I knew Lisa was right, but I also knew that Mama would never accept money from us, if she could help it.

"I told y'all, he had a checkin' account." Mama pointed to the breakfront. "He kept ever'thang up yonder."

This cabinet of ugly dark wood contained the family's most important knickknacks, including my favorite, a rusted music box with glass emeralds that played "I Love You Truly." The breakfront also housed Mama's wedding gifts—her patterns of Syracuse china, Imperial Candlewick crystal, and Reed & Barton silver—that she brought out for Christmas dinner. On top of it, only a square wicker basket remained. My sisters had already brought down the rest.

"And he did his figurin' sittin' right there," Mama continued, shaking her finger at me. I shifted in the desk chair, felt its wheels slide dangerously. So that was why Daddy had kept it next to the table. Since he'd retired, the dining room had doubled as his home office.

"He wrote out checks from a big ole leather book. I seen him do it many times." Mama added, "Usually, he whistled," as if this detail would convince us of the truth of her assertion.

"There's no leather checkbook here," Lisa said, rifling through the papers. "No checkbook of any kind. Just junk. Like everything of Daddy's, pure junk." She drew her chair back from the table.

Debbie flicked the top off another envelope. "I have to assume that even Daddy had a checking account. Just keep looking. There has to be a statement." But Lisa drifted off into the living room, where I heard her ordering Elizabeth to take a bath.

I moved out of the unreliable desk chair to her empty seat. Picking up an invoice from Southern Bell, I was startled to find Daddy's slanted signature on the envelope's flap, *S. T. Nicholas Jr.* It read like "St. Nicholas," and again I thought of what Uncle Sam had said. Daddy had also held onto bills from the gas and electric companies, and on each he'd signed his name and printed a date, which I assumed was the day he'd paid it.

Then I pulled a sheaf of papers from a large manila envelope and began to study them. "What's this? Something from AT&T. It's kind of inscrutable. Why would Daddy get mail about stocks?"

"Just do the best you can," Debbie told me, not looking up. "I've got plenty here to keep me busy."

"Y'all stop fussin'," Mama said. She handed Debbie the letter she'd been trying to read. "Here. I can't make heads nor tails of this 'un, neither."

Debbie took the letter from her. "This is from Daddy's cardiologist in Jackson," she said. "He had his pacemaker checked over the phone just three days before he died. It was working fine." She waited for Mama's reaction, but the irony seemed lost on her. Mama just picked up another piece of mail to examine through the looking glass.

Then Debbie turned to me, her voice a little softer. "He got a lot of mail from AT&T. Just ads, I think. Don't bother to open them."

For the rest of the morning, we sorted through the papers. As Debbie predicted, most were offers for credit cards and cable TV, petitions from Catholic Charities, more ads from AT&T. We discovered that Daddy had had a Visa card, though he'd only used it once a year, just enough to keep it active; that he'd bought car and house insurance from Farm Bureau; and although Medicare had paid the majority of my parents' doctor bills, he'd purchased supplemental coverage through Physicians Mutual. His income tax returns showed that when he'd retired from Great-Uncle Dan's car dealership, Daddy's salary had been less than $10,000 a year. Since then, he'd received a monthly Social Security check of $660. Mama had been correct on this point: They'd lived on a paltry sum.

"That's that," I said, heaving the papers into the kitchen garbage pail. We still hadn't come across a bank statement, and now even Debbie was willing to admit that Mama had most likely been wrong about the phantom account.

We broke for dinner when Gerry and Joel and Elizabeth came to the table. I hadn't even changed out of my pajamas. After a meal of leftover funeral food, just when I was thinking of crawling back into bed for a nap, Mama announced, "We're goin' to take a ride downtown, to pay a call to the bank."

Mama put on slim navy slacks, the ill-fitting beige jacket she'd worn when we arranged Daddy's funeral, and pointy black loafers that looked as if they pinched her toes. I knew she'd be disappointed to discover that Daddy had no money in the bank, but I didn't say anything, figuring that while we were downtown we could open a new checking account in her name. I'd take my own checkbook along to help fund it, if she'd let me.

Joel stayed with Elizabeth, and the rest of us filed down the front steps. This time there was no discussion about which of the cars we would take, because right away Mama ordered us into the Oldsmobile. She wanted, she said, to "air it out." Gerry drove, Mama beside him in the front seat, with Debbie, Lisa, and me in the back. Sandwiched between my sisters, I felt the car's cloth lining fall around our heads, just as it had in my dream.

As we approached Grandma's, I saw Aunt Pauline and her daughter in the bed of a pickup, which was parked close to the back porch. The truck's tailgate was down, and they were loading it with cardboard boxes. In the five years Grandma had been in Martha Coker, Daddy had preserved her house as if she would return to it one day. During the winters, he'd gone over to light the heaters to keep the pipes from freezing, and during the summers, he'd mown the grass for as long as his weakening legs allowed. While Daddy was alive, his siblings had humored his obsession to keep the house like a Nicholas family museum, but Pauline was already emptying the contents so she could make good on her promise to put the house up for sale. She was bundled against the cold, and as we drove past, she waved cheerfully with gloved hands.

Gerry rounded Goose Egg Park, and I stared into winter barrenness, the skeletal branches of the big elm, the mottled brown bark of the crape myrtles. We passed the Stop 'n Go, bleak in a different way, with barred windows, fortified metal doors, and a parking lot stained with motor oil. I couldn't bring myself to tell Mama and my sisters about my conversation with my aunt during the funeral reception, so they didn't show any concern on seeing her at Grandma's back door. But I was overwhelmed at the idea of selling the family homestead, the place Grandma loved most, the place we all loved most. What would Pauline say when Grandma pleaded, "Take me home"?

Finally we came to downtown, and Gerry parked at the intersection of Broadway and Main, where Yazoo's two banks faced off against one another—Delta National, a white brick box with a sign that flashed the time and temperature, and the redbrick Bank of Yazoo City, supported by exuberant flying buttresses.

We got out of the Olds and stood beside it. Mama, who seemed to sense my mood, turned to me. "Don't sull up now, Treesa."

She looked from one bank to the other, trying to decide which to enter, then made for Delta National. Banking Yazoo-style still relied on tellers, not machines. Delta National had recently cashed a check that my aunt Willie Belle had written at the grocery store, even though in a fit of absent-mindedness she had signed not her own name but "Mrs. Jitney Jungle." When she asked why the bank had accepted the check, the teller had replied, "Oh, Willie Belle, we knew it was you who wrote it." Daddy had also been well known to the tellers because he'd kept the books for the Yazoo Motor Co. Every day at ten o'clock he would get up from his desk, walk the few blocks to the bank, and deposit Great-Uncle Dan's money. Usually, he'd be whistling. Mama had been right about this detail: Daddy had whistled while he banked.

Mama bypassed the waving tellers and rushed to take a seat outside the vice president's office. "Mama," I whispered when I caught up to her, "since all we're going to do is open a checking account, I don't think we need to see the vice president."

She looked at me and muttered a solitary "Naw."

Then the vice president appeared out of his corner office and extended his large red hand to Mama. "I was so sorry to hear. Everybody loved to see Sol June coming. He sure was a character!"

Mama smiled as he pumped her arm up and down.

"How can I help, Miz Florence?" he asked.

"No need to bother you," I jumped in, "we're just here to open a checking account."

He started toward his office. "One of our people can help you with that, but if I can do anything for y'all, just let me know."

But Mama blurted out, "I'd like to speak to you a little minute, please. Sol June got any money in this here bank?"

I shushed her. "Mama!"

The vice president walked back to where she sat. He smiled, then said in a friendly way, "Why, Miz Florence, your husband was a regular! Surely, y'all knew."

Then Debbie stepped forward. "May we speak to you in private?"

"Of course, come on in," he answered, making a sweeping gesture in the direction of his office. We took seats in front of his mahogany desk, where a brass lamp with a green glass shade pooled yellow light.

"Now," he said, "how can I help y'all?"

Debbie asked, "What kind of account did our father have?"

"And how much?" Lisa put in.

"Let me run the numbers," he said, getting up. "And I'll be right back with y'all."

I looked at Gerry, who raised his eyebrows. "It must be the checking account Mama mentioned," I said. Lisa let out a low giggle, but Mama only crossed her legs, tapping her bottom foot.

When the vice president returned, he was trailing computer paper, the kind with sprockets on the sides. "The accounts are up to date as of this morning, including interest on savings," he said, turning the printouts over to Debbie.

"Savings?" I asked.

Debbie began to read the sheets, then handed them to me. With Gerry looking on, I scanned the pages and passed them to Lisa, who gave them to Mama. "Well," she said. She'd stopped tapping her foot and stared straight ahead.

"These accounts are under my father's name," Lisa said. "Are there any others? Is there one under my mother's name? Or Debbie's, Teresa's, or mine?"

"No, that's all we have." Then he added, "I'm sorry. But what else can I do for y'all? I know this must be a difficult time."

"You've helped us more than you know," Debbie said. We stood to leave—all of us, that is, except Mama.

"Come on," I said, tugging her up by her jacket lapel.

On our way out, the tellers waved at us again. "Y'all come back now," one called.

We lingered in front of Delta National. Lisa began hopping up and down, and the farmers driving by in their dirty pickups turned to stare. "Hot diggedy!" she squealed. "Daddy had money in the bank!"

We stepped off the curb toward the Oldsmobile, but Mama grew roots on the sidewalk. "Naw, naw, naw," she said. "Y'all don't git in that car. We're goin' into this here other bank."

Debbie, her hand already on the door handle, protested. "Why?"

"I'm goin' to ask them, too."

She said this so defiantly that I knew there was no point arguing with her, yet I tried anyway. "Where would he get more money?"

But Mama only replied, "You don't know your daddy, Treesa." Then she ambled across Main Street in her pointy shoes, and we had no choice but to follow her into the Bank of Yazoo City.

Sixteen

A broad-faced, middle-aged man came right over to greet Mama, who didn't say a word; she just nodded and let Debbie do the talking. My sister asked this vice president if we could speak in his office, and after we were seated, if he could advise us about the status of Daddy's accounts. I was convinced we were making fools of ourselves, until he said he would print out the up-to-the-minute balances. After he left, it was my turn to tap my feet.

"Hold them legs still, young'un," Mama told me. "I feel higher 'n cat hairs, and you're shakin' the whole place down." Then she drew a piece of Juicy Fruit out of her pocketbook and began to chew.

"Daddy couldn't have saved a lot more on his salary," I said.

"Treesa, I'll lay you a dollar to a dingbat he had money in this here bank." She turned to Gerry. "You're thinkin' this family don't got all its noodles cooked, ain't you?"

"Not at all," he replied, giving us the benefit of the doubt.

When the vice president returned, he was smiling and waving a piece of paper. "Here are the figures for checking and savings," he announced.

We stared at the total. Finally Mama said, "Well, really."

Debbie asked if Mama had check-writing privileges, something we'd forgotten about at Delta National. But the vice president said no, the accounts were in Daddy's name only.

"That money ain't mine," Mama said flatly.

"Mama, it will be," Debbie answered, not stopping to explain.

We stumbled out of the bank, across Main Street, and into the Oldsmobile. Debbie pulled a notepad and pen from her handbag and started computing. Altogether, she announced, Daddy was worth nearly six figures. Then she returned the pen and pad to the bag and shut the clasp with a *snap*.

"Wow," I said. "Wow."

After that stroke of insight, no one said anything. Gerry drove the car in the gutter, the way Daddy used to, at five miles an hour. We passed the courthouse, St. Mary's rectory, and the First Methodist and Presbyterian churches, staring out the windows as if we'd never seen these places before. We passed the fancy Victorians on Grand Avenue—Dr. Moorhead's, behind its wrought-iron fence; the Clarks', with its wraparound porch; the Ericksons', with its stained-glass windows.

Then I realized something surprising: I wasn't angry that Daddy had hoarded money while he made us live like paupers. I wasn't angry that he'd kept it a secret. What I felt was relief—Mama would be taken care of. And I thought of what Mama had said to me, that I didn't know my daddy. Just where had he gotten all that money, on his salary? Finally I asked, "Mama, what do you think?"

"What do I think?" she repeated. "About what?"

"About everything. Where did he get the money?"

"I don't know," she said, still looking out her window. We were passing King's Daughters Hospital. "Except that he pinched ever' penny he could. He was good at it."

I asked, "Do you think he stole from Great-Uncle Dan?"

She twisted in her seat to face me. "Naw, naw, naw. Your daddy was not a thief. He pinched ever' penny he could rake his hands on, and we did without anythin'."

But I still didn't see how that could account for it. "Why did he have money in two banks?" I asked. "Was he paranoid?"

"Naw," she said. "He was weird."

We rode by the Stop 'n Go, and I noticed that now the afternoon sun was shining golden on top of the decrepit building. "Mama, do you know what it means to be paranoid?"

"What?"

"It means to have delusions."

"Naw. He was just weird."

"Anyway, who cares where he got the money?" Debbie said. "Just be glad for Mama's sake."

Lisa added, "And think what she can do with it."

Gerry pulled the Olds up into the yard, and we got out, slamming the heavy doors. We made our way to the front porch, where Joel and Elizabeth were sitting in the broken-down café chairs. Lisa ran to tell them what we'd discovered.

In less than an hour, everything had changed.

In the living room, Mama took up her seat in the La-Z-Boy. By midafternoon, the temperature had warmed up enough that we could cut the gas heaters off and open the front door. Joel, Elizabeth, and Gerry were fooling around on the porch. Lisa went off by herself to Mama's bedroom, while Debbie stretched out on the corduroy couch. Mama seemed tired, too, and I volunteered to brew a pot of coffee. She nodded, and I went into the kitchen.

A few minutes later I heard a muffled bang, then a yelp coming from Daddy's bedroom. I ran to the entrance—we all did. Mama had slid the mattress off Daddy's box spring, and it was wobbling at the foot of his bed like a giant slice of Jell-O.

"What are you doing?" I shouted, afraid she'd hurt herself. But Mama was standing calmly next to the denuded bed, pointing to a brown canvas pouch on top of the springs.

"Look a there," she said. "There's somethin' in that thang."

I stared at the money bag, then at her. She'd put on a tone of surprise, but she must have known about this. She'd always made up Daddy's bed, and she had a lifelong habit of flipping mattresses so they wouldn't "wear out in one place."

Before anybody could move, I grabbed the bag and whacked it on the floor, but I couldn't dislodge the lock. "Give it to me!" someone yelled. "Let me try!" "I can do it!" Then Joel yanked the bag away from me and ran off to get Mama's pinking shears.

When he couldn't cut through the heavy canvas, we set about ransacking Daddy's room. "The key has to be here someplace," Mama said vaguely. I looked around: The bedroom was a mirror image of the Toy Room, complete with old front door. Daddy's bed took up most of the space, but there were also two tall, broken-down bureaus, a low cedar chest, and a small table. His junk was everywhere: on the tops of the furniture and on the floor, spilling from under the table and bed. Over the ragged, dirty wallpaper, with its pink fleur-de-lis design, he'd plastered monkey calendars, an army of chimps pushing tiny lawn mowers, typing at tiny typewriters, eating at tiny tables, and playing tiny games of golf, each dressed in a tiny outfit appropriate for the activity.

We crowded next to Mama in front of the taller bureau, and she began opening the drawers as fast as the warped wood allowed. An ugly clutter revealed itself: the flotsam and jetsam of machinery and of our childhoods, Daddy's coin collection heaped like pirate's booty. Great-Uncle Sam had said that Daddy was a saint, and there certainly was something otherworldly about this mess in his room.

"How we ever goin' to find that key?" Mama asked.

Then we stationed ourselves in front of the other bureau. In the middle drawer, Daddy had thrown keys of all styles and sizes: skeleton keys, rusted keys, shiny keys, house keys, car keys, keys with labels and keys without. One said *73 Buick,* although we'd never owned this particular vehicle. There were little plastic boxes of keys, dozens and dozens of them neatly stacked in a corner. Inside each one, resting on black foam like a crown on a velvet cushion, lay a lovely gold key commemorating a different antique car.

But one key, with a paper tag, stood out from the rest. On the front was printed an inscrutable *F,* but on the back, punched out in white letters on a blue plastic label, was the word *SACK.* Joel inserted the thin key into the lock and after some jiggling worked the bolt free. Then he unfolded the top and opened the long, deep bag, pulling out a rubber-banded wad four inches high. He counted the money and counted it again. Finally, his pronouncement: two thousand dollars.

Joel extended the stack to Mama. She took it and ran off to her bedroom.

Exhausted, the five of us dragged Daddy's mattress back onto the box spring, and Debbie and I made up the bed again, drawing the white cotton spread over the two pillows. We plopped down on top, with Elizabeth curled up in Lisa's lap, and I leaned against the headboard. I never thought that even Daddy would hide money under his mattress. And Mama said he wasn't paranoid?

When she returned a minute later, I asked her what she'd done with the cash.

"Put it up yonder," she replied.

"You put it in your underwear drawer, didn't you?"

She hung her head. "I got to have some money to live on, Treesa."

Debbie nudged her. "Mama, all the money we found today is yours."

But she wouldn't raise her eyes.

"You know that, don't you?" Debbie asked.

"I don't know nothin'," Mama said.

Then Debbie pulled a folded-up piece of pink paper from her jeans pocket. "I came across this in one of the drawers."

Mama took the paper from her and slowly opened it. From where I sat, I could make out the typewritten message:

Clear 4 times to the left: Stop on 10
Turn to the right past 18 two times and stop on 18
The third time
Turn to the left past 45 one time and stop on 45
The second time
Turn to the right as far as it will go
Open seys me.

I wanted to laugh. *Open seys me.* Daddy had kept a beat-up manual typewriter next to his place at the dining room table, and I imagined him typing out the message with two fingers, cackling over the last line.

Mama let the slip fall onto her lap. "Well," she said. By now I realized that Mama said "well" when she couldn't say anything else. She'd said it a lot today.

Debbie gave her a sideways glance. "What's it to, this combination?"

"Why, to his safe, of course."

"Where's the safe, Mama?" I asked. The day after Daddy's funeral had become a treasure hunt, and it wasn't over yet.

Mama turned toward me. "The Bon Ton," she answered, referring to Great-Uncle Sam's defunct café. She, too, was full of secrets, and you had to ask exactly the right question to pry them out of her.

"Did Daddy have a key to the place?" I asked.

"Well, sure," she drawled. "Your daddy had keys to ever'thang. Look up on that cabinet in the dinin' room in the brown wicker basket."

She'd hardly gotten the words out when the others rushed from the room. Then Mama sighed and left, too.

"Well," I said to Gerry.

"Well," he said to me. "Well, what?"

"Well, nothing." I looked at my watch: four-thirty. I knew that there was no electricity in the Bon Ton and that we had about an hour of daylight left to try to open the safe. I went out into the living room, Gerry following. There was Mama, already holding the key.

Seventeen

Mama walked to the rack in the hall, picked off her beige car coat, and struggled into it. Then she went to stand in front of the television. Debbie slipped on her black leather jacket and joined her there. I rushed to get my coat, too.

"You ain't goin'," Mama told me. "None of you is goin' except for Debbie."

"Why can't I go?" I asked. Even if this turned out to be only a fishing expedition, I didn't want to miss it. As a child, I'd liked fishing.

"Because I said so." When we were little and Mama used this tone with us, there was zero chance of getting her to change her mind. However, there were three techniques that could be tried, arguing, wheedling, and trickery. I skipped right to wheedling.

"Please, ma'am," I begged.

"Quiet, young'un, you're goin' to drive me to Whitfield!" Mama snapped, summoning up the specter of the state mental hospital. Then as she picked up her purse she relented. "Well, git in that car, but stop your whinin'."

I took Mama's elbow and guided her down the front steps. The late afternoon sky had turned to powder blue, the clouds blown like feathers in the evening wind. Across Calhoun, I heard raucous twittering coming from the leaves of the two magnolias next to St. John's Methodist Church. Hundreds of small black birds took flight as we slammed the Oldsmobile's doors, swooping and dodging like a school of fish around the church's steeple.

"Them birds," Mama spat out. "Look at that windshield!"

Debbie turned on the wipers, then drove us quickly down Calhoun in the fading daylight. On West Broadway, she made the U-turn before the railroad tracks as Daddy always used to, parking the Olds directly in front of the café. We stood on the sidewalk under the rusted Bon Ton sign, which had once glowed with green and red neon. I handed Debbie the key, and while she fiddled with the lock, I glanced beyond the tracks toward the old Rose Oil, where Brother used to work. Across from the station, several elderly black men rested on a wooden bench, their heads turning this way and that as they watched the cars driving to and from the Delta.

Thirty years ago, walking through the Bon Ton's heavy door, we would have been met with the warm smells of boiled coffee, fried catfish, and sweet potato pie. There had been a long counter with stools, chrome and Formica tables, wooden café chairs, and red leatherette booths, each with its own jukebox. Now the Bon Ton's furnishings were gone, but the floor still had its tiny white octagonal tiles and the ceiling its pressed tin, though the tiles were cracked and filthy, the tin rusted with leaks. I looked over at Mama; she pointed, and we picked our way through the trash on the floor to the back of the long, narrow space.

We came to what had been the kitchen. It was creepily dirty, with industrial-sized pots and cooking implements lying on the greasy stovetop. The safe resided in a corner, and it was massive, with the words *Wells Fargo* painted on the front in gold block letters. I could understand why Daddy hadn't kept this behemoth in the tiny duplex, but how had he managed to drag it into the back of the Bon Ton Café?

Debbie took a position directly in front of the safe, while Mama and I stood behind, trying not to disturb her concentration. She pulled the slip of pink paper from her jacket pocket and with dexterous fingers slowly rotated the dial, pausing after each turn to read Daddy's instructions aloud. But the safe wouldn't open. She tried again, this time maneuvering the knob more quickly. Then she dropped her arms and stared at it.

Mama said, "Huh."

The kitchen gave onto the dark alley, where the daylight had already disappeared. I kicked at some rubbish around my feet. "Should we just give up?" I asked.

Debbie shook her head, then placed her ear next to the safe as though listening to a patient's heart. By now she knew the combination well enough that she could spin the dial smoothly. After each rotation I could hear a faint *click, click, click.*

"Open says me," Debbie pronounced, and the big metal box obeyed.

"Well," Mama murmured, "that was harder to git into than I thought."

We peered inside. I could make out three deep shelves and three fat folders. Debbie reached in and grabbed a red accordion file. "Let's see what this has in it," she said. Then she laid it on top of the safe and began leafing though its contents.

"That's gen-u-ine leather," Mama marveled, fingering the expandable folder. It was the most enthusiasm she'd shown about anything all day. "And it even has a snap to close it up real good."

Debbie read: "Kohlmeyer & Co., New Orleans, Louisiana, members of New York Stock Exchange . . . Harris Trust and

Savings Bank, Chicago, Illinois, midmarket investment and corporate banking."

"It ain't nothin', is it?" Mama asked.

"Too soon to tell," Debbie said. She went on flipping the pages, reading to herself. After a few minutes, she looked up. "He was speculating in stocks." She held out a handful of documents illustrated with fine black-and-white engravings. "These are stock certificates. International Mogul Mines, Timber Realization, Lorado Uranium."

I repeated the strange names. "Do you think they're worth anything?"

"I don't know yet," she said. "But on this one, Deer Horn Mines, Daddy wrote, 'Wallpaper.'"

"Maybe for once he was thinking about papering the house," I suggested.

"Huh, that ain't likely," Mama said.

Debbie ignored us. "Listen to this. Here's a letter from Atlas Tile and Brick Co., Inc., from back in '57. 'Enclosed is your certificate for our company stock. As a new stockholder you are to be congratulated upon your business acumen in taking advantage of this opportunity to share in a new Mississippi industry that holds every promise to give you excellent return on your investment and benefit our state as a whole.'"

"Atlas Tile and Brick?" I asked. "Whoever heard of them?"

"Yeah, it ain't nothin'," Mama said.

"In the 1960s, he bought a hundred shares in Lucky Stores, Inc., for $1,607.48. I don't know if he got lucky with them," Debbie chuckled. "But look at what he wrote about Braniff Airways. 'Cost $1,330.00. Sold $1,913.39. Capital Gain $583.39.' And here's something more on Atlas Tile and Brick. Eight years after Daddy purchased the stock, the company merged with

Mississippi Industries, Inc., and it netted fifty cents in cash for each share surrendered. He had a thousand." She closed the accordion file. "He was making bits of money here and there."

"Bits of money," Mama parroted. "Here and there."

"It's how he funded his accounts," Debbie said.

"How he funded his accounts," Mama repeated. Then she asked, "What accounts?"

"Daddy was buying stocks," Debbie explained. "Sometimes he made money, and he would take the profits and buy more stocks. Sometimes he would deposit the profits into his bank accounts, the ones we found this afternoon."

"Un-huh," Mama said.

I looked at my big sister. She was right: It was fishing, pure and simple. I thought about how Daddy had enjoyed taking us on the occasional fishing trip. We'd set off in one of our clap-trap cars to buy bait from a shack that advertised *Worms and Cokes*. Then he would drive us to a muddy pond that smelled as if something had died in it, where we'd sit for hours on the grassy edge, holding a cane pole and hoping. When the red and white eyeball float would bob up and down, indicating that a fish was nibbling, Daddy would patiently reel it in for us. Most times he'd pull in bream, a fish he said wasn't worth scaling. The way Daddy practiced the sport, fishing was pure experience. He could sit at it for hours, and we often did. But occasionally, one of us might bring in a catfish bristling with whiskers and attitude. This we took home for Mama to cook with hand-cut French fries even tastier than those served in the Bon Ton. You started with something small, and maybe you got wallpaper, not walleye. But you kept on; you had to be patient. Sometimes you ended up with something of value. "Put the line right back in that same spot, Teresa," he'd say. "Not the minnow. Don't be afraid to use the baitworm." He knew the habits of fish, that there could always be another catch.

"What's in the other two files?" I asked.

"More of the same," Debbie guessed. "His old records. It's getting dark. Let's take them and go."

"No, let's look now," I said. "Maybe there's something good."

Mama pulled out a folder, this one a plain gray file, and several tattered envelopes spilled to the floor. I reached down and picked up the one closest to my foot, surprised to see my own handwriting of thirty-five years ago.

"What's this?" I asked.

Mama shrugged. "Open it."

I turned the envelope over in my palm, struck by the sense of almost remembering. The letter, folded in thirds, was written in faded pencil on a piece of blue-lined paper.

"It's my letter to Santa!" I exclaimed. "All our letters to Santa."

"Read them," Mama told me.

"No, let's take them home with us," Debbie said. "We'll read them tonight with Lisa. It's too dark in here now."

She reached to remove the last folder from the safe, and the three of us leaned against the door to seal it. We'd come seeking more of Daddy's fortune, but all we'd found were these worthless stock certificates and our letters to Santa Claus. Well, at least now we knew how he'd managed to save his money.

Then, as we were walking toward the front of the café, Mama pointed to the last folder and asked, "What's in that one?"

We were standing next to the plate glass window, which was covered with a film thick as petroleum jelly. Debbie turned the file sideways. "The label says AT&T." She pulled out a sheet. "What's this?"

I read the first paragraph over her shoulder. "He owned three hundred shares. So that was why we'd found all those envelopes from AT&T in his mail."

Mama asked, "That's the phone company, ain't it?"

I looked at her and nodded.

"Well, that's too much sugar for a dime. Ever since I was a telephone operator with Southern Bell back in the 1940s, I wanted to own me stock in the phone company. That's right smart." She trundled out to the car without another word.

From the doorway, I looked back into the café. Once again, I could see it full of customers, the men in white, short-sleeved cotton shirts, the women in paisley shirtwaist dresses, resting on the backless stools in front of the counter, sipping coffee. Great-Uncle Sam standing next to the cash register, ready to refill the white porcelain mugs. Then Debbie motioned me ahead of her, and we stood side by side while she locked up. Across Broadway, the white fluorescence of the Kentucky Fried Chicken flickered and came to life as cars lined up at its drive-through window.

On the way home, as if reading my mind, Debbie said, "We'll figure out what the stock is worth when we get back to the house."

I was sure we would, and I was sure it would be worth a small fortune.

Eighteen

In the front yard, Mama stopped long enough to kick at some dry sycamore leaves, wide like the palm of a hand, and watched as a gust of wind rolled them in the air. Glancing up at the wispy clouds, she announced, "Mare's tails this evenin', rain tomorrow."

She made her way up the front steps and into the living room, where she dropped down into the La-Z-Boy. The room was lit only by the lamp next to Mama's chair, on whose shade I'd painted long ago, on a bored afternoon, a pair of bright red lips. Gerry had parked himself on the velour love seat, as near the light as he could get, with Shelby Foote's three-volume history of the Civil War. Elizabeth was playing another game of solitaire on the floor, while Lisa and Joel reclined on the corduroy couch. Joel asked Mama what we'd found in the safe.

But she only said, "Well, we blew the popcorn bag wide open."

Debbie sat on the love seat next to Gerry, crossed her legs man-style, and started to elaborate. As soon as she mentioned the three hundred shares of AT&T, Joel went to the table next to Mama's chair and began rummaging though its two tiers, alternately holding up a mini hair clipper, a beat-up paperback copy of *Ivanhoe*, and a plastic bottle of Hex-a-Clens that Daddy had kept for disinfecting his toenails.

"What you doin'?" Mama asked.

"Looking for a Jackson newspaper, so I can figure out the value of the stock."

"Well, there ain't one in this house," Mama told him. To save on expenses, Daddy had only ever bought the Jackson paper on Sunday.

"We'll have to wait until the morning when we can buy a *Clarion-Ledger*," Debbie said. "Mama, no matter what the stock is worth, you can just hold onto it for now."

But Mama wasn't listening. She wasn't even gazing at the television screen, but at the wall above it. Then she started pulling at the flap of skin on her neck, a sure sign that she was worried. In fact, I thought she'd seemed worried ever since we'd left the Bank of Yazoo City earlier in the day.

We spent the rest of that evening, the last we'd have together, reading our letters to Santa. On the envelopes, I recognized Debbie's neat penmanship, Sol's messy printing, Lisa's round baby scribbles. I unfolded one of my letters and strained to make out my own words. "More than anything else I want Tiny Chatty Baby. She is fifteen inches tall and says eleven different things."

"And you got her, too," Mama said. "Remember?" Of course I remembered: The doll was lying face-up on the floor of the Toy Room.

The rest of my letters were compendiums of more Sears-inspired wants: a Casper doll and a Coca-Cola box, a play stove and a refrigerator. Then I pulled out one of Sol's.

Dear Santa Claus, I would like a Give-a-Show Projector. Also a Snow Cone machine. Don't forget a Bop-a-Bear. An Electronic Pistol Range. Get me a bike, too. Lego too. Bugs Bunny. The Rocket Ride. Penny the Poodle. Army Set. A record Player and records. Air Plane. Vac-U-Form. Guns. Riffle. Electric train. (or key train). Dirt Digger. Race car set. Big Bruiser. A Boat and Truck. Dirt Scraper. Dump Truck. Car Garage. Army Set. Machine Gun. Your friend, Solomon Nicholas

I could imagine him sprawled beside me in front of the gas heater in the living room, also furiously copying from the Sears, Roebuck catalog.

Mama sounded proud. "We didn't have much money, but Santa brought just about ever'thang y'all ever wanted." I had to admit, Mama was right: We'd had fine Christmases, even after we'd moved into the duplex. Every year, a fresh-cut cedar tree, trimmed with fat, colorful lights, including Frosty the Snowman and Santa, and the tin angel, which Daddy always made a ceremony of placing on top. Before the holiday, he would give each of us a Christmas club check for twenty-five dollars, which we'd use to buy presents. Undoubtedly, he'd saved this money bit by bit, like he'd saved the rest.

Mama flinched. "Well, I guess we had more money than I thought. At least, your daddy did."

"Let me see my letters," Debbie told me, and I handed her a pile. "I wrote to Santa on behalf of Clemmy," she said, sounding surprised. "'For Christmas please bring Clemmy some stockings, some good shoes, and some house shoes.'"

Then Clementine Williams seemed to rise up before us in her rolled Supp-Hose and her man shoes, clad in a shirtwaist dress with an apron wrapped around her pillow-shaped middle and a do-rag on her head. Our "black grandmother," who'd helped take care of us when we'd lived at Grandma's, and who used to frighten us by saying that the knobby growth next to her pinky was a sixth finger. She'd lived up the street from us in a bungalow the same vintage as Grandma's, but instead of carpets on the floors, hers had undulating linoleum. Instead of oil paintings on the walls, she'd hung Joe Louis posters. Her house had smelled of being closed up for too long and of something so foreign that I'd associated it with Clemmy's Negro-ness. Clemmy had also taken care of Daddy when he was a boy, and now I remembered how Daddy had looked in on her during her old age, bringing her little presents, including the jug of wine he bought each Christmas.

I opened Lisa's lone letter and tried to get her to look at it.

"It's on Santa Claus stationery," I cajoled.

"It's nothing but scribbling," she complained. "Why didn't he save any of my later ones, when I could write?" She'd often pointed out that there weren't many pictures of her in the brown camera bag, either. But when I thought about her childhood, I didn't think she'd been given short shrift. I thought about how she'd been Mama's favorite, the only one of us she'd named.

I collected the letters and carefully placed them back in their folder. I knew it wasn't a coincidence that Daddy had kept them in his safe, with his most important papers.

The next morning, the weather was pleasantly stormy, light showers and a breeze from the Gulf. Mama had been right about the coming change. At daybreak we congregated at the dining table, Debbie and I in the café chairs, Lisa in Daddy's desk chair. We were waiting for the customary batch of send-off biscuits. Whenever any of us left, Mama baked biscuits, and now she was at the kitchen counter, kneading milk, Crisco, and self-rising flour in her biscuit pan, a dented aluminum bowl with six-inch sides.

Joel had gone to the corner Shell station to buy the *Clarion-*

Ledger, and awhile later he came in carrying a copy and announced, "The stock is worth $15,445.42."

Mama was standing in the doorway to the dining room, holding the plate of hot buttered biscuits. "That ain't mine," she said.

Elizabeth asked innocently, "What isn't yours, Grandmother?"

"The money," Mama said, dropping the plate on the table. She wiped beads of sweat from her forehead and fanned herself with the bottom of her apron.

So this was what she'd been working herself up to since yesterday. "Oh, Mama, you can't be serious," I groaned.

She sat down next to me. "I mean what I say, young'un. That money ain't mine." Then she asked, "Don't nobody want a biscuit?"

But nobody did. Debbie tried arguing with her. "Mama, a lot of times when the husband dies he's left money in his name, and then when things are settled, the wife gets it."

Mama only said, "Naw."

"It's a lot of money, Mama. You can't just refuse it," I insisted.

She said, "It's little of nothin'."

I stared at the uneaten biscuits. "Mama's cream puffs," Daddy used to call them. A jar of homemade fig preserves rested on the table, and Lisa opened it and dribbled syrup onto a biscuit top. Then she said quietly, "Mama, you could use the money to fix up the house."

Fix up the house. From the first time she'd seen the duplex, Mama had urged those words on Daddy. Finally, several years after we moved in, he bought a five-foot-high stack of lumber, the Lumber Pile, which he dumped near the privet hedge and

proudly photographed us in front of. When it began to rot, Daddy covered the Lumber Pile with a plastic sheet. But Mama kept urging those words on him. Then in July 1964, Daddy gave in and hired Mr. Tyson, but only to paint the outside of the duplex. For weeks that summer, ancient, skinny Mr. Tyson came to us in his painter's pants, a loose shirt, and a floppy hat. When we sat down to eat in the dining room at noontime, Mama made sure he had a plate of the same in the shade of the chinaberry tree, along with iced tea in a jelly glass. When Mr. Tyson finally finished painting, Daddy took his picture and put it in the brown camera bag with our family photos. Mr. Tyson—not even Clemmy—was the only black person ever to find his way in there.

Of course we all knew that Mama should use some of the money to fix up the house. It was what she'd wanted her whole life, what we'd all wanted, and still wanted. We could remove the extra doors, demolish the steps to nowhere, tear down walls and enlarge the kitchen. We could install sheetrock and lay new flooring, reroof, even build a brick foundation. We could buy air conditioners. A new place began to take shape: It would never be a showcase, like Grandma's, but the duplex could become fit for habitation. But could Mama bring herself to do it? She no longer had Daddy to go against; he'd even left her enough money. But fixing up the house contradicted what Daddy had taught us, that we didn't need anything better, and what we'd concluded, that we didn't deserve anything better.

"It just ain't my money to use," Mama was saying. "If your daddy had meant for me to have it, he would of told me about it."

"Mama, I'm sure he wanted you to have it," I said.

"Then he would of put it in my name, Treesa. I won't touch it. Not them stocks, neither. Y'all eat."

As if we felt like eating. "Mama, you are so stubborn," I said.

"Stubborn as an ole biddy. I don't take nothin' from nobody. Never have, never will."

This made me think of Mama's stories about her uncle Will, and how after her daddy died she'd hated accepting his meager charity. For the rest of her life, Mama had worked hard for the little she'd ever got; it was her scrap of dignity. To her, accepting Daddy's money, which she hadn't even known existed, would be like taking charity. It seemed no amount of arguing or wheedling or trickery was going to change Mama's mind or assuage her anger at Daddy for keeping the money a secret.

After a while, she reached across the dining table to part

the window curtains. "The storm come close around us, but ain't goin' to last," she said. Debbie got up to wash in the Pink Bathroom, Lisa to collect their bags. When they were ready, we went outside to the front porch. The rain had let up, but the cars were still crawling on the slick-wet street. We milled around, unsure how to say good-bye.

Then Gerry suggested we take a photograph. Mama said to go into Daddy's closet off the living room and get the Polaroid camera he used with Erin. There, Gerry found not only the Polaroid but also a shopping bag of film packets that Daddy had purchased in a Kmart special. While he loaded the camera, I read the copy on the packet. *The Polaroid Instant Camera makes it easy to capture those spontaneous moments, share the fun, and enjoy the smiles, instantly!*

Gerry assembled us in front of the door. Mama and I, the tallest, went to the back, and without thinking I draped my arm around her shoulders. When Gerry pressed the button, the photo slid out and we gathered around. Out of a swirl of greens and blues and reds our faces materialized, showing wistfulness, relief, boredom, detachment, worry. Another moment, another snapshot to throw into the brown camera bag.

My sisters hugged me. "No matter what Mama says," Debbie whispered, "make her go to the bank and put that money in her name. Then work on her. Get her to use it to fix up the house. You can handle her." I nodded, but I wasn't so sure.

"Good luck," Lisa said.

"What are y'all sayin' about me?" Mama asked.

"Nothing," I lied.

They got into their cars, and I waved as hard as I could with both hands, just as Grandma had whenever I'd left home after a visit. I would drive down Thirteenth Street, and she would run out onto her back porch, pumping her arms up and down.

And I'd wonder about that moment after I turned the corner, when she walked back to her kitchen. Now as I watched my sisters disappear from sight, I understood her letdown.

Mama sighed. "Y'all goin' in four more days."

I looked over at Gerry, then back at her. I told her, "I'm going to stay with you."

She glanced from one to the other of us.

"It's true," I said.

"Well, that'd be mighty fine with me," she said and padded back into the house.

Gerry turned and walked down the steps toward the Sol Boy sycamore. The rain had barely penetrated the tree's tangled canopy, and I sat down in Erin's swing. He began to push me higher and higher, until I heard the limb creak.

He took the ropes to slow me down. When I'd nearly come to a halt, I dragged my feet and then twisted around until I was looking up at him.

"How long are you going to stay?" he asked. He didn't seem angry; he didn't even seem surprised. His Yankee reserve, Grandma would have said.

"I don't know," I answered. "I have to help Mama."

He asked, "Are you going to be okay? You've always hated being in this house."

True, I'd be left with Mama in the duplex, the window shades drawn to the sills, pink curtains pulled together in the middle; the outsized couches and Cyclops-like television and everywhere the sprawl of junk; the stained ceiling and the walls with their picked-off paper. When I closed my eyes, I could still see the geography of the bald spots in the dining room, the shapes oddly reminiscent of the mid-Atlantic states: New York, New Jersey, Pin-sla-vania. That's how Mama said it; she'd never been able to pronounce the place where Lisa and I had

gone to college. It was above the Pennsylvania-shaped patch that Daddy had hung the plastic sign, *God Bless Our Home*.

"I don't know," I said.

He shrugged. "Let's go inside." Then he handed me the Polaroid he'd taken on the porch.

In the living room, I went straight to Daddy's closet and took out the brown camera bag, its plastic top spotted with mold. I opened it and began to thumb through the old black-and-whites. I stared at us on our birthdays, our big-eared smiles behind white cakes and candles, posed at the dining room table in front of the peeling patches of wallpaper. Had I been happy then, or angry and sad? When I looked at these photos, I thought I seemed happy, but I couldn't remember any happiness after we'd moved into the duplex—not on our birthdays, not even on those fine Christmases.

Mama had said to me outside the bank, "You don't know your daddy, Treesa," But she had used the present tense, not the past. Once, a few years after Clemmy died, Lisa had asked Mama the whereabouts of her daughter, Little Clemmy, and Mama had replied, "Well, right now she's dead," as if tomorrow Little Clemmy would be right back with us. Now Mama spoke the same way about Daddy, as if I could still get to know him. As if I could accomplish through memory what I'd never been able to do when Daddy was alive.

Part III

We Rode, Remembering

Nineteen

Mama soon found out what it was like to buy a can of tuna. The next morning, when I asked her if she wanted to visit Glenwood Cemetery, she said no, the Jitney Jungle.

The Jitney is only two blocks from the house, but we drove anyway, Gerry parking as close as he could to the store's entrance. Mama went ahead through the automatic door, then stopped to take in the bright reds and yellows and oranges of the potato chip bags, the muted browns and blues of the bread and cake packages. Maybe, like me, she was remembering the Nicholas Cash Gro., that narrow, dimly lighted space with its plain metal shelves.

I took a cart and pushed it toward the produce aisle, Gerry and Mama lagging behind. Over the lettuces and cabbages, a tiny misting machine moved back and forth, refreshing the greens. Mama stuck her hand beneath the sprayer. "Look at that thang!" she cried.

We turned the corner into canned goods, Mama scrutinizing labels as she went. "I ain't never bought groceries before, just a carton of milk. A lot of ways your daddy wouldn't let me do anythin', but he wasn't mean about it. What did he say?" She was referring to the store manager, who was making an announcement over the loudspeaker.

But I hadn't understood the garbled message, either. Mama tilted her head, waiting for him to repeat it. "There he went again. 'Miss Piggy is callin' on line three.'"

"Mama, he said, 'Pork special in aisle three.'"

She turned to Gerry. "Miss Piggy only calls the Piggly Wiggly," he told her. Mama nudged me aside and ambled down the aisle with the basket.

"Don't tell her that," I said to Gerry, "she might believe you."

We caught up to her in front of the canned fish. "So many kinds of shrimp," she sighed. "Tiny shrimp, small shrimp, medium shrimp. Even broken shrimp. How is it with tuna?"

"There are two decisions to make," Gerry explained. "First, you have to choose between white or light."

"What does it mean, light?"

"Light means dark."

"Well, why don't they just say that? What do y'all buy?"

"White," Gerry said.

"I think Daddy bought light, but I want to try white."

"White it is, then." Gerry reached for our brand.

"Is that all there is to it?" she asked.

He held up the label for her to read. "No, you've got to decide between oil and water."

"Which is better?"

"I like water," he said.

"Then give me water. Now is that all there is?"

Gerry nodded. He tossed the can into the basket.

"This ain't so hard. Let's go look at the milk." We stood for a long time in front of the dairy case, while she ran her finger over the stickers on the plastic jugs. "Daddy bought whole, but I'm gittin' 2 percent. It's goin' to take me a little while to realize what I want."

We left the store with a cart full of staples. I was relieved that Mama had taken this little step, but I was anxious for her to take the bigger one of returning to the bank to put Daddy's money in her name.

That had been Thursday. Mama seemed able to engage in only one activity each day, so Friday I tried to convince her to go to the bank. But she put me off, maintaining that she had to dry a load of clothes at the laundromat. On Saturday she wanted to visit Daddy's grave. Stricklin-King had already taken down the tent, and only two stands of spent gladiolas remained. "I got to buy him his stone right quick," Mama said. That day she broke her pattern and engaged in a second activity, keeping her standing appointment at Miz Pie's beauty salon. We'd come full circle, a week to the day since Daddy had died.

Then Sunday, Gerry left. He got up early, washed quickly in the White Bathroom, and ate a sizable number of his send-off biscuits. The three of us gathered on the porch, and he hugged Mama and told her he'd always be ready to help with whatever she needed. She went back into the house, and I walked him down the steps to the rental car.

"You're going to catch cold, wearing your slippers in the yard," he said.

"Call me tonight when you get to New York," I told him.

He got into the Prizm and drove down Thirteenth Street, and I watched him round Grandma's corner onto Grand Avenue. Then I realized I'd forgotten to wave good-bye with both hands. For a long time, I stood looking after him.

The Sunday-morning street was quiet except for the electric jabber of a blue jay. Through the trees, I could just make out the windows at the back of Grandma's house, wide and still as staring eyes. I decided I would pay a call there to find out what my aunt had removed a few days before in the pickup.

When I went inside the duplex, Mama was slumped in her La-Z-Boy, watching a Tarzan movie with the sound muted. The window shades and curtains were drawn, the lamp was switched off, and the place reeked of gas heat.

"Treesa," she said, "I ain't goin' to Mass today." I told her I was spending my morning over at Grandma's, and she seemed as taken aback by my declaration as I had been by hers. "There ain't nobody in that cold house. Why would you want to?"

I began rummaging in the brown wicker basket for Grandma's front-door key. There I found several coins, one of which had been run over by a freight train, a favorite prank of ours when we were little; four nail clippers; a blue sachet, smelling of lavender; and eight unmarked keys. Since Grandma's door opened with an old-fashioned skeleton key, it was easy enough to pick out. I said a hasty good-bye to Mama.

I turned into Grandma's side yard, walking past the remains of last summer's wisteria vine, and went up the four steps to the front porch. The roof of the old house rose far above me, and I stood for a moment looking through the slender white columns toward Goose Egg Park. Then I inserted the skeleton key, but the rusted lock wouldn't budge. When I bent to peer through the keyhole, I couldn't see any obstruction, only a tiny view of the center hallway. I finally managed to open the door and get inside. It had been five years since I'd been in Grandma's house.

Old, damp air hung in the high rooms, and when I crossed from the center hall into the living room, mustiness emanated from everywhere—the embroidered rugs, the mauve couch and armchair, even the long side table with its turned legs and inlaid wood. Atop this table rested one of Grandma's treasured figurines, a cowboy on a bucking horse. Next to the gas fireplace, the glass-fronted shelves were still filled with curios—

the wooden backscratcher, the pink and green shot glasses, the lady bud vase with its long neck and rhinestone choker. At least in Grandma's living room nothing had been altered, except that a fine layer of dust covered the many surfaces, and cobwebs stretched like hairnets from the sills of the floor-to-ceiling windows.

I returned to the hallway, which was filled with early morning sunlight streaming through the transom. But as I walked toward the back bedroom, the light became filtered, as if passing through deep water. When we'd lived here, this had been my parents' room, and my grandparents had slept in the romantic front bedroom with its rose-pattered wallpaper. But after we'd moved out, they had changed to this quieter room, away from the traffic on Grand Avenue. It had a wall of windows looking onto the screened porch where Grandma and I had sat side by side in the glider, shelling peas. It was also here that we'd admired sunsets and once Grandma had claimed we were seeing the aurora borealis, come down from Canada.

I passed Grandma's vanity, with its can of Aqua Net hairspray, carton of cotton balls, and bottle of mineral oil, and went straight to the bird's-eye maple bureau. I wanted to reassure myself that Grandma's collection of costume jewelry, purchased over many years from the Marylena Shoppe, remained intact. Grandma had no fine jewelry, at least not any more. One day after Grendaddy died, as she sat dozing behind the counter at the grocery straight up on a metal stool in front of the chewing tobaccos, she'd had her engagement ring and watch stolen out of her purse.

The bureau had a row of small drawers at the top and four larger ones at the bottom. I pulled out one of the top drawers, and there they lay, the white cardboard boxes. Some were square and contained the brooches; others, long and shallow, held the bracelets; and still others, the smallest and most arresting, accommodated her earrings. I began by opening a large box and so rediscovered the purple bracelet, an inch-wide band of base metal studded with violet glass. I fingered the piece and returned it to the layer of protective cotton.

Then, one by one, I looked inside all the boxes. There were bangle bracelets, a dinner ring made of rhinestones, and a star-shaped red glass brooch; there were boxes and boxes of earrings, most of them clip-on, since Grandma had pierced her ears at the age of seventy. I could remember not only every piece of jewelry but the many occasions on which Grandma and I had performed our careful examination of them. The last time had been Christmas when I'd been a senior in college. That day, we'd gone so far as to remove all the drawers from the chest and place them on her bed, where we'd sat for hours, trying on the jewelry to the gentle hiss of the gas heater. Now I closed the drawer, relieved at having found the precious baubles. As long as Grandma's belongings stayed together, there was still a possibility that she might return to her house.

But my aunt had been packing boxes into the pickup. What had she taken? I decided to check the bedroom closet. I opened the door, and an empty shoe bag swung out ominously; I had known this bag to be filled with Grandma's best heels. When I looked inside the closet, I could see clear to the faded blue wallpaper. Everything was missing, even the hats.

There were three closets in the house, one off each bedroom, and Grandma had kept her clothes in all of them. I went to the others: Gone were the racks of pert sundresses and softly draping frocks, of practical shirtdresses and pantsuits; gone, too, were the dozens of other shoes, pumps of patent leather and faux alligator, sandals and house shoes. I especially mourned the hatboxes, the black and white with the legend *Bee Hats;* the

Tiffany blue and white with the Marylena Shoppe logo; the tan and blue with a New York street scene. My aunt had cleaned out Grandma's closets.

For a while I lingered in the doorway of the front bedroom, taking in the stale air. Then I shut the closet door and, climbing up onto the four-poster bed where I'd slept as Grandma's overnight guest, lay down on the cotton spread. In a corner of the room, the rose-patterned wallpaper had fallen over on itself, exposing the lath. On the floor, I saw a small parcel wrapped in pink gauze, one of the sachets Grandma had liked to keep with her clothes. I knew how much she loved this house, how much she wanted to return to it; I knew because I'd never wanted to leave it, either. Closets were only the beginning, and Pauline would most likely return in the coming days to continue her work. I listened as the traffic picked up on Grand, the Baptists hurrying toward their eleven o'clock service. I rolled off the bed, determined to do something for my grandmother. At the very least, pay a call on her in the nursing home. After all, it was Sunday, the customary day in the South for visiting.

I walked the six blocks to Martha Coker, past the Jitney and the Goose Egg. Several drivers in their Sunday finest waved from passing cars, the way they do here, unpeeling one or two fingers from the steering wheel. When I came to King's Daughters Hospital, I turned into the side street where the nursing home was located, on the corner of Calhoun, across from the hospital's emergency room entrance.

Inside the home, it was a slow Sunday morning. The sitting room lacked its regular inhabitants, who had yet to be washed and dressed and settled in their wheelchairs for the day. Only one attendant guarded the nurses' station, and she directed me toward the hallway on the right.

I found Grandma's room, paused in front of its blond wooden door, then knocked. When nobody answered, I gave the metal handle a little push, and the door glided open. Grandma shared the ample room, where two white curtains and a small sink divided the space. Her roommate, a severely wizened lady on whose face another ten years could scarcely have made a difference, lay in bed covered by a thin sheet. She was asleep in the near darkness. I could see the outline of her wasted body; her legs ended below the hips.

In Grandma's half of the room, the blinds were wide open and her big-screen TV blared cartoons, but she lay in the hospital bed like an upturned turtle. She couldn't see the television, which was situated on a desk to her right, because she wasn't able to shift in its direction. Even so, the bed's side guards were fully extended, penning her in. She was perfectly still, with her glasses off and her eyes shut.

I stood and waited for her to sense me. Finally she opened her eyes, though she didn't look at me but at the ceiling. "Hi, Grandma," I said, leaning so close that my face was just inches above hers. I searched the bedside table for her glasses and fitted them onto the bridge of her nose, watching as recognition spread across her features. To touch her was to remember, how we had once kissed on the mouth every time we greeted. I'd never thought it strange, because it was how we'd been with each other back then.

I cranked her bed to a forty-five-degree angle, and we began to talk. Or rather we tried to talk, because we had to contend with the Parkinson's and her deafness. I yelled to make myself heard, but even then she understood only part of what I said. Her eyes gave the only clue: If they stayed big and round like silver dollars, I knew she hadn't comprehended.

"How's my house?" Grandma asked.

"Fine."

"What?"

"Fine!"

"Take me home with you, Treesa."

I decided to start all over again, to shake her off track about the house. "How are you, Grandma?"

She blinked, so I knew I'd gotten through to her. "The food here is terrible," she said. "I'd give anythin' for a plate of jolly-jolly-jing-jing-jing."

I looked at her. "Grandma, I thought you didn't like Lebanese food."

"Hmm?"

"I said, I thought you didn't like jadra." That was our other name for imjadara. I couldn't bring myself to use Grandma's term for it.

"What's that?" she asked.

I sighed. "You know, jolly-jolly-jing-jing-jing."

"Oh, I liked that. It was the meat I couldn't stand, because it made me break out." She said this as if revealing a secret, though I'd heard all my life about her supposed allergy to beef. "And I loved sap soup. Could you make a bowl for me, Treesa?"

I shook my head. "Nome, because it's winter, and there aren't any good tomatoes. Don't you remember?"

But Grandma seemed to have gone far back in time. "He done me dirty," she said. "He done me dirty, dirty, dirty, dirty, dirty."

"Who, Grandma? Who did you dirty?"

She stared at me with blank eyes. "He did. Your grandfather." Then she repeated the entire sequence, adding an extra "He done me dirty" at the end. And so we continued, yet she wouldn't explain, no matter how many times I pressed her.

After a while she fell silent, and I let my eyes wander around her room. Other than the desk and television, there was the bedside table with pill bottles and skin lotions and color photos of her great-grandchildren, and three small, falsely cheerful stuffed bears. Then I looked back at Grandma and saw that with great, slow effort she had managed to bend her right elbow, so that her forearm extended into the air, with the index finger pointed. Halfway up, the limb had become arrested.

"I've got an itch," she explained.

As I was struggling with exactly how to help, the door swung open, and Pauline came in. She was fresh from church, and having inherited Grandma's taste in clothes, looked elegant in her suit, jacket, and scarf. We exchanged "heys."

"Mama, why haven't they gotten you up out of this bed?" She picked up the hairbrush from the bedside table and pushed it through her mother's thick hair, rigid with yesterday's Aqua Net. "Just look at you."

As Pauline worked on her, Grandma's blue eyes got even bigger and rounder, and she rolled them at me in an exaggerated, comic way. She'd given up trying to move the suspended arm. Finally Pauline lay down the hairbrush and reached into her handbag for a pen and a long sheet of paper.

"Mama, put your name here with this ink pen," she said, trying to fit the implement into Grandma's raised hand. But it slipped down her palm and onto the bed.

"She can't hold it," I said. "What is it you're trying to get her to sign?"

"It's the paper for her house," Pauline answered, lowering her voice. She tried again to position the pen in Grandma's fingers but with the same result. "You know, to give us the power to sell."

Grandma's eyes, rounder than ever, moved first toward Pauline then toward me, and her right arm began to shake from elbow to hand.

"Here, Mama, I'll hold the pen while you sign." But Grandma couldn't write her name even with assistance. "Then just make your *X*," my aunt told her. While I stood watching, helpless as my grandmother, Pauline guided the disobliging hand. She returned paper and pen to her purse and said, "You're my witness, she made the *X*."

"Me?"

She leaned over to kiss her mother. "Mama, I love you, but I've got to go." Grandma blinked.

Given what I'd just seen, I couldn't stay, either. "Wait, I'll go out with you," I said.

As I went to kiss Grandma good-bye, she managed to turn her head toward me. I was afraid she was about to burst out with "Take me home" again, but instead she launched into the "He done me dirty" refrain. "That's how come I didn't cry at his funeral," she concluded.

I kissed her on the cheek. "Bye, Grandma."

I caught up to Pauline under the eave of the building, and we went down the sidewalk together. Through half-drawn blinds I could see the patients' possessions jumbled on the windowsills, their lotions and pills and family photos and stuffed animals.

"Can I have a ride home?" I asked.

We got into Pauline's car, and she drove a block in silence. I couldn't bring myself to mention to my aunt what I'd just been a part of. Besides, there was no point. We had to sell Grandma's house to keep her in Martha Coker.

Finally I asked, "Why does Grandma say Grendaddy did her dirty?"

Pauline seemed about to tell me something, then thought

better of it. "I don't have any idea. But if there's anythin' y'all want out of that house, you better go ahead and get it now. I'm goin' to call Mashburn Realty tomorrow. Of course, we won't tell her."

She let me out at the corner of Thirteenth and Calhoun, then pulled into her carport next door. I watched as she went into her house, that neat ranch with bars on all the windows and doors. For the first time, I noticed how stooped she was when she walked.

No, of course we wouldn't tell Grandma that we were selling her house, the place most important to her in all the world. I looked down the block: The bungalow's windows stared back at me. That house had witnessed everything, including whatever secret thing had happened between my grandparents.

Twenty

When I came through the front door, Mama was still sitting in the La-Z-Boy, feet propped on the swing-out stool, watching Bob Hope and Bing Crosby caper across the silent television. Though the living room clock showed twelve-thirty, she hadn't done anything about fixing dinner, and I was sure she hadn't taken her insulin, either.

I lowered the flame on the heater and sat down on the couch opposite her. "Mama, are you just going to sit in your La-Z-Boy all day?"

She kept on staring at the TV. Finally she said, "Ain't a La-Z-Boy."

"What do you mean?"

"Just ain't."

"What is it, then?"

"A Bassett."

How could I not have known the make of her much-loved chair, where she spent every possible moment? She liked doing four things in it: reading, watching TV, solving word puzzles, and napping—five, if you counted "just sittin'." If the telephone happened to ring, she would answer in her slow voice, "Mhello," and when the caller inquired how she was, she would reply, "I'm in my chair," meaning everything was as right as it could be.

"I thought it was a La-Z-Boy."

"Maybe you don't know as much as you think." She took hold of the chair's lever and snapped the footrest down, as if to punctuate her retort. Then she looked at me. "I have to talk to you," she said. Her mouth began working, but only gibberish came out. "Well, I . . . but then . . . go on . . . it ain't . . . so . . ."

"Mama, are you okay?" I was afraid she might have had another stroke.

She took a swig from a glass on the table, and I noticed two empty Coca-Cola bottles. Had she drunk too much soda?

"Mama, do you need to take your insulin shot?"

"Naw, naw, naw," she said.

"What is it, then?"

"Well." She glared at me through the half darkness. "Treesa, can you keep a secret?"

Did everybody in this family have a secret? I had been going to tell her about Pauline putting Grandma's house up for sale, but when I got home and saw her looking so glum and remote, I couldn't bring myself to do it. Now, with Bob Hope and Bing Crosby as my witnesses, I made Mama a promise. "Of course I can."

She thought about what I'd said. "Well, after you left, there come a knock on my front door."

"Who was it, Mama?"

"Who?" She eyed me doubtfully. "Are you sure you can keep a secret?"

"Yes, I can."

Finally she told me, "A li'l ole gray-haired gentleman."

I laughed. "This little old gray-haired gentleman, did he have a name?"

"Well, of course he had a name, but I can't tell you what it was."

I sighed. "What can you tell me, Mama?"

"After I heard all that racket, I looked through the window, and there was this li'l ole gray-haired gentleman before my screen door. I recognized him from St. Mary's, so I went ahead and unlocked the doors. He was dressed up so nice, in a white suit and striped tie. He asked me if he could come in. Treesa, I let him inside." Then she lifted her chin and smiled proudly.

I shifted in my seat, imagining the vision he must have had—of the poorly lit, overheated living room, of the awful furnishings in the duplex.

"Where did he sit?"

"Right where you're sittin'. First off, I asked him if he wanted a Coke, and he said yes, so I got up and fetched him one." That explained the two empties on the table. "I told him I was sorry to hear about his wife's death and asked after his family, how they was gittin' on."

"His wife just died? How do you know?"

"Was in the church bulletin three weeks ago. He said to me, 'That's exactly why I come to see you. It has to do with my wife. I believe she would want me to. I've got a list of the ten newest widows from the church, and I'm talkin' to each one.' Well, I sat there stunned."

Mama leaned forward in the chair, and I could see she was troubled. I felt suspicious of the stranger. "Why can't you tell me his name?" I asked.

"Just can't."

"Because you can't remember?"

"Of course I can. He asked me not to tell. You know, because of what he did next."

"What was that?"

She peered at me. "Are you sure you can keep a secret?"

"Mama, please just tell me what happened."

She started speaking quickly, for her. "Well, he reached into his suit coat pocket real slow and drew out a long white envelope. Then he laid it right here on the table. I could see the green peekin' out."

"Go on."

"He said, 'You take it. You're a widow, and I know you can use it. My family has money. If I told you how much we have in the stock market and how much in the bank, it would surprise you. And I know my wife would want the poor widows of the church to have some of it.' He gave the envelope a push in my direction. There was a little smile on his face."

"And then what happened?"

"I said to him, 'I can't take money from you!'"

"How much was in the envelope, Mama?"

"He just kept talkin' about his wife, and how she would have wanted it, and he said I should leave it on the table for a while and think about it."

"How much money, Mama?"

She sank back in her chair. "You have to promise not to tell. Promise, because when that li'l ole man got up to leave, he put a condition on me. He said, 'There's one thang you have to do. You must promise never to tell anybody about what happened here today.'"

"I promise! But how much did he give you?" I went to the table and took the fat envelope in my hand.

"Well, I don't know. A bunch of bills. Promise never to tell a soul! Oh, what am I goin' to do, Treesa?"

I opened the envelope. "It's five hundred dollars."

"What am I goin' to do?" she wailed again.

"What if you write him a thank-you note?"

She shook her head. "Couldn't do a thang like that."

"So why didn't you just tell him to take it away?"

"Well, I couldn't hurt his feelin's."

"Then you have to keep it. Put it toward fixing up the house."

She crossed and uncrossed her legs. Now I understood why she'd been sitting in the dark living room with the sound off on the TV: She'd been fretting about money. After a lifetime of deprivation, money was coming to her from all sides, even from strangers, and she wanted none of it.

"Did you hear me?" I asked.

"Of course."

As I sat holding the cash, my suspicions about the little old gentleman vanished. I could accept that to him, Mama was simply one of the church's newest and neediest widows. He wanted nothing from her.

After a while, I asked again, "What are you going to do with the money?"

She shrugged, turned up the sound, and watched the end of her movie. Afterward, she took the envelope from me and put it on top of the television. Then she fixed herself a pimento cheese sandwich, which she ate in the Bassett, thus initiating a sixth activity in her beloved chair.

Twenty-one

The next morning, I woke up to the mean stares of my dolls, which were still strewn on the floor beside the bed in the Toy Room. It was Monday, and judging by the traffic on Calhoun, rush hour in Yazoo. I threw back the quilts and went to find Mama, but she wasn't in her chair. I walked around the back of the house: her bedroom, the Junk Room, the tiny kitchen. Then I looked out the front door and saw that the Oldsmobile was missing from its spot in the yard.

Where could she have gone at eight A.M.? I sat down in the living room to wait. An hour clicked by, then another, finally three. I was thinking about calling Willie Belle at the sheriff's office to see if an accident had been reported, when I heard Mama's soft footsteps on the porch. She crossed the room and collapsed in her chair.

"Where did you go?" I asked.

She picked up a church bulletin from the table and began to fan herself. "To visit your daddy," she said. "It's hot in here, Treesa. Cut them heaters off."

I did as she asked. "The entire morning?"

"I had a lot to tell him."

I was alarmed that Mama would stand at Daddy's grave for three hours. "What did you say all that time?"

"Just thangs."

"Like what sort of things?"

She dropped her improvised fan. "Well, I told him that you're stayin' with me, and that today we'll be buyin' his tombstone."

That was the last thing I was planning to do today. "But, Mama, we have to go to the bank."

"What for?"

"To put Daddy's money in your name."

"Naw, can't do that today. Got to buy the tombstone."

"Well, what are you going to pay for it with?"

"The mattress money, of course." She gazed into her lap. "I don't want Daddy to have to wait."

I thought of the twins, who'd waited twenty years for their marker. I asked, "If we buy his tombstone today, will you go with me to the bank tomorrow?"

"All right, Treesa," she finally said.

"And will you put Daddy's money in your name?"

She sighed. "All right. But I'm not goin' to use it."

"What about the cash from the little old gentleman?"

"I ain't sure I'm keepin' that."

I shrugged. At least I'd gotten her to agree to go to the bank with me.

After dinner, we got into the Oldsmobile and headed for the monument works at the top of Broadway, the longest and most treacherous hill in town and over the years the site of numerous traffic accidents. When I was growing up, stories would run wild about So-and-So's car careening out of control on Broadway and coming to rest in the yard of one of the historic houses that lined the street. But this afternoon, the Oldsmo-

bile struggled to make it up the hill. It started to strain near the County Health Department, and by the time we reached Sarah Cooper Lear's house, we were barely moving.

"Press the pedal down hard," Mama instructed. I did as she said, but nothing happened. I looked out my window at Miz Sarah's fine wrought iron fence and stained glass windows.

"Isn't this where Daddy had his accident?" I asked.

"What accident?"

"You know, in the Soap Box Derby."

It had been one of the great disappointments of his life. When Daddy was twelve years old, he built a wooden racer, which looked like a rocket with the sides cut out. On July 27, 1938, he entered the Mid-South Soap Box Derby, and he would have won that day if his wheel hadn't fallen off. Daddy had often showed us the yellowed photo from the *Herald*, which he'd preserved in clear plastic, with its caption: "Solomon Nicholas Jr. was leading by 100 feet in Yazoo Class B first heat when he lost control 24 feet from the finish line." You could see the racer heading into the large crowd, and one panicked boy darting to escape its path. You couldn't make out Daddy's face, only his outstretched arms trying to force the car back into the middle of the road.

Mama repeated, "Press on the gas."

I pushed the pedal to the floorboard, but the Oldsmobile didn't respond. Cars began to pass us, and from behind a trucker sat on his air horn.

"Put it in neutral, and rev it up real good. Then pop it back into gear."

I looked at her, amazed she knew just what to do. This time the Olds lurched forward, dark smoke billowing from its tailpipe.

"This car is a piece of junk if ever I seen one," she said.

We got to the ridge where Broadway widened, its stately older homes ceding to a forlorn cluster of low commercial buildings. Outside the monument works, gray and pink granite slabs were lined up like used cars. I pulled off the road and parked, but Mama didn't budge. "I got to choose a stone," she said dolefully.

Finally, she got out and began wandering among the tombstones. There were upright, slanted, pillow, and flush-to-the-ground models, with many different kinds of lettering. Some had a photograph of the deceased or a carving of an angel or a twelve-point buck. I thought of Daddy and his monkeys, but I supposed that not even he would have wanted a primate on his grave.

"Treesa, do you think I should git a monument with a vase?" Mama was patting a receptacle of pink granite.

"I don't know. Why would you want one?"

"So y'all can put flowers in it, of course."

"Let me get somebody to help you decide," I said.

I picked my way into the office, where I found a salesman. "We want to buy a memorial for my father," I told him, "and my mother may want a vase. What do you have to choose from?"

He reached for a sample book and motioned me back outside. After he extended his condolences to Mama, he thumbed to a page and read the cost of a single low stone with a vase. "Warranted forever," he said, showing Mama a glossy black-and-white photo.

She scrutinized the picture. "But I want a double-wide."

He looked at me for clarification, but I didn't know. "Mama, what is it exactly that you want?"

"A double-wide."

I took her by the elbow. "You mean a double marker?"

"Ain't that what I said?"

"You want to buy your own tombstone?"

"May as well, long as I'm here."

I dropped her arm. "Now do you understand what she wants?" I asked the salesman.

He started flipping through his samples again. "Something like this?" he asked, holding up another photo.

She took it from him, turning it this way and that. "Naw, naw, I don't want a low stone. I want somethin' that sits up. And I want a vase in between Daddy and me. Show me what else you got." She handed him back the book.

"Follow me," he said. We walked to the edge of the grounds, stopping a few feet away from an auto repair shop. "Ma'am, would you like this monument, by any chance?"

It was a simple tombstone in gray granite, upright on a narrow rectangular base, with a Grecian urn separating the two sides. "It's a classic. Comes to seventeen hundred dollars. But it's less without the vase," he added quickly.

"I don't want to scrimp on his stone," she said. "What do you think, Treesa?"

"Whatever you want, Mama."

She fretted because the salesman said the perpetual warranty didn't cover vandalism. Or maybe we wouldn't put fresh flowers in the vase often enough to justify the expense. "Please don't use them plastic ones," she told me. But in the end, she decided to buy it. She gave the salesman the wording for the markers: On the left side, she would have them carve *Solomon T. Nicholas Jr.*, with his dates of birth and death; on the right, *Florence Hood Nicholas*, and her birth date. Then she pulled a stack of bills from her jacket pocket, peeling off seventeen hundred dollars from the wad of mattress money.

When we climbed back into the car, I shifted to face her. "Why did you decide to buy your own tombstone?"

"Well, I don't want y'all to have to worry about it later."

It was such an unselfish thing to say that I didn't know how to answer. As I turned away from her and started the Oldsmobile, she startled me by placing her hand on mine. "Just one more thang."

I stopped the car. "What's that?"

"When my time comes, there's one thang you've got to tell Buster King for me. Tell him, when he lays me out in my coffin, that I don't want him to put no makeup on me. I won't have people in this town starin' down at me and sayin' how good I look."

I nodded, feeling the tightness in my throat. Then she took her hand away, and we made for home. On the way I thought, Daddy never got to have his classic car, but now and forever, he would have his classic tombstone.

Twenty-two

On Tuesday, the day we were finally supposed to go to the bank, I woke up to the discordant symphony of the old black telephones Daddy had peppered throughout the house. Where was Mama, and why didn't she pick up? I was beginning to revise my impression that she just sat in the Bassett all the time. Lately, it seemed she was out of her chair more than she was in it.

When I got to the wall phone in the hallway, the line was dead. Then as I was replacing the receiver, the back door slammed, and Mama came in. I thought I could smell tobacco smoke wafting off her clothes. She'd quit the habit thirty years before, but after the funeral she'd taken it up again. Several times a day, Mama sneaked out to visit Dot Knot, the widow who lived next door, and the two of them smoked together in her backyard, hiding like schoolgirls under the broad leaves of the fig tree. When I'd tried to discuss Mama's new-old vice with her, she'd snapped, "Leave me alone, young'un. I didn't tell you what to do when you was a teenager." And it was true. During all my fights with Daddy, she hadn't come to my side, but neither had she taken his part against me. So I left her to smoke, though I worried about the effect on her already precarious health.

"This morning we're going to the bank, and we're taking that money from the little old gentleman with us," I said, pointing to the envelope that was still on top of the television.

"You haven't mentioned him to nobody, have you, Treesa?"

"Nome," I lied, since I'd told Gerry about the mysterious visitor in one of our nightly phone calls.

"You didn't tell Willie Belle, did you? It'll be on that police scanner all over town if you did!"

"No," I said truthfully.

Then she frowned. "You told Gerry, didn't you?"

"Well, I might have."

She wailed, "It's goin' to be all over New York City!"

"Gerry's not going to tell anybody, and even if he did, they wouldn't understand what he was talking about."

But I couldn't persuade her that everyone in New York wouldn't soon find out about the little old gentleman. Twice the population of Yazoo could fit inside Madison Square Garden alone, but to Mama New York was just another small town. Gerry and I had once gone to watch the Mets play, sitting behind the dugout near the first base line. She and Daddy had happened to catch the game on television, and every time a left-handed batter had come up, we'd appeared on the screen. Now whenever she watched the *Today* show or any broadcast from New York, she expected to see us in the crowd.

"Mama, want to know what Gerry said about the money?"

"What?"

"That you should put it in the bank."

She mumbled, "Accept money from a complete stranger. Gerry says I should. But Law, what's next?"

I left her to mull it over and went to wash up. When I returned, she was at the dining room table, writing. "What have you got there?"

She scraped the paper into her lap. "Nothin'."

"Let me see."

She pulled up a piece of ecru stationery. "Well, it's a thank-you note to that li'l ole gent."

"Really? Does that mean you've decided to keep his money?"

"I might could, so I don't hurt his feelin's. First I got to write him this, but, Treesa, I can't think of what to say."

I sat down next to her. "What have you got so far?"

She sighed, holding out the note for me to read. "Dear Mr. Raeburn, thank you." I saw her dismay as she realized what she'd done.

"Don't worry, Mama, I won't tell anybody his name."

"Promise, Treesa?"

"Promise. And what you have is fine. After all, it's hard writing a thank-you note for something you're not supposed to mention."

"I can't even sign it. Supposin' somebody was to see it? They might wonder why somebody like me was sendin' him a thank-you note."

"Now will you go ahead and deposit his money?"

She nodded, then got up from the table and trundled off to her bedroom to change her clothes.

An hour later, we took our places in the Oldsmobile, I sliding behind the steering wheel, Mama settling herself on the passenger side. Parked in the early spring sun, the car smelled of sweet, warm plastic and of fabric soured by the leaky roof.

I turned to Mama. "Where are we going?"

"To the bank," she answered.

"I know that, but which one?"

"Why, Delta National, of course."

In the cavernous main room, light seeped through the vertical blinds. There were no other clients, and most of the perimeter offices were dark. A teller attended a car at the drive-through window, while two others chatted quietly over a low partition. Mama and I waited behind a velvet rope until one waved us over. She had a pleasant face and, according to her brass nameplate, was named Mary Sue.

"Why Miz Florence, the last time you were here you didn't even stop to say hello." She meant our visit when we'd discovered the first of Daddy's hoards. Then Mary Sue leaned toward Mama and said sweetly, "Sol June was a favorite of ours. We miss him. How're you doin'?"

Mama replied that she was just fine, thank you. She held up a small key in a plastic pouch. "Can't somebody let me in, please, ma'am?"

"What are you doing?" I whispered. "Aren't we going to put Daddy's money in your name?" But Mama went on waving the little key in the air.

"I'll get the door," Mary Sue said. Then she disappeared behind a wall, and Mama ambled around the corner, leaving me alone at the teller's post.

"Well, come on," Mama called out.

I followed her voice and found them both standing before the barred door that led to the safe deposit boxes. Mary Sue brandished a long key chain. "Just a minute. I'll get this lock to work if it's the last thing I do today."

Finally she got the door open, and we went inside the alcove. Mama handed her key to the teller, who scanned the rows of tan boxes. "Y'all want to look at it here or take it out yonder?" she asked, inclining her head toward the main room.

"Right here is fine," Mama answered.

Then Mary Sue pulled out a thin metal ledge from the wall, rested the safe deposit box on top, and left.

"What are you doing?" I repeated.

Mama flipped back the lid and began thumbing through dozens of envelopes. "What I'm doin'? Examinin' Daddy's safe deposit box."

"I can see that," I said, confused, "but how did you know he had one?"

"I know your daddy."

"What are you looking for?"

But she only peered over her glasses, mouthing return addresses, pulling out certain envelopes and setting them aside. There was such a slow, mesmerizing quality to the way she worked that for a moment I almost forgot why we'd come.

Finally I said, "Mama, give those to me."

She handed the envelopes over. All of them were from the same Massachusetts insurance company. "Daddy had insurance?" I asked.

"Treesa, I figured he must of bought himself a burial policy, but it weren't in his bedroom or in the Bon Ton. He put it in here."

"Mama, if you knew Daddy had insurance, why didn't you mention it?"

"First thangs first," she said cryptically.

Soon we had a stack of envelopes, because of course Daddy had saved every bit of correspondence from the company. And of course Mama was right. She tapped the folded policy lightly against her palm. "Buster won't mind waitin'," she said. All along, she'd been counting on this money to pay for Daddy's funeral.

Just then Mary Sue came back, and Mama told her we were finished. As the teller reshelved Daddy's safe deposit box, I could hear the bank stirring, the employees returning from their dinners at Stub's or River-Bend Catfish House. After Mary Sue locked the iron door behind us, she inquired of Mama, "What more can we show you today?"

"We still want to put Daddy's money in your name, don't we?" I asked. To my relief she nodded.

Mary Sue gestured us toward one of the offices. "Why don't y'all wait over yonder, and I'll ask one of the ladies to help you."

We took seats in front of a metal desk. I examined the print on the wall behind it, a large woodcut of a duck, while Mama leaned her chin on her hand and sighed loudly. Then she took an envelope out of her purse.

"Like you told me, Treesa, I'm goin' to deposit the gift from the li'l ole gentleman."

"Uh-huh," I nodded.

"And I'm goin' to deposit Daddy's Social Security and the leftover mattress money." She twisted in her chair to stare at her pointy loafers. "But the way I figure it, I don't need Daddy's money. I got nearly fifteen hundred dollars with these, and I don't have bills for more than that."

"So you're not going to put Daddy's money in your name?"

"Yeah, I am, but I ain't goin' to use it. I'm savin' it for that day when I have to go into the nursin' home."

"Mama," I groaned.

Then a middle-aged black lady joined us. Mama handed over Daddy's death certificate to her, and she helped Mama fill out the paperwork to transfer his savings. As we walked out past the teller windows, Mary Sue called over, "If there's anythin' more you need, Miz Florence, just call me. I can help you over the phone."

Mama waved at her. I followed her out the door, but she stopped and faced me.

"I just hope it ain't too hard," she said. "Writin' out checks. Treesa, will you show me how?"

"Of course," I said.

"You ain't mad at me, are you?"

She stood close to me on the sidewalk, wearing the beige jacket that barely fastened around her middle and the loafers that I knew must pinch her toes. But there was so much dignity in the quiet way she held herself.

"Of course I'm not." I was disappointed, though. All those years when we were growing up, Mama had thought—we'd all thought—that if only we had money, everything would be okay. Now Mama had it, and she was determined to live as if the money didn't exist.

As we rode past Ricks Library, she called out, "Stop over yonder," gesturing toward the post office. I made the U-turn around the Confederate Monument to park in front of the one-story white building with the town's zip code emblazoned on its front.

"What are you doing now?" I asked.

She waved the Crane's stationery. "Got to mail the li'l ole gent his thank-you note." I watched as she slowly walked over to the metal slot and dropped it inside.

Twenty-three

Not long after, Mashburn Realty placed a crooked metal sign in Grandma's front yard, next to the linden tree on whose gnarled roots I'd so often played as a child, pretending they were a scale for telling my weight and fortune. Several times I'd started to tell Mama that we had to sell the family homestead to keep Grandma in Martha Coker, but I hadn't been able to say the words. Now that the sign had gone up, I had no choice. I sat down on the edge of the love seat in the living room and muted the television. That was why Pauline's pickup had been parked so often at Grandma's back steps, I explained. She was emptying out the house.

Mama looked at me. "Well, what about all her thangs?"

"When I ran into Pauline Sunday at the nursing home, she said we could have anything we wanted," I told her.

"Huh," Mama exhaled.

After dinner, she dug the skeleton key out of the brown wicker basket and told me to get my coat. Together we walked down the block to Grandma's. As far as I could remember, the only other time Mama had returned there in the thirty-five years since we'd moved out was when Grendaddy died in 1976.

The old front door opened more easily for Mama than it had for me only a few days earlier. When we stepped inside, I saw that the house had changed dramatically: My aunt had cleaned out not only the closets but most of the furniture and knickknacks. Gone were the dining room's elegant mahogany table and the front bedroom's romantic four-poster, not to mention the plain pine table in the breakfast room where we'd lingered over dinner in the afternoons and the faux-leather reclining chair where Grandma had watched television in the evenings. Only the living room's prickly mauve couch and chair and my grandparents' bird's-eye maple bedroom set remained. Mama and I moved slowly through the disordered rooms, our footsteps reverberating off the high ceilings. Throughout the house, forgotten curios and a chaos of scattered linens were turned out on the floor. Grandma would have been appalled.

Mama chose for herself a gold-leaf mirror, several oil paintings, an art deco chandelier, and a high desk with a pull-down front. She said that Grandma had promised this desk to her a long time ago, but she hadn't had a place to put it in the duplex. I asked her what she planned to do with it now, since there still wasn't room for it, but she only said, "I got somethin' in mind." Then Mama asked me what I wanted for my keepsake. I went straight to Grandma's bureau, found the square white box with the purple glass bracelet, and took it for myself.

We left the house, and for the last time I locked the front door with the skeleton key.

Mama and I walked out the side yard and down the block. She was studying the neighbors' houses as if she'd never seen them before. When we reached Mrs. Carter's, she stopped.

"That yard is full of staubs," she said, pointing toward the brown winter grass.

I searched Mrs. Carter's wide lot. "Mama, what's a staub?"

"Well," she answered, "they're not really staubs, they just look like it."

Later that afternoon, while I was hanging out our laundry,

I saw Pauline sitting in a green plastic chair under her carport. I called over, telling her what we'd selected at Grandma's and asking her not to dispose of the things until we'd had a chance to move them out. She nodded.

Then I approached the privet hedge that separated our houses. "Pauline, what's a staub?"

"A what? Never heard of it."

She said she wanted to ask my advice. She didn't know what to do with Grandma's bedroom suite, because nobody wanted it. And that's how I came to be the one who suggested that she consign it to the local antiques store. Later, I would see it there, the double bed my grandparents had slept in for so many years, laid out in fine, white linens, with a price tag of eight hundred dollars. The dresser and bureau, emptied of the costume jewelry, sat alongside.

Soon after the for-sale sign went up in Grandma's yard, one of the Piggs made an offer on the house, and so did someone from Graball Road who wanted to move it far out into the country. But even though Grandma's welfare depended on it, my aunt wouldn't sell to just anybody. Bad enough that the homestead had to be sold, but she didn't want it to disappear off the lot. And so the old house continued its vigil of sitting and waiting for the next thing to happen.

A few quietly eventful days passed. Mama and I went to the Bank of Yazoo City, withdrew the rest of Daddy's savings, and put that into her account, too. I showed her how to make out checks and watched as she struggled to write the amounts for the telephone, electricity, gas, and cable bills in her spindly handwriting. I also tried to explain how to balance her new checkbook. Every morning, Mama took to sitting at the dining room table to practice with what she had taken to calling "my book." One day, the payment arrived from the insurance company, and Mama wrote a four-thousand-dollar check to pay for Daddy's funeral.

Then time seemed to change and grow languid. Always, the nights came slowly. Nothin' much happened, that was how Mama said it. Johnny didn't visit from Jackson; not even Cindy and Erin visited. Gerry called, but he seemed a world away. I didn't hear from anybody else in New York except from my boss at the publishing company, who phoned to sympathize, not to pressure me to return. Mama and I existed in a kind of isolation, with just each other and the TV for company, our only friends Marshal Matt Dillon and Ben Cartwright.

Napping provided us escape from the slowly turning days. There were two kinds: Bed naps commenced with lying down and might last all afternoon; chair naps were shorter and took place in front of the television. I liked to stretch out on the double bed in the Toy Room and drift on the sunlight filtering through the pinholes in the yellowed window shades, while Mama's favorite place was in her recliner.

Once she dreamed that she was in the Bassett watching television while Daddy fixed them lunch. He was whistling as he sometimes did, and the dream had seemed so real that when she woke up, she went looking for him in the kitchen. When she didn't find him there, she went to the cemetery. She'd taken to driving off by herself in the Olds each day, after the two o'clock showing of *Bonanza*. I would probe her about these excursions, but she would only complain that I asked too many questions.

One Thursday, to get us out of the house, I suggested we have dinner in a restaurant. Mama agreed, and we cranked up the Oldsmobile for chicken and dumplings at Stub's, which quickly became a habit for us. The self-service restaurant came alive just before noon but was deserted by one, the chocolate chess pie tray empty in the refrigerator case and the stainless-steel vats of grease cooling in the kitchen. It seemed the entire town came—Mississippi Chemical laborers in jeans and T-shirts and office workers in dress shirts and ties; judges and dentists, including Mama's, who dined in his blue scrubs; dirt-clad cotton and catfish farmers; thickset black ladies in fancy hats and calf-length shirtdresses whose stockings swished as they walked. The hearse from Stricklin-King would pull up, and the driver would run inside; he ate quickly. The Lions Club met in the banquet room. Once we even saw the mayor, and Mama tried to persuade him to cut the top off the giant hackberry in her backyard. She was afraid that if we got another ice storm, like back in '51, the tree's huge limbs would fall onto her house. He promised, just as any good politician would, but nobody ever came to trim the tree. There was no ice storm, either.

After dinner at Stub's, we would drive out Highway 49. Mama wanted to see where she'd been raised and to visit the Midway Primitive Baptist Church and her parents' graves. While she studied their tombstone, I would wait at a distance. She didn't speak, except maybe to comment that their marker needed a good cleaning or that the pink and purple plastic flowers adorning their plots could use replacing. When she finished paying her respects, we would climb back into the Oldsmobile.

We might stop for a Coke at Midway Grocery, where Mama said Grandma Hood had traded fresh eggs for school paper sixty years earlier. Nowadays, the little store sold soft drinks, candy, and peanuts in a locale so remote that the ice cream truck didn't even stop. But it was a busy place, with farmers parked out front in muddy pickups, hanging from windows to chaw while their dogs sniffed each other's tails. Inside, a hand-lettered sign by the pay phone read, "If what you have to say takes longer than three minutes, I suggest you go see the person you intend to call."

Those weeks we took many trips into the gentle hills around Midway and Benton. We would ride, and Mama would talk. Something would set off her memory—a bend in the road, or the way the sunlight filtered through a stand of trees, or a lone brick chimney—and she would relate snatches of her long-ago life. About her great-uncle J. A. Hood, who had fancied himself a poet. On July 7, 1875, he wrote to a young lady of his fancy: "Dear Miss, it is with pleasure that I take my pen in hand to drop you a few lines to tell you how I love you. I love you better than anything in the world except fried gosling." But J.A. was a man so mean that people drew straws to decide who would kill him. Afterward, they found in his pocket the small leather book where he jotted his poems, which to this day bears the knife lick.

Or Mama might speak of Myrt and Mattie, the "kissin' aunts," from whom she "would run like a turkey." How once Grandma Hood tried whiskey and "chased the stove all day." That Mama had kept a crippled hen for a pet, but Grandma Hood got tired of it underfoot, so one Sunday there was a fine plate of chicken and dumplings on the table. Our drives loosened Mama's memory, so these recollections might slip out.

Mostly she talked about Daddy. She talked about our poverty—not just the scarcity of money, but the lack of spirit and hope. She reminded me how she'd applied for a job at the local Head Start program. She didn't mention it to Daddy until the day before she was supposed to report, and when he found out, he blew up. He couldn't stand that she would be outside the house, taking care of black children rather than us, even though by then we were well up in school. So Mama phoned in her resignation even before beginning. But that wasn't enough for Daddy: He gave her the Silent Treatment.

At least once, Mama had thought of leaving him. I was able to recall the warm night when I cowered at the foot of her bed with the lights out, a young girl in baby doll pajamas, while she lay perfectly still. I could remember her saying how the Catholic religion bound them together and besides, where was she to go with four children?

But when we were nearly grown, she did finally defy Daddy and take a job. She was briefly a part-time switchboard operator at King's Daughters Hospital and for several years a typist at Amco, a manufacturer of farm equipment. She had used her small salary to buy her bedroom set and the Bassett. I hadn't even remembered Mama's jobs, which she'd gotten as I was starting college, but hearing her talk about them now, I knew how hard it must have been for her to go against Daddy. When she was laid off from Amco, she retreated to the house and her chair.

Mama talked, and I listened. I took in the rhythmic quiet of our drives, the lulling sound of tires on pavement, the deserted roads with their clean light and long shadows. In the distance I saw the muddy Mississippi creeks with their white sandy banks; I saw the farmers and their spring machines lumbering in the arc of their fields. I had come to Mississippi thinking I could just forget Daddy. Mama had told me I didn't know him, but now I realized I hadn't known my mama, either. As I took in her words, I felt pride and sadness, and anger receding. We rode, remembering. It was our way of grieving.

Twenty-four

One Sunday morning, Mama decided to fry a chicken. She hauled the phone out from under her Bassett and invited Cindy and Erin to eat with us, then turned on the television. Although she hadn't gone back to Mass, saying she didn't like to sit alone in the family pew, she'd devoted herself to another ritual: She watched *Meet the Press* and had even gotten on a first-name basis with the anchor. This morning when the show finished, Mama complained about the Republicans. "I just don't like the way they talk," she sighed, handing off the clicker to me.

I watched as she shuffled into the kitchen in her house shoes, heard the refrigerator door squeak open and water running in the sink as she started to cut up a chicken. Mama always cooked a whole fryer, which she would first scour inside and out with cold water. Then she would carve it up with a butcher knife, sculpting dainty pieces, including the much-prized wishbone, which we called the "woolly bone." She would flour and fry everything—even the neck, back, gizzard, and liver—in her big black cast-iron skillet. There was no point in offering to help her, since she wouldn't have accepted.

At eleven-thirty, Cindy and Erin came over. We hadn't seen them in the three weeks since Daddy's funeral, but Cindy had called to say she'd made other babysitting arrangements. Now her parents took care of Erin while she worked afternoons at Murphy's Florist.

She sank down on the corduroy couch. "I know I look like I been rode hard and put up wet," she said. Her light brown hair, which she'd drawn into a stringy ponytail, was still damp from her shower.

Erin grabbed the remote from me and stood in front of the television. She began flipping channels, flying past a Tarzan movie and Sunday preaching. "The picture's green," she complained. "Will y'all ever get a new TV?"

I shrugged. Then the kitchen door swung open, and Mama appeared, holding a large fork and wiping her forehead with her apron tail. "Y'all want some sweet tea?" she asked breathlessly. Frying chicken was hard on Mama, because she stood over the hot stove so she could turn the pieces just as they browned. When Cindy shook her head, Mama went back into the kitchen, Erin tagging behind.

I took the opportunity to ask about Erin's health. "There ain't nothin' new," Cindy said as she pulled a cigarette package and a disposable lighter from her quilted bag. "Mind if I smoke?" I shook my head, and she lit up, taking a slow draw but letting the smoke out quickly. Then she waved the cigarette, as though she could sense my disapproval. "I think I'll go outside with this," she said.

A moment later, Erin bounded back into the living room and flopped down in the Bassett. She wiggled her feet and arms and turned her head from side to side; then she rocked furiously, staring at the ceiling. I knew from Daddy that aspects of the duplex frightened her, especially the black cloudlike stains left by the leaks in the living and dining room ceilings. Her obsession with them had in turn obsessed Daddy, who'd been afraid she might stop visiting. Not that he'd done anything to fix them.

"Where's my mama?" Erin asked, and I inclined my head toward the porch. But instead of going to find her, she picked up the remote and gave the TV another once-over.

Finally Mama called out, "Dunner! Y'all come on!"

Erin jumped up and ran into the dining room, and I went to get Cindy. She was slouching in a rocker that she'd pulled into a wedge of sunshine, her feet propped on one of the porch's narrow columns.

"Dinner's ready," I said, and she stamped out her cigarette. As I followed her inside, I glanced across the yard toward St. John's. The members of the congregation—middle-aged, small-town folk with soft bodies and average expressions—were ambling to their cars, which they'd parked up and down Calhoun Avenue. It was just noon.

In the center of the dining table, Mama had placed the platter of chicken, a pyramid of flaky, bronze pieces. She and Erin were already seated, and I took my place next to Mama so that Cindy could occupy Sol's chair at the end. Erin rushed through the blessing Daddy had always recited, then helped herself to the potato salad. This was one of the few foods she would eat, along with canned English peas, mashed potatoes, and jolly-jolly-jing-jing-jing. Daddy had introduced her to all the Old Country dishes when she was a baby. Though she ate cubbie, she put catsup on it, as if it were a Middle Eastern hamburger. She wouldn't touch sap soup, convinced the salad was made from weeds—actually, mint that grew around the faucet in Grandma's backyard.

Mama fanned herself with a paper napkin, then poured herself a glass of tea and placed a lone chicken liver on her plate. Cindy didn't take much, either. I helped myself to the woolly bone, which I ate in a few bites. When I was finished, I extended the bone toward Erin and ordered, "Pull." She yanked hard, just as her father always had in these contests, and came away with the longer side.

"I won! Now Grandma can get a new TV instead of that crummy green one. Won't you get a new TV now that Granddaddy's gone?" Even she realized that he'd been the one who'd held back progress in this house.

Mama asked, "Green? Maybe they's some knobs we can turn."

Erin let the split woolly bone drop onto the tablecloth.

I said, "I don't think that TV is going to be fixed with any knob."

A few feet away, the disparaged Zenith blared in the living room. This was like every Sunday dinner we'd ever had as a family. There was a sense of nothing much happening, either inside or outside the house, of the world slowed down and grown quiet except for the drone of the television. I took a slice of Sunbeam bread and tore the middle from the crust, then started mopping up crumbs as large as pennies from the bottom of the chicken plate, pushing them into the doughy bread and squeezing it into the shape of my fist. We'd called this a "crumb sandwich," and I began to eat it slowly, savoring the perfect blend of taste and memory.

Mama went on fanning herself with the napkin. "A new TV," she mused, taking up the conversational thread of ten minutes ago. She drained her glass of tea. "Well, I don't know 'bout that. But I decided to git my house painted."

I lowered the crumb sandwich. "What did you say?"

She cut into the chicken liver on her plate and took a little bite. "I said, I done made up my mind to git my house painted."

I could hardly believe it: After wishing for so long that Daddy would fix up the house for her, Mama was finally going to do it for herself. Then everybody started talking all at once. Cindy wanted Mama to buy a clothes dryer, which she promised that her father, James, would install, so that Mama wouldn't have to go to the laundromat in winter. Erin asked, "Grandma, what about a new livin' room couch, to go with the new TV?"

But, I had a terrible thought. "You said you're going to get the house painted. You mean both the outside and the inside, don't you?"

Mama was fingering her empty tea glass. "Naw, just the outside."

Erin dropped her head onto the back of her chair. Cindy asked, "But Miz Nicholas, what about the rest that needs doin'?"

Mama stood to clear the dishes. "Can't do no more. That's all I can afford."

"But you've got all of Daddy's money!" I burst out.

She muttered, "Naw."

"Well, just how are you going to pay for painting the house if you're not going to use his money?"

She was scraping our plates onto hers. "Well, with the li'l ole gent's, of course. You wanted me to use it, Treesa."

Cindy looked bewildered, but I didn't stop to explain. "It costs more than five hundred dollars to paint a house," I told Mama, thinking of mine back in Bronxville, which we'd recently painted for five thousand.

She glanced at me out of the corner of her eye. "I know that," she said coyly. "It costs six hundred if it costs a day."

I sputtered, "Mama, how could that possibly be enough to paint this house?"

"Well, I got me a price for that," she sniffed.

I couldn't imagine Mama soliciting an estimate, much less believe that she'd found somebody who'd quoted so little. "Who from?"

"Why, Mr. Tyson, who done painted the house back in '64."

"Mr. Tyson!" I thought of his photo in the camera bag, his brown face wrinkled as a walnut shell. "How could he still be painting houses? He must be close to ninety years old."

She stopped stacking dishes to calculate. "Naw, he's closer to a hundred. But he's still paintin' houses." Then she walked off into the kitchen.

"How's he going to climb up on a ladder? Answer me that!" I yelled after her.

She called back, "All I know, young'un, is that I'm goin' to git my house painted, and Mr. Tyson's goin' to do it."

I heard her turn on the rusty taps, the water running in the sink. "Aren't you worried he's too old to take on a job as big as painting this house?"

She cut off the water and poked her head into the dining room. "Naw, that ain't what worries me," she admitted. "What worries me is he has cancer."

She marched to her chair, and the rest of us followed. I looked at her with exasperation. "If you hire him, you better not pay him until he's finished!"

"Well, Mr. Tyson's goin' to want a deposit," she said, picking up her book of word puzzles.

Cindy and Erin left as soon as they decently could. When

they'd gone, Mama lowered her puzzle book and said quietly, "Treesa, don't worry so much about ever'thang. You always was the biggest worrier, even when you was little."

She was right. I was a worrier. And call me silly, but I worried about hiring a hundred-year-old man with cancer to paint her house. And in her fixation on ancient Mr. Tyson, we'd lost track of the real issue—her refusal to use Daddy's money to fix up the duplex from roof to foundation. I shook my head at her, not that she noticed.

She was full of plans. Spring would come, and with it her birthday and Mr. Tyson. He would paint the outside of the house, just as he had those many years ago. Once again, he'd sit in the shade of the yard, and she'd bring him dinner and iced tea in a jelly glass. Not only that, when he was finished painting, she would have him move the china cabinet from the dining room to make way for the writing desk she'd claimed at Grandma's. Why, maybe Mr. Tyson would like to have the old cabinet! One day, she'd put up the fine mirror and the paintings and the art deco chandelier, but not just now.

As she talked on into that time she called evening, really afternoon, I couldn't help but wonder if our visit to Grandma's hadn't inspired Mama to this. After all, once it took root, I knew Grandma's house to be a hard place to rid from your imagination.

Twenty-five

As the afternoon deepened, the day turned black dark. A thundercloud hung in the western sky; soon the temperature would drop and the wind pick up. Mama yawned, stretched for the remote, and reduced the TV's volume. Before she could settle into her chair nap, I got the Oldsmobile key from the wicker basket. "I'm going to visit Grandma," I told her, and she sent me off with a wave of her fingers.

I drove the few blocks to Martha Coker without meeting another car, diagonal parking in front of the nursing home. But I waited, preparing myself for my visit with Grandma. Finally, I made my way down the concrete walk toward the entrance, past the neatly trimmed holly hedges and the slender pines. What would I say to Grandma when she asked about her house? I would lie and say nothing.

In the entryway of the nursing home, I paused to examine the scene. As usual, the ablest of the residents were keeping company in the large, open room, with the ladies off to the right and the gentlemen to the left. I located Grandma and went to stand in front of her. She wore a beige duster with a frilly nightgown poking out from underneath and a soft, stark-white sweater on top. A cheerful blanket lay in her lap, with stripes of yellow, blue, white, green, and red. Next to her wheelchair was a straight-backed leather chair, and I took a seat. Grandma's gaunt blue eyes, encircled by her large plastic glasses, found mine, and the appearance of sweetest joy filled them. When she arched her eyebrows, I realized she was signaling me closer. Did she want to give me a kiss on the lips, our greeting of old? I bent toward her.

"My butt hurts!" she shouted.

I drew back. My grandma didn't talk this way. I'd never heard her use strong language, at least not in English. She'd often discharged a word that sounded like *hotter,* which we understood to mean "damn." But this habit of hers had been grounds for laughter, a prim-mannered southern matron from Holmes County, Mississippi, swearing in Arabic.

She looked at me imploringly. "Treesa, pull me up by my armpits." Unable to shift her weight, she was confined to one position in the wheelchair, forced to suffer the discomfort of immobility. I thought back to my last visit, when I'd found her in bed, also unable to budge.

I stood up in front of her and tried to do as she requested. As bony as her arms and shoulders were, her lower body was a load, and I couldn't raise her. Finally I sat back down, and she scowled, disgusted with my failure. We weren't getting off to a very good start. Then it began.

"How's my house?"

"Fine."

"Take me home. I'm goin' back there and never comin' out again."

"Nome, I can't."

The lady to our left, who'd been watching us intently, began to wail, "No, no, no," as if echoing my denial. A nurse with a starched cap perched on her bouffant hairdo came over to comfort her with a few soft words, without effect. And so we went on, Grandma begging to go home, and her companion chiming in with her "nos." I glanced through the window into the courtyard just outside where we were sitting. The early spring flowers, the hyacinths and tulips and daffodils, drooped in the rain, as fat drops danced on the stone patio like stubby men. I would go mad listening to these two old ladies.

Grandma stopped asking about her house when her right hand began to shake. The tremor started small but moved up to include her entire arm before gradually ebbing. When she resumed speaking, she changed the topic to Grendaddy. "He done me dirty," she said. "Dirty, dirty, dirty, dirty, dirty." She twisted her mouth into the camel lips, then relaxed them and started back with the rant. After she said the word *dirty* exactly five times, she formed the lips again, alternating rant, lips, rant, lips. Then she said, "That's how come I didn't cry at his funeral" and was finally quiet.

I asked, "Why do you keep saying that about Grendaddy?"

Her eyes grew so round they seemed to fill the space defined by her glasses. There is a photograph of my grandparents taken during their courtship, sometime in the early 1920s. They are seated on the running board of a Model T. Behind them you can see the car's plush ribbed seats and its oversize steering wheel, and beyond, the thick foliage of a warm Mississippi day. She is wearing a flapper dress with a lacy skirt and a scalloped hem. Her hair is bobbed, and she has bangs. He is dressed in a light-colored suit and is holding a straw hat with a wide band. His dark, foreign looks contrast sharply with her fair features. Although their shoulders are touching and he has inclined his knee slightly toward hers, they look like strangers.

When I knew them in the 1950s, they still seemed strangers to one another, still a study in contrasts. They could be summed up by the way they wrote: She used a ballpoint pen and had painstakingly regular handwriting; he a pencil, and his English was full of mistakes. Despite their differences, I believed they'd loved each other because they'd slept together in their double bed surrounded by the romantic rose-patterned wallpaper. Yet they did criticize each other, he calling her the Old Battle-Axe, she complaining about the way he repaired things with bailing wire and shoe polish and bubble gum. Moreover, Grandma thought he had no gumption. Her proof was that the grocery store had failed during the Great Depression.

But I doubted that these shortcomings of his could infuriate her so much that she would rant like this eighteen years after his death. Was she mad at him for dying first? Did she resent him for leaving her alone all those years in that big house with no other companion than Penny Girl, their hairless fice terrier?

I thought back to the cold way she'd described Grendaddy's death to me, shortly after it happened. He'd been sitting in the wide center hallway, watching television. At eleven o'clock, he appeared in the doorway of their bedroom, awoke her, and told her he was dying. She rose and helped him the few feet to his recliner, asked him if he was in pain. When he replied, "No, no pain," she'd said, peeved, "Well, then, what do you mean, sayin' you're dyin'?"

Yet before the ambulance could arrive, even before my father could run down that silent southern street, Grendaddy was gone. "You could see this pallor come over him," she'd said to me, no softness in her voice. Reaching up with her hand, she'd pulled an invisible shade from her forehead down to her chin. "He changed colors, and these great big ole balls of sweat broke out on him."

Now I asked her again. "Why do you keep saying that about Grendaddy?"

"He done me dirty," she said.

I stood up to distract her from the rant that I knew was about to begin again. "Grandma, let me wheel you around the corridor." I released the brake on her wheelchair and pushed her past the other residents.

"That's the men's side," she objected, gesturing toward the patio with her index finger.

"What?" I stopped, momentarily confused.

"The men's side," she repeated, directing the wayward finger more accurately and sounding appalled.

"Yes'um," I said, and took her down their side anyway.

As we got under way, she didn't protest again. Although the men's corridor was a mirror image of the women's, and like theirs illuminated with fluorescent lights and equipped with waist-high grab bars, it was new to her and prohibited territory. She swiveled her bony head back and forth, excited to be taking it in. Since most of the men were back in the sitting room, nobody was around, and we dashed along. I pushed her faster until I had the impression that we were flying together in the open cockpit of an old-fashioned plane, our scarves beating in the breeze. Then we came upon a spacious lounge with two fake-leather club chairs and a wide-screen television. With a flourish, I wheeled her in front of the TV, fastening the brake on her chair. Though the volume was turned up loud, after a minute she complained, "I can't hear the thing," and I pushed her even closer, until her face was just inches away.

Something magical was happening. Grandma stared at the television and then laughed, a deep chortle rising from her belly. The phrase *tickled to death* came to mind. She had often said she was tickled to death by one tiny thing or another, such as her favorite comic strip, *Beetle Bailey*. I stood back and admired my handiwork: I'd made Grandma laugh again, laugh in the old way, and all it had taken was a little trip down the men's side.

Then she shouted and pointed her crooked index finger again. "That nigger, she's done good by herself!" Startled, I looked at Grandma, then at the TV. Oprah was on the giant screen, advertising her daily television show.

I explained as patiently as I could. "Grandma, that's Oprah. You know, Oprah, from Kosciusko." I thought if I reminded her that Oprah was a fellow Mississippian, she might relent. "Oprah, Oprah," I repeated like a chant. "Our state treasure, Oprah."

"Nigger," she said, staring at me.

I glanced around to see if anyone had heard. I wanted to rap Grandma on the top of her crusty head, wheel her back to the front, park her, and leave her there. I released the brake and began pushing her slowly toward the sitting room. In the hall, we passed a black attendant, who smiled cautiously at Grandma. I was beginning to understand. The staff must have hated her.

When we got to the entrance, Pauline was there, looking for her mother. "Here she is," I announced, my voice sounding overly bright. "We've been for a ride." I wanted to hand Grandma over to her and run, but it was five o'clock, and I was caught. Pauline was insisting I stay for supper. She'd already had the staff set three places for us in the dining room.

We situated ourselves at my grandmother's usual table, close to the kitchen. Those residents who were able to sit up and eat slowly filed in. Others, such as Grandma's roommate, had to receive trays in their rooms. The servers, two large black ladies wearing hairnets, began distributing plates. They placed one in front of Grandma, and we stared at the gooey food.

Then Grandma looked at me. "Where's yours?"

"Nome, thanks just the same, but I'm not hungry," I answered.

Nevertheless, the next time a server ambled by, Grandma requested plates for Pauline and me. My aunt didn't pay hers any attention but started to talk. Grandma's supper also remained uneaten, congealing as it cooled. The staff began moving among the other tables, helping some of the more infirm to cut their food. Then I realized that Grandma couldn't eat, because she couldn't manage the fork and knife. When nobody came over to us, I figured they thought we'd help Grandma, but neither Pauline nor I did.

Finally I asked, "Grandma, do you want something?" She only stared. "To eat?" I shouted. "Eat, eat, eat?"

She continued looking at me with those round, vacant eyes then said in a most unladylike but entirely lucid way, "I don't want to eat this crap."

Pauline continued to talk. Grandma randomly placed a finger on the side of her nose, and a nurse came over and chastised her for "not eatin' a thing." As soon as the servers cleared, Pauline got up.

"You're not goin', are you?" Grandma asked. "Don't leave me here. Take me home."

"Mama, I've got to go. I'll see you later this week."

I also stood. "I've got to leave, too." We left Grandma sitting alone at her table, waiting to be pushed back to Room 115.

Something was dispelled that day, something that would not come again. As I left, I had the impulse to cry: Like Grandma's laugh, that chortle I'd resurrected so briefly, my urge rose from the stomach, but I stopped it in my throat, preventing it from going any further. I lost Grandma that day, lost her for good. I'd always known, deep down, what she was like, but it wasn't until that day that I let myself admit it. What was it she'd used to sing to me? *Any bags, any bones, any bottles today, it's the same old story in the same old way.* Same old story, same old way.

Twenty-six

The sky was on the move again. The black birds returned one afternoon at five o'clock, massing like a dark cloud over St. John's.

"What in the world is happening?" I called to Mama from the porch.

But she didn't answer me. She was in her Bassett with the telephone next to her, waiting for Mr. Tyson to call to tell her when he'd start painting. Yet the phone hadn't rung, and she'd grown worried. She had no bother over birds.

Early the next morning, I came upon her in the door of Daddy's closet, pulling his shirts off their wire hangers, piling them on top of the love seat cushions. I fingered the polyesters and flannels and pulled out a red and white wool plaid that I remembered him wearing back in the late 1950s.

"What are you goin' to do with that?" Mama asked suspiciously. She was finally weeding out his clothes, and she didn't want me second-guessing her.

"I'm going to take it home with me," I told her.

She seemed surprised. I hadn't mentioned leaving before. "At some point I've got to go back to New York," I said matter-of-factly, trying to ignore her disappointed expression. I pointed toward the castoffs. "After dinner, if you like, I'll take these to St. Mary's."

"Naw, ain't no need. They'll come git 'em. Just fold 'em up in a box."

She worked on his closet for a while longer. At eleven o'clock, just when I thought she'd quit to cook dinner, she went to Daddy's bedroom. Except for the three nights Joel had slept there, the room had remained sealed off, its door propped closed with a baseball bat. Now Mama paused in front of it, wielding a broom and a black garbage bag. Then she reached for the gold-spray-painted doorknob and marched inside.

I tagged behind, watching her. "What are you about to do?"

"Clean out Daddy's room."

"Right this minute?"

"I don't know no better time." From the doorway, we considered the prospect: Daddy's bed, the only orderly spot, with its white spread pulled taut. The two bureaus, the blanket box, and the table. The sealed-off front door. Brown and black curtains in a geometric design, the peeling pink fleur-de-lis wallpaper hung with the monkey calendars. And of course, Daddy's junk, piled on the furniture and poking out from under the bed. Mama stepped over a mop and bent down to look at a stack of posters under the double windows, advertisements for the county fairs that had come each fall for as many years as I could remember. On each poster, in the lower right-hand corner, Daddy had penned his name in his slanted handwriting, *S. T. Nicholas Jr.* I thought again how it read like "St. Nicholas" and of what Uncle Sam had said at the funeral, that if anybody would go to heaven, it would be Daddy.

"He pulled these off the telephone poles," Mama said. I had the impression that at least this odd practice of his had tickled her. "You remember them fairs, Treesa?" And I did—how when the weather cooled and the cotton went to gin, these broadsides would appear, crudely illustrated and printed in fluorescent inks. Then would come our long anticipation of the chosen day, when we would finally climb into whichever vehicle happened to be working and Daddy would deliver us to the fairgrounds. As we turned onto Airport Road, the carnival would announce itself with the mesmerizing lights of the Ferris wheel.

Now I stooped to read one of the posters, which had alternating yellow and red block type that grew bigger toward the bottom. *The Absolute Finest in Family Entertainment,* it promised. I observed that beneath his blue ballpoint signature, Daddy had added the date he'd pried it off the pole.

"Crumple these up and stuff 'em in this here trash bag," Mama ordered.

"I can't do that," I told her. Daddy had been trying to make permanent the fleeting days of traveling fairs, and throwing away the posters seemed just plain wrong.

She eyed me ominously. "Do as I say, young'un."

I separated out six of my favorites, then pitched the others.

"Over here," Mama commanded. She was standing next to his bed. "Reach down and take ever'thang out from underneath."

I dropped to my hands and knees and dragged out old-fashioned black telephones and fat-stranded mops and clear plastic containers. These last, about three by four and an inch deep, had originated from Patenotte's Grocery and had once been full of pimento cheese. He'd washed the containers, about thirty in all, but left them with their labels intact.

"What a pack rat," Mama said, ramming pimento cheese containers into the garbage bag. "While I do this, Treesa, take all them mops outside. There's more out front. He hung mops in the bush he planted for you. Put 'em all in the gutter for the garbage man."

I gathered together the half dozen mops from under the

bed, then went out to the side yard. My namesake shrub, about six feet tall, grew in an oval shape, with dense, evergreen leaves. I removed another six mops, which he'd draped with their wooden handles pointing down. But instead of obeying Mama, I walked back to the front door and yelled, "Don't you want to keep any of these?"

"Naw," came her sharp reply. I pitched the mops into the street.

Back in Daddy's bedroom, Mama was loading up the bag with telephones. "You got all the mops out of the bush?"

I nodded.

"I'm goin' to git that thang cut down," she proclaimed.

"Why?" The Debbie gingko, the Sol Boy and Lisa Maria sycamores, these she wasn't talking about annihilating.

"Because them li'l black birds sit and eat them berries, and then they doody on my car."

She handed me the garbage bag. "Take this out, and on your way back bring me an empty one."

"Don't any of these work?" I pointed to the nest of wires, receivers, and phone bodies protruding out the top. She smacked her lips, as if to say, *How ridiculous*. Again, I made my way to the street.

This time when I returned, Mama had her back to me, examining something. On the floor at the foot of Daddy's bed was the torso of a female mannequin. Except for a tartan scarf wound tightly around her neck, she was naked. But that wasn't all. There was a row of these ladies set up under the windows, and they were all naked, except for the tractor caps he'd placed on their bald heads.

"Where did you find them?"

"Humph," Mama responded, somewhere between mad and embarrassed.

"They were under his bed?"

"And hidden under the table."

"What should we do with them?"

Finally she said, "We'll put 'em in the trunk of the Oldsmobile and this evenin' cart 'em to the dump." I knew it wouldn't do, adding them to the pile for the garbage man.

"Grab some of 'em," she said.

We carried them out on our hips, two by two, and lined them up on the front porch. With Mama standing beside me, I opened the trunk of the Olds.

"Oh, my God!"

"Get the Chevrolet key," Mama snapped. I did as I was told. But it, too, was full of the busts.

Maybe it wasn't time for reflection, but I thought of Grendaddy. How once he'd placed a mannequin in the grocery store window. But he'd dressed his, not only in Debbie's Girl Scout beanie but also in the uniform shirt. One day, a black couple on their way through town had pulled up in a gold Cadillac. The lady wanted the dummy to put up in her living room, and Grendaddy reaped a bonanza of $7.50 for it.

I asked, "Mama, what does it all mean?"

She said, "It means we have to load up the back of Sol's truck."

This we did, piling the dummies helter-skelter, their half smiles going in a dozen different directions. I covered them with more black garbage bags. Later on we'd visit the dump, but for now Mama wanted to return to Daddy's bedroom. Though it was way past the hour for dinner, she wouldn't be stopped. Every last trace of Daddy would be thrown out, the years of his accumulations.

It was time for the bureaus. From that day when we'd

searched for the key to the money bag, I knew we'd find Daddy's coin collection—Indian head pennies, buffalo nickels, Roosevelt and Mercury dimes, and silver dollars. We also found Debbie's high school slide rule and a crumpled 1973 Buick calendar (commemorating the 1903 Model A, the 1933 Model 33 56C, and the 1963 Riviera). Spent flashcubes, twisted electrical wires, plastic caps, motor condensers, screws, sparkplugs, marbles, nails, a package of Listo Lead (black no. 162), and his childhood red and green spinning top with a large glob of glue holding the stem to the base. There were forty-year-old passbooks from Delta National and the Bank of Yazoo City, exhorting, "Save Regularly." Letters from Heber Ladner, Mississippi's secretary of state in the 1950s, authorizing Daddy as a notary public. A red and blue pamphlet from the White Citizens' Council protesting the integration of King's Daughters Hospital in the 1970s.

I dropped all of it, minus the coins, into the garbage bag. We would make quick work of this, doing away with Daddy.

Then in the bottom drawer I saw a flimsy, handmade book, bound with a yellow cord and decorated with holly boughs and a tiny black-and-white illustration of a manger scene. At the top, printed in block letters, were the words, "TO MOTHER," and at the bottom, "AND DADDY." I turned to the first page. "I have a Christmas surprise for you," my father had written to his parents in 1933. "I am offering my Masses, Holy Communion, and all my prayers on Christmas Day for you. I hope the Christ Child will bless you."

The booklet also included two essays, two pages of writing practice, and a drawing of an apple. I started to read out loud, deciphering Daddy's young handwriting, more upright and rounder than his adult slant, careful in the way of a boy who has just learned. His essay "The Fair" began, "The fair was supposed to bring a circus but they brought the baby airplanes instead. I rode on the whip. One night I saw a white man and a colored man box. One night my daddy was going to let me go to the fair but he gave me only twenty cents. My mother gave me a dollar bill."

I glanced at Mama. "It's funny to think of Daddy, when he was only eight, writing this," I said.

She looked at me quizzically.

"You know, it's hard to imagine what their life was like at home, Daddy and Grandma and Grendaddy." Had he been a mama's boy? Was that why he'd addressed the book to his mother, with his father's name added at the bottom, like an afterthought? Was Daddy, like Grandma, critical of Grendaddy? Was that why he'd mentioned how much money they'd each given him for the fair?

"Look a here," Mama was saying. That same drawer was full of our baby shoes—Debbie's Baby Janes, the black patent leather shiny after forty years; a pair of Sol's desiccated brown baby boots. There were polished white shoes and pastel knitted booties. Then Mama pulled out a cigar box and handed it to me. It was light brown and smelled of sweet cedar wood. The engraved label, green, gold, black, and pink, said, *Perfecto Garcia & Bros. Finest Cigars.*

I sat down on Daddy's bed and opened the box. Inside I was surprised to discover a miniature copy of my birth certificate. The orange nametag off my Challenger bike. A holy card from my First Communion, May 13, 1962. A white handkerchief embroidered with Daddy's name. A tarnished money clip with a Buick affixed to the front. There was also a brittle newspaper clipping, a photograph of Johnny and me from May 20, 1972, when we'd won a journalism prize given by the *Memphis Com-*

mercial Appeal. I'd thought Daddy hadn't approved of my writing for the high school newspaper, but he'd saved the article, and when he'd made up this box, he'd put it with the rest of the things that were to be my keepsakes from him.

By now the sunlight in the room had traveled from the two side windows to the three panes above the duplex's old front door. Mama took a seat beside me, the half-filled garbage bag deflated at her feet. "One for each of y'all," she said. "Open 'em."

Inside Debbie's, Daddy had placed a receipt from the Wood Street Grocery dated April 15, 1952, for a nine-inch, two-layer cake with one candle and the inscription, *H.B.D., Debbie.* In Lisa Maria's, he'd put her gold-tinged baby hair, coiled inside white envelopes. He had kept not only her earliest curls but also her adolescent clippings, the most recent from June 22, 1975, when she was sixteen years old.

Then Mama handed me Sol's cigar box. Daddy had saved a lock from his first haircut and his first lost tooth. He'd saved the commemorative cards from his First Holy Communion and his Confirmation and had even kept the little clip-on ties Sol had worn—white for the Communion, black with gold spots and stripes for the Confirmation. At the bottom of his cigar box was a laminated, tasseled copy of his obituary, headlined, "Solomon T. Nicholas III, Pipe Fitter."

I looked at Mama for her reaction, but she was studying a piece of lined paper. Over her shoulder, I read the date written in longhand: October 30, 1954. It was an invoice from King's Daughters Hospital, addressed to her:

Room from 10-26 to 10-30	36.00
Nursery 1 @ 2.00, 3 @ 2.00	8.00
Delivery room	10.00
Anaesthetic	10.00

Medicines	22.70
Oxygen	32.50
Lab and Dressings	7.00
Total	126.20

The line for babies' beads, which would have been put around their wrists to identify them, was blank; apparently there had been no need. Just as my parents had always said, one of the twins had lived one day, the other three.

I took the invoice from Mama and turned it over. On the back, I recognized Daddy's handwriting. He'd printed twelve Bible verses in blue ballpoint. From John 3:16: "For God so loved the world, that he gave his only begotten Son, that whosoever believeth in Him should not perish, but have everlasting life." And from Corinthians 6:2: "For he saith, I have heard them in a time accepted, and in the day of salvation I have succored thee: Behold, now is the accepted time; behold, now is the day of salvation."

Mama laid the invoice on top of Sol's remembrances and sighed. "When I die," she said, "promise y'all do somethin' for me."

"Promise you what?" I stood up and began to unload the contents of the garbage bag back into the drawers. "You already told me not to let Buster put any makeup on you when he lays you out."

"Well, I got more to say, Treesa."

I sat down again and felt her weight sagging on the mattress.

"I want you, Debbie, and Lisa to divvy up the crystal, china, and silver. I want Erin to have my birthstone ring, because she was born in March, too. And promise me that the only flowers at the funeral are the ones y'all put on my coffin."

I nodded, remembering that when I'd ordered the arrangement for Daddy, she'd insisted I buy only ones for the coffin, too.

"And one more thang. Promise me y'all visit my grave."

I thought of the trips we'd made to her parents at Primitive Baptist Church in Midway and of her visits to Daddy in Glenwood. I nodded again.

Mama had gotten all of her final wishes out. As we turned to go, I noticed another naked dummy, her protruding beige bosom peeking out from the blanket box. Mama saw her, too, but said nothing.

A week passed, and time worked its way ineluctably toward March and Mama's birthday. Meanwhile, she still waited for word from Mr. Tyson. Then one Friday afternoon, my boss telephoned, causing Mama to jump. He said if I was coming back, I'd better come on. He'd taken a month off for his father's illness and death, and I'd been gone now just over four weeks.

Afterward, I went out onto the front porch and sat in the rocker, while Mama settled herself to nap in the Bassett. There wasn't much traffic, but whenever a car or truck did happen by, the driver would wave at me. I propped my feet up on a porch column and watched as a curl of papery white bark slipped off one of the sycamores. The foliage was budding on both trees and soon would stretch a verdant rooftop over the yard. I knew I had to go back inside and tell Mama I was leaving, but I couldn't bring myself to do it, not just yet. Then a late-model gold Buick pulled up into the yard, and Uncle Sam strolled down the sidewalk toward me. He had on a dark blazer and a checkered shirt and was holding an envelope in his hand. I hopped off the porch, and when I kissed his cheek, a shy smile lit up his moon-shaped face.

Uncle Sam asked after Mama, and I told him she was napping. I invited him to sit with me on the porch. "What are you doing over this way?" I asked him.

"I had some business to take care of with the Nicholas Trust," he said. These were the properties still owned by the family, including the defunct Bon Ton Café and Nicholas Cash Gro. and the Army-Navy.

"You know, your daddy managed the trust."

"I didn't know." Just another thing I hadn't known about my father.

He nodded. "Uh-huh. He was the treasurer."

"Does the trust have much income?"

"Not for years," he told me. "I have this check for your mother. To pay her Sol June's salary for January."

"Oh, really?"

"Just seventy-five dollars."

"Oh," I said.

"I guess I'll manage the trust from here on out."

"What do you mean, from here on out?"

"We're tryin' to sell the buildings," he explained.

"Oh," I said again.

A whiff of Uncle Sam's Old Spice wafted toward me. I'd been waiting a long time to ask him this question. "Do you remember what you said to me about Daddy, at the funeral home?"

"What's that, sugar?" He peered at me over his black-framed eyeglasses.

"You said my daddy was a saint."

"I did?"

"And that if anybody would go to heaven, it would be him."

He chuckled. "Honey, I can't remember the half of what I say these days."

I was disappointed, because I'd hoped that he would tell me something I didn't know about Daddy. But as it turned out, his remark was just one of those things people said; he didn't think Daddy was a saint any more than I did.

Uncle Sam must have sensed my disappointment, because he added quickly, "Your daddy may have been a little unusual, but he was a good man."

For a while longer, we sat side by side. Finally I asked Uncle Sam to tell me where each of his eight children was living nowadays, and one by one he rattled off their names and the cities to which they'd moved. Then he left. I didn't know it at the time, but I'd never see him again.

When I went back inside, Mama was in her chair, holding her chin in her palm.

I asked, "What's the matter?"

"You was right, Treesa," she said, not bothering to meet my eyes.

"What do you mean, Mama?"

"I called Mr. Tyson."

"And what did he say?"

She sighed. "Mr. Tyson's done died."

I sat down next to her on the love seat.

"That's how come he didn't call." She'd talked to Mr. Tyson's daughter, who'd informed her that the painter had passed on a few days ago, sitting in his own chair.

I reached for her hand. "I have more bad news."

"What?" She looked at me anxiously.

"I'm leaving Sunday."

"Well, I knew you was eventually." Then she glanced off, and I felt that she had left me. Well, at least now Mama could write a check and buy canned tuna. But I feared that Mr. Tyson dying was the end of her ever fixing up the duplex. That she wouldn't use Daddy's money, and that she would always be one of those people who wouldn't take nothin' from nobody.

I released her hand and went into the Toy Room to pack. I was going back to New York with six posters from the county fair and Daddy's baggy work shirt, which still had the yellow cleaner's tag stapled to its collar. I couldn't have said why I wanted these useless things of my father's, just that I wanted them and wanted them badly. As I put them into my suitcase, I keep thinking of what Mama had said: "You don't know your daddy, Treesa." If I'd learned anything about Daddy over the past month, it was that he wasn't as simple as he'd seemed. He'd had a secret financial life, he'd saved our baby hair, and he'd liked to collect busts of naked women.

That Sunday, just as we were about to say good-bye, Mama surprised me by pulling a wrinkled paper from her pocket. "I keep this in my underwear drawer," she said proudly and wistfully. As I began to read the faded writing, I recognized the note I'd written that day I'd left for college twenty-two years before. It didn't say much—only "Don't be sad at my going"—but Mama had kept it all these years. I remembered how little emotion I'd felt then, when I was so excited to be getting out of Mississippi. Now, as I left her again, alone and in that house, I felt the old guilt return. But I also felt something new. Now, as we stood on the front porch hugging good-bye, a large part of me wanted to stay with her.

Charlene, the lawn lady, gave me a ride to the airport. But as I boarded the plane that would take me to New York, I knew I would be coming home again soon.

Part IV

Buryin' Daddy

Twenty-seven

We circled over the city. This time, I wasn't cheered by the endless stretch of sodium lamps twinkling orange in the twilight across the five boroughs of New York. The same car service picked me up at the airport, and as the driver headed toward Westchester, I looked out at the city's tired street corners, capped with mounds of black snow and bits of stray garbage. After a long day of travel, I walked into the always-waiting house and Gerry's embrace.

I went right back to work. I took with me the six posters from the Yazoo County fair, put them in simple black frames, and hung them in my office. To my surprise, they delighted my sophisticated colleagues, and I found myself explaining how Daddy had pulled them off Yazoo's telephone poles, signed and dated them, then hidden them in his bedroom. During the interminable meetings, I also found myself thinking about Mama. I would trace her daily paths, from her bedroom to the Pink Bathroom to the Bassett, and remember the conversations we'd had in the dim light of the living room—how she'd struggled to explain her views even about something simple, such as why she preferred Pa's buckskin to Little Joe's pinto. "Naw, it ain't that I don't like Little Joe's horse. The thang is, I just like the color of Pa's better." How, after the two o'clock showing of

Bonanza and before the three o'clock *Gunsmoke*, she would "porch walk" to get out of that house, shuffling the length of the narrow overhang in navy felt slippers, stopping to admire the tiny green lizard who lived under the concrete steps.

Mama still didn't call me, but I took to calling her every morning. Now I knew her habits—that she got up at four, when the first freight train shook the town, and that as soon as the sun rose, she went outside to wash off the Oldsmobile's windshield. She hadn't yet cut down the offensive Teresa shrub, whose messy berries were sustaining a growing flock of spring birds. But she'd sold Sol's '81 GMC pickup to Brother, and she planned to sell the '60 Pontiac, the '63 Chevy, and the '67 Buick to a fellow named Osborne, who lived down the street and restored old cars. Soon the Olds would be her only vehicle.

By the time I called her, Mama would be in the Bassett, sipping Maxwell House. She'd answer the telephone by the second ring.

"Awful early to call, ain't it?" she'd say.

"How'd you sleep?" I'd ask.

The day of Daddy's funeral, she'd told me that she didn't need the deadbolt I'd had my cousin Alan install, but even with the new lock, Mama hadn't had the peace of mind to sleep well. She decided that the side yard between her bedroom and Aunt Pauline's carport was too dark, so one day, when she ran into the mayor in Stub's Restaurant, she asked him to put up a light. And not just any light, but a forty-foot-high sodium-vapor street lamp. She had to pay the city five dollars a month for it, a sore point with her, but I pointed out that if you considered the amount of illumination it threw off, it was a bargain. Mama had been sleeping better ever since.

I could see that she was changing her habits little by little, starting to adjust to life without Daddy. Weekdays after the westerns, Brother would pick her up, and they would drive to Stub's for coffee. Despite his diabetes, my uncle would also order himself a honey bun, which would be delivered to the table still in its cellophane package. On Sunday afternoons, Mama would visit Kmart, where she roamed the long aisles, checking out the prices of moisturizers and cartons of Coke. Afterward, she'd stop by the Shell station to buy the *Clarion-Ledger* from the vending machine. Sunday was the only day she took the paper, which she wanted mainly for the funnies, because Daddy, too, had enjoyed the adventures of Snuffy Smith, his wife, Loweezy, and their baby, Tater.

After I got back, whenever I worked in our garden, I took to wearing Daddy's red and white wool plaid shirt, which smelled of cleaner's fluid and felt scratchy and strange against my skin. My habitual sleeplessness worsened, and so began the evenings of sitting alone in the dark. I would lie on the couch in the living room, staring at the pin oak's emerging leaves, which were eerily illuminated by the neighbor's porch lamp. For the first time in a long time, I had a compulsion to write—about Mississippi, about the past, about my family—but I couldn't do more than scribble some disjointed thoughts. The tiny leaves got bigger. Once or twice, Gerry and I talked about making a change, moving into the city. A seemingly endless stream of dinner guests occupied the time, keeping the mind from straying too much.

Always I came back to those evenings alone. While Gerry slept his punctual sleep, I kept trying to set it all down. But it was as if there were a well inside, deep as wells are and smelling of rain and old dank places, only water could not be drawn. And so I continued the evenings of sitting alone in the dark, dry-eyed, with only the leaves and the wish to write.

✦ ✦ ✦

Then early one morning, Mama called.

"Treesa, I got to talk to you right this minute!"

I threw back the quilt and sat on the edge of my bed. "What is it?"

"It's gone!"

"What's gone?"

"The Oldsmobile!"

It took her awhile to explain what had happened. That morning, when she'd peered through the fan-shaped window over the front door, she'd seen only an oil spot on the Bermuda grass. She'd run out onto the front porch, then back into the house and called the police. Then she'd called me. "It just wasn't there, Treesa," she kept saying. I, too, was shocked that somebody would steal the Oldsmobile—because I couldn't believe that anybody would want it. Two days later, when the police still hadn't recovered it, I called my cousin Danny at the Yazoo Motor Co. and told him we were in the market for a used car.

"Your mama's a tall woman, and she needs something big," he advised. "There's something on the lot I think she'll like. I'll have Donald bring it around to her."

Danny made it easy to buy a car over the telephone. That same day, Donald delivered the 1990 Ford Crown Victoria, handed Mama the keys, and told her to take it for a test drive. The car, with power windows and air-conditioning and royal blue velvet seats, enthralled her. The Ford cost forty-five hundred dollars, and I was surprised that Mama let Debbie and me pay for half of it. The rest she would make up with the insurance money from the Oldsmobile, plus the proceeds from the truck, Pontiac, Chevrolet, and Buick.

She was happy with the acquisition. "We ain't never owned us no Ford before," she repeated proudly. But she was still shaken by the theft of the Olds and afraid the thief might come back. Donald, who'd worked with Daddy for many years, bought Mama a security gadget called the Club and taught her how to use it. He also installed a motion-sensor light on the side of the house where she parked. But Mama would still get up from her chair to look out the window throughout the day, checking on the Ford as if it were a newborn.

With Mama's seventieth birthday coming up on the first day of spring, I told my boss I'd be taking a few days off, and three weeks after leaving Mississippi, I returned. At the Jackson airport, I rented a car and drove Highway 49 north toward Yazoo City. The season had deepened, and the hardwoods that grew close alongside the road wore gentle shades of green and seemed to wink in the light wind as I passed. The dogwoods flowered stark white, and the redbuds gaudy, purple, outrageous. Everything was memory—the softness of the greens and the persistence of the breezes that I knew would bring the traveling storms and maybe the tornadoes.

I got to Yazoo City in midafternoon. When I turned onto Thirteenth Street, I was startled to see Grandma's wisteria with its clusters of purple flowers hanging like thick grapes; it had been a long time since I'd seen this vine in bloom. On our corner, all of Daddy's dilapidated cars were gone, with only the gleaming white Ford Crown Victoria parked on the grass. And someone had finally cut down the Teresa shrub, leaving behind a skinny, foot-high stump. But the duplex's clapboards were still unpainted, the porch still covered with detritus.

Mama was sitting in the Bassett as I came through the door, but she reached up to hug me. "Where's Gerry?" she asked.

I'd come alone, I explained, since the visit was only over a long weekend. She looked disappointed.

"What have you been doing?" I asked, taking my accustomed place on the green and white velour love seat.

"I ain't been doin' nothin'." She grinned broadly.

"Have you talked to anybody today?"

"Naw."

"Is anything new?"

"Ain't nothin' new."

She made a fist and rested her mouth on her fingers, then announced brightly, "Well, two days ago, we had us a tiny little rain."

Minutes clicked by, and we continued in companionable silence. Only occasionally would we break into conversation, and just for a line or two. I asked about Erin and Grandma, but there was no further news about what was ailing my niece, and there'd been no other offers on Grandma's house. More minutes clicked by. Then, as if the news of my arrival had already spread, the telephone rang. I reached for the Touch-Tone beneath the Bassett. Willie Belle was inviting us to a fish fry the next day in celebration of Mama and Brother's birthday.

Mama had me drive the new/used Ford Crown Victoria to the birthday supper. "Ain't it nice, Treesa?" she crooned. As we glided along the torn-up macadam on the old Vicksburg highway, the Ford conducted itself in every way like a luxury automobile. From the high road, I could see the Yazoo River in the distance, where it curved to meet South Main. We went past a run-down house here, a trailer there. These were lonely buildings with no one about, only rusting cars and abandoned farm machinery.

A few miles south of town, I turned into Willie Belle and Brother's gravel driveway and guided the Ford to the carport in back of their brick ranch. It was odd, seeing Sol's truck parked under there. Then a motion-sensor light flicked on, and a beagle, one of Brother's many hunting dogs, began to bark.

"He ain't nothin' like Pup Dog," Mama said about the nondescript beagle. "Pup Dog, now he was a dog."

Pup had been a smooth-hair fox terrier, a "station dog" that Brother had bought for five dollars and who'd lived under the counter at the Rose Oil. Pup Dog was also the town dog, and if cousin R.B. or a friend or neighbor had a hankering, he'd invite the dog to climb into the cab of his pickup, and off they'd go to Jackson. As town dog, he even rode with the street sweeper. But he was true to his master; once he found his way between Brother and a rattlesnake, and afterward he wore his wounded face with pride. He survived getting hit by a car and kidnapped by a drunk, and he talked, at least once. One day when Willie Belle was about to get into her car, Pup Dog begged to go, but she told him he couldn't. He sat down and yawned, and the noise he made sounded like "I am." Mama was right: Dogs these days just didn't measure up.

We entered through the back door, which opened into a combined kitchen and den divided by a laminate counter where my aunt kept her police scanner. Brother lounged in his vinyl reclining chair, and as I bent down to hug his neck, I was struck by the contrast between his thin shoulders and protruding belly. To Mama he said gruffly, "Hello, Suster," and extended his hand, but he didn't say "Happy Birthday." Probably it was just another something understood between twins.

Willie Belle was in the kitchen frying catfish and hush puppies. Mama went to help her, and I took a seat beside Brother. The den was ordered, with a neat leatherette couch, a low coffee table, and even an entertainment center for the TV and VCR. There were family photographs in gold frames, including a handsome one of Brother in his Marine uniform. I vaguely remembered the story of how he hadn't graduated from Benton High with Mama in 1944 but had gone to war, where he'd fought in the Battle of Iwo Jima. Brother's attention was on the television, though every now and again he lanced a question at me about Gerry or the weather up in New York.

Willie Belle finally called us to supper, and we took seats on the bar stools at the counter. Brother mumbled a few words to Mama, and they all laughed.

When they talked among themselves, even I couldn't make out their accents and shorthand. "What's so funny?"

"Naw, it ain't nothin'," Brother said, but with a twinkle in his eye.

I asked one more time, and he relented. "You know, Suster and me, we started up goin' to Stub's ever' afternoon for coffee. And them waitresses thought I'd done got me a girlfriend." Then they all laughed again.

Willie Belle had baked them a lazy chocolate cake, a Hood family favorite, with cinnamon in the icing. Brother said, "Suster, we'll just have us a little piece. It ain't ever' day we turn seventy."

Afterward, Brother went back to his chair. I stayed at the counter sipping a cup of coffee while Mama helped Willie Belle wash the dishes. Then Mama giggled.

"Now what's so funny?"

Willie Belle half turned toward me, her hands still submerged in the dishwater. "What your mama got for her birthday."

"And what was that?"

"A pair of pretty pajamas from Miz Black's," she answered. Mama began to laugh harder.

"That's nice," I said to Willie Belle. "But why is it funny?"

"It's who they're from."

"Okay, who?"

"Your daddy." She went back to washing the dishes.

Mama tried to explain. "Well, last year he gave me a sale purse from Miz Black's, and I didn't much like it. Anyway, I needed a pair of dressy pajamas. Me and Willie Belle, we have us a pact. If she finds me, she's to put a pair of dressy pajamas on me before they take me away in the am-bu-lance. I don't want to go to Buster's in no scrubs." Debbie had left a set of green surgical scrubs at the house that Mama had taken to sleeping in.

Just yesterday, Mama had said that "nothin' was new." But some things were new, though change was coming slowly, like the blooming of the spring flowers and trees. In Mama's selling Sol's truck and the derelict cars, in the theft of Daddy's Oldsmobile, in the acquisition of the Ford and the pleasure she took from it, even in her cutting down my namesake shrub; in Mama's altered routines, coffee with Brother during the afternoons, shopping at Kmart on Sundays. She seemed able to accept these changes and sometimes even went looking for them. During the weeks I'd stayed with her after the funeral, when we'd gone riding together, she'd been looking behind. Now the past was receding like a car in a rearview mirror, and Mama was looking straight down the road in front of her. But there was one more thing she had to do to shed the past: She had to tackle the duplex. I knew this, sure as I knew anything.

Twenty-eight

I knew what Mama needed to do to put Daddy behind her, but it wasn't so easy to see what I had to do. In New York I found a therapist and spent my lunch hours talking about Daddy, about how I'd felt muted by him and rebelled against him, even when I was five years old. My therapist was a sympathetic woman who told me that I was stuck in childhood anger, but it all seemed too theoretical. So I kept on going to Mississippi, first in May, then again in July, both times for long weekends, both times by myself. Charlene, the lawn lady, would meet me at the Jackson airport, driving the Ford Crown Victoria, with Mama sitting shotgun.

Just as spring came early to Mississippi, so did summer. In May, along about six o'clock each evening, the sun would penetrate the tightly drawn window shades of Mama's living room. This was the hottest time in the duplex, which not only didn't have air-conditioning but didn't have ventilation because the windows wouldn't stay up. I would sit on the love seat in cutoff shorts, trying not to stir up any more heat by moving around.

"If you'd just use some of Daddy's money," I'd tell Mama, but I'd stop before adding the family catchphrase, "to fix up the house."

"I done lived here for thirty-five years, and another hot one ain't goin' to matter," she'd retort. But I noticed she made constant use of a long-handled fan from Stricklin-King Funeral Home. "Git up off that love seat and do somethin'," she'd tell me, though her aspirations for herself weren't very great.

Mostly we sat, and when we had to eat, mostly we fixed ourselves cold-cut sandwiches from Patenotte's. Once, I cooked dinner in the appalling kitchen, preparing spaghetti with garlic, olive oil, and fresh tomatoes, and Mama invited her next-door neighbor, Dot Knot, who was becoming her best friend. It was odd having Dot occupy Daddy's place at the dining table. She and Mama marveled over sauce that didn't contain meat, Dot even lifting up the strands of pasta, searching for it. Yet they both liked the "foreign" dish. I heard them say as much as they went off together to smoke under the leaves of the fig tree.

Oddly enough, the weather in July proved more tolerable, with long afternoons when the air would cool and the strong west wind blow in a stray shower. That weekend when I was home, Johnny called from Jackson to say he was coming to Yazoo City. He wanted to walk on his friend Sam's cattle farm, which was located just outside of town. Would I like to go with him? I hadn't seen Johnny since Daddy's funeral, though we'd kept in touch by telephone.

"Do you good to git out of this house," Mama said. Daddy had always been suspicious of Johnny, accusing, "You're not meetin' that boy again, are you?" But Mama would say, "Johnny's a nice person." That was how she'd thought of him then and how she still thought of him.

I went to wash up in the Pink Bathroom and in the shard of mirror examined my face. It hadn't changed all that much since I was a teenager; there was even a blemish on my right cheek. Crossing the hall to the White Bathroom, I opened Daddy's cabinet, where I found the unguents left over from our adolescence—a bottle of half-used Regular Strength Zemo, dried-up calamine lotion, and a Zapzyt cleansing bar, still in its original box, which promised to "clear acne pimples and prevent new ones." I scrubbed with the brown, medicinal soap, then ran my hands through my hair.

When I heard Johnny's knock, I took one last look in the mirror and went to let him in. We embraced in front of the television, and he walked over to Mama, bent down, and hugged her neck. He told her he was sorry about Daddy.

"Would you like to come for a ride with us?" Johnny asked.

She shook her head. "Naw, y'all have a good time. I'm goin' to fix myself a glass of cornbread and milk."

We started out, and as I was closing the front door I glanced back and saw her padding into the kitchen in her navy scuffs.

Johnny had parked his Nissan Stanza on Thirteenth Street. As we got in, his dog, a black chow, leaned forward from the back seat and stuck her head between us. He called her name, Licorice, then started the car and drove toward downtown.

It was midafternoon, and the heat had built up, bouncing off asphalt, hanging in windless trees, tormenting innocent children who would rather be out riding their bicycles, not whining at their mamas in air-conditioned houses. Then at the foot of South Main, Johnny made a sharp left in the direction of Ridge Road. We passed a bungalow perched on a low rise, partly hidden by a line of cedar trees, and I twisted in my seat to look. The old house had the same lines as Grandma's but was carefully painted, with a well-tended lawn.

"Lisa Hill's place," Johnny said. "Do you remember her? She lived there when she was little, and after her grandmother died, she moved back in with her husband and kids."

Lisa and I had attended grammar school together at St. Clara's. Since I'd only met Johnny in ninth grade, when I'd transferred to the public high school, he wouldn't have known of our friendship, that I'd captioned the back of her School Days photo *Best Friend in Fifth Grade*. She'd had hair the color of light honey, which she'd worn in an old-fashioned braid straight down her back. Many nights I'd slept over with her, sometimes in that house so like Grandma's, sometimes in her father's camper trailer, which smelled of oil and leather and tight, dusty corners. In the surrounding woods, in the bottom of the deepest ravine, we'd become blood sisters, Lisa jabbing first her thumb on a thorn tree, then mine. We grew apart when she entered the public school a year before I did. I'd last seen her twenty years ago on another stifling summer day, when I'd run into her in the parking lot at Mrs. Black's store as she sat in a car, holding her firstborn on her lap.

Johnny dug in his shirt pocket for a cigarette. "I know I should quit," he said.

We continued past other houses, some inhabited, some not, at last coming to a stretch of deserted road. He turned onto a rutted path and stopped before a metal gate. With the dog following, he walked to the gate and pulled it open. She scooted ahead, while Johnny climbed back in the car and drove us through.

Where the path ended under the scraggly limbs of an ancient pear tree, we could just make out the ruins of a foundation and chimney, encumbered by vines. "I've always thought I'd like to build a house here," Johnny said.

The day was still hot, but the afternoon breeze had come up. In the distance was a small pond. "Let's see what the beaver's been doing," he suggested. We got out of the car and pushed our way through the tall grass toward the dam. The dog stomped in the mud, impatient for us to take some action against the animal.

"You're not going to break it up?" I asked. "Look at all the trees he's killed." Their remnants were scattered around, pathetic, chewed-off stumps protruding from the water's edge.

"No," Johnny answered. He knelt, examining the structure of bark and leaves. "Isn't it amazing?"

After a while, we walked up a hill and looked out over the fields, but there was still no sign of the cattle. When the dog circled back to the dam, we sat down to wait for her.

I looked at Johnny's boyish features, framed by his thick, graying hair. Whenever he and I got together, we talked about our past. About how we'd met in Mr. Moore's general science class, passing notes until the teacher drew a ring on the chalkboard and made Johnny stand with his nose in it. About how we'd dragged Grand, dreaming of leaving. How he was going to be an architect and I was going to write.

He said, "It's nice of you to be spending so much time with your mama."

"She needs me right now."

"Probably you need her, too, at a time like this."

"You're right."

"Do you think you'll ever come home to live?"

I shrugged. "I've lived in New York almost as long as I lived here."

"You remember what Truman said?" Johnny was always quoting our favorite writers.

"No, what?"

"'All southerners come home sooner or later, even if it's in a box.'"

We both laughed. "Well, I've always planned on that at least."

He tore off a piece of the long grass and twirled it in his fingers. Then he asked, "Remember sophomore year, when

Mrs. Davis wanted to meet you after she read one of your themes?"

Helen Dick Davis was a writer and the wife of Mississippi novelist Reuben Davis. I'd met her long after her husband died, when she graded our student compositions. During many hot afternoons like this one, I'd kept company with Mrs. Davis on her screened porch, listening to her talk about writing.

"Remember what she told you?" Johnny asked.

"That working on the school newspaper was a waste of my talent."

"Yes, but what else?"

"I don't remember."

"That you were meant to write about this place."

When I didn't answer, he got up and went to collect his dog. I saw his figure recede, heard him hollering. But I stayed awhile longer before walking back to the car.

Johnny was already there, surrounded by dozens of the cattle, which were milling in anticipation. "They associate cars with feeding," he explained. "When Sam comes in his truck, he hauls food in the back." Johnny placed my hand on a steer's muzzle, and I tentatively stroked the broad, rough nose. Then he clapped to scare away the insistent cattle, called his dog, and motioned me inside the car. He drove home past Short Creek. Beyond the church and cemetery, the road changed to hard-packed gravel, and the woods came right up to its sides. Though I'd taken it many times, I'd forgotten where it would come out.

Afterward, when I remembered that day, I thought Johnny was right to remind me of what I'd meant to do. But he'd been wrong about one thing. Truman Capote never made it back to the South: He'd been cremated, his ashes buried in California.

Twenty-nine

In August and September I stayed in New York, but instead of writing, I began long-distance running. Weekend mornings, I jogged on a path along the Bronx River, ten or so miles, then I spent the afternoons recuperating in our backyard. We kept a wrought-iron table and chairs on the patio next to a small fishpond, and I would rest while Gerry tended the garden, a twisting border of phlox, coreopsis, hollyhock, foxglove, and coneflower.

On the cordless telephone, I would call Mama for news of home. I daydreamed about buying Grandma's house and living in it, just as my childhood friend Lisa Hill had done with her grandmother's. Gerry and I would fix it up, repapering the bedrooms with romantic rose-patterned wallpaper and renovating Grandma's garden. There, in her house, I would write the books Johnny had said I was meant to write.

But I couldn't bring myself to dial Pauline and make the offer. Instead, I bought more furniture for the house in Bronxville, and when I'd filled it with as much as it could hold, I began buying knickknacks: hand-painted dishes from Italy, a French mantel clock, a lamp fashioned out of an ostrich egg, two butterflies from a shop in Paris, a nineteenth-century painted vase, a tortoiseshell candelabra, a mahogany ogee mirror. The list went on.

Then on the last Friday in September, while seated on the terrace, I received a phone call. It was Mama, saying that Brother had died early that morning of a heart attack, the latest victim of the Hood heart. On Saturday I flew to Atlanta and met Debbie in the airport, where we boarded the same flight to Jackson. She drove fast through the ribbons of hills outside Yazoo, and we got to Stricklin-King just as the service was about to begin.

We took seats next to Mama near the front of the chapel. She smiled at us, then turned away to face the lectern. But I kept on looking at her, trying to judge how she was taking her twin's death. From behind, I could hear quiet footfalls and low voices as the room filled with mourners. Then Great-Aunt Natalie marched up to Brother's coffin and pronounced, "Rest in peace, Lawrence. If anybody deserves it, you do." There was a brief eulogy, and afterward we gathered on a ridge in Glenwood, and on that hot October day, in a strong, dry wind, we buried Brother. There were speeches, and sunlight blurred the faces; I believe someone folded a flag and handed it to Willie Belle, and I believe she clutched it to her. My attention wandered, because Brother's October funeral made me think of Sol's, even though his had taken place after the fall rains had started. If I searched, I could just make out his plot and Daddy's at the bottom of the hill, beyond the thicket of trees. Finally, the sheriff's deputies came forward to hug my aunt, and Brother's ceremony was ended.

Mama drove herself to Willie Belle's house in the Ford Crown Victoria, slowly negotiating the old Vicksburg highway, while Debbie and I followed in our rental. There were vehicles parked everywhere, even on the well-tended front lawn. Mama pulled off the gravel and found a spot near the woods, and we squeezed in behind her. My aunt and uncle had liked this house because of its isolated setting, far from the road, away from the neighbors. But I couldn't see Willie Belle living out here now, all by herself.

We got out and picked our way to the back door. Mama took a seat on a stool at the kitchen counter, but Debbie and I mingled among the crowd in the family room. They were telling stories about Brother. That a former governor of Mississippi, Bill Waller, had once referred to him as "the biggest politician in Yazoo County," because people asked him how they should vote. That Brother knew the county better than anybody and that he loved to ride it. On many a Sunday afternoon, he and Willie Belle would strike out with her driving; together they must have covered every one of the back roads. That Brother also loved his garden. Each year, he had to have a vegetable plot as big as a football field, with corn and watermelons and tomatoes and beans, most of which he gave away. Once Mama and Willie Belle, who were his helpers, hoed up a large plant, believing it was a weed. After that, he would repeat wistfully, to tease them, "I had me a sage plant once."

Finally, Brother's younger son, Lee, spoke up. He wanted to tell about deer hunting with his father. They'd gotten separated in the woods, and Lee, who was still a boy, had come running back, calling out, "Daddy, Daddy, I saw a damn bear! There's a damn bear!" To which Brother had replied, "Son, watch your language."

Everybody laughed, and for a few minutes there was silence. To mourn is to remember, to remember, forget.

Then Mama motioned me over. I stood beside her, but she nodded to signal me even closer. Evidently she, too, had a memory to share, but she didn't want to say it out loud. I bent down, put my head right next to hers.

"Brother said somethin' to me about you."

"What was that?" I drew back to look at her.

She whispered, "He said you have a big heart, Treesa."

I had to glance away. My own father had never said that about me. When I was able, I asked her, "Why did he say that?"

But she only shook her head.

After a minute I asked, "Well, when did he say it?"

"After Sol Boy died."

Again Mama motioned me to bend down. I expected she was going to explain, but she whispered, "My keys are out yonder in the car."

At first I thought she meant she'd left them in the ignition. But then Daddy's funeral reception came to mind, when we were all stranded on the front porch. "You locked them inside, didn't you?" She nodded firmly.

I went to talk over the problem with Debbie. We took a wire coat hanger from a closet, unwound it, and made a hook with one end. Then we went outside to study the Ford Crown Victoria. My sister carefully threaded the hanger between the glass and the doorframe on the driver's side, trying to pull up the lock. She'd managed to open Daddy's safe in the Bon Ton, but the Crown Victoria proved too much even for her skilled fingers. I stared at the stalwart vehicle, longing for the simple-to-steal Oldsmobile. I was unsure what to try next, so I went to ask Willie Belle. She called over a deputy, who easily unlocked the door with a slim jim. That was the only thing Mama did that day to show us how much she was hurting.

When I'd been home during the summer, I hadn't gone to see Grandma, not after she'd called Oprah a nigger. But the Sunday after Brother's funeral, I decided I had to pay her a call.

Martha Coker's bright lobby was crowded with its wheelchair-bound residents, but Grandma was not among them. At the nurses' station, I was told that Mrs. Nicholas had chosen to rest in bed for the day. Was I familiar with her room number?

I nodded. "One-fifteen, on the women's side."

The nurse seemed taken aback. "There's no such thing."

"What do you mean?" I was surprised myself.

"We don't have a 'side' for the women. Most of our patients are women."

So that had been another of Grandma's delusions, like Mrs. Worley being "Miz Lafitte, kin to the pirates from Louisiana." I walked down the right-hand corridor and pushed the door open; she lay on her back in the hospital bed, dead asleep. The television was on, transmitting watery images and soft murmurs. The two thin white curtains that divided the room pulled on ceiling tracks like those on a child's train set, and I drew them tight. I wanted some privacy from the legless lady, who lay directly opposite Grandma, though she, too, appeared to be sleeping soundly.

I went to Grandma and peered down at her. The white spread was tucked around her body. Her light brown hair stood up stiffly from its residue of Aqua Net; her eyes were closed and her glasses off, one of the nurses having placed them atop the clutter on her bedside table. Grandma's broad face looked pale and vulnerable against the hospital-white pillowcase, and her exaggerated features—hooded eyelids, ample forehead—were startlingly like Daddy's. Her nose even hooked slightly, though she wasn't Lebanese. She was making little *poopoo* noises with her lips.

"Grandma," I whispered. She didn't stir, and I said her name more loudly. When she still didn't wake up, I shouted, "Vashti!" and watched as her eyes popped open. Then I worked her spectacles onto the bridge of her nose, slipping them gently behind her ears.

With fanfare, she raised and lowered her eyebrows. "You know," she said, "Grandpappy rode with Jesse."

"Jesse?"

She chuckled. "Yes, sirree, durin' the war. And Jesse even came by the house afterward and invited Grandpappy to go out West with him and his boys."

Grandma's family home near Coxburg, which I'd last seen circa 1970, came to mind: the gravel walkway to the cabin's low front porch; the few rooms, nearly vacant of furniture and smelling of something sharp and indefinable, maybe the country itself; the worn red linoleum floor; the dark kitchen with its wood-burning stove and a hand pump for drawing well water; the lonely path to the outhouse.

"But Grandpappy had sense enough not to get mixed up with those outlaws. Otherwise, I might not of had the good fortune to be born in the state of Mis'sippi."

I had no idea if any of this might be true, but I thought she was gearing up for a rant. I could tell by the inquietude of her right index finger, which she held trembling next to her jaw. Yet she said softly, "Mama, she was cousin to Jeff Davis."

She was talking about Tenner Lee Long Pettus, and on this point I was inclined to believe her. More than a century later, the president of the Confederacy was still an unpopular figure in his native state, because he had lost the war for us. Nobody in Mississippi would admit to being kin to him unless it was unavoidably true.

For a while she lay still. Then she came out with one word: "Hulda."

"Who's Hulda?" I asked.

"Hulda," she repeated. "Hulda, Hulda, Hulda, Hulda, Hulda."

This time, I couldn't distract her by wheeling her down the "men's side." I could only nod and wait. Rants, like the weather, had to run their course. But unlike when I'd last seen her, she didn't ask anxiously, *How's my house?* or beg, *Take me home.* Nor did she rage about Grendaddy. She just repeated the one inscrutable word. Then she dozed off, right in the middle of a string of *Huldas.*

Here in the home, life was a question of waiting—to be bathed, for a tray in your room, a portable toilet, somebody to put you on it. In this place of nicked walls, of tan linoleum floors flecked with the black scuffmarks of the nurses' hasty footsteps, in this place almost without life, sleep was the only release. In this place, the murmur of the television, like a mother's heartbeat, reminded you that you were not in the world but that the world existed outside you. In this place—not even a room, a half room—halfway between life and death, Grandma slept toward death, quietly; maybe it didn't hurt too much, gradually closing down, inch by inch.

She shivered, and I pulled the white bedspread all the way to her neck. What if I weren't here to pull the covers up, providing just the smallest comfort, the difference between an acceptable and unacceptable existence? Was I the one keeping her alive this afternoon?

She opened her eyes again. Now she seemed to recognize me.

"Who's Hulda?" I asked.

"Our ole dog. Mine and Vesta's and Hop's." She was speaking of her siblings and when they were little.

Then she rolled her eyes. "What a life."

Vashti Elma Pettus Nicholas. I couldn't bear knowing she was conscious of what her life had become. I quickly said good-bye and left the room, but I waited on the other side of her door until I collected myself enough to walk past the nurses' station.

When I arrived back at the house, Mama and Debbie were in the living room, Mama in the Bassett, Debbie on the corduroy couch. The television was turned off, and it seemed I'd interrupted their conversation.

"How was Miz Nick?" Mama asked as I took my place on the love seat.

"Okay."

"Did she ask about her house?"

"No, she didn't mention it."

"Did she complain about your grendaddy?"

I studied my mother, so unusually full of questions. She almost never went to the nursing home, so what did she know of Grandma's rants? I asked, "Mama, why does Grandma say that Grendaddy 'done her dirty'?"

But she only picked up a felt-tip pen and a paperback, *Large Print Word Finds*, adjusted her glasses, and began hunting. It struck me ironic that she, who had such trouble coming up with words, would be obsessed by these puzzles.

"What are you talking about?" Debbie asked.

Not bothering to lower her book, Mama scolded me, "You always did ask too many questions, young'un."

The next day Debbie and I left. But I wondered about Grandma, how long my visit had stayed in her mind, which was now able to recall only her deepest past. And I wondered about Mama, what secret she knew about Daddy's parents that she wasn't divulging.

Thirty

After Brother died, Willie Belle bought security bars for her doors and windows and began sleeping with a pistol tucked under the mattress of her canopy bed. Then came the news that Dot Knot had lung cancer. When Mama told me, I recalled Dot's rasping voice, rough from the years of her habit. She wasn't sick for long, but before she died she proposed to Mama that Willie Belle buy her house so that they could live side by side.

So even before my aunt sold her ranch house on the old Vicksburg highway, she bought Dot Knot's. Willie Belle replaced the buckled wooden floor in her new living room. She trimmed the foundation shrubs into neat green balls and installed a patio door with curlicue bars. In due time she moved in, bringing with her the white '81 GMC pickup, which she kept permanently parked under her carport. Thus my brother's truck found its way back to the Nicholas family block.

Now Mama was flanked by her sisters-in-law, Pauline to the east and Willie Belle to the north. Since Daddy's death, Pauline and Mama had begun to engage in a bit of fence-hanging. The privet hedge, which for years had separated our yards, was cut down, and whenever Mama hung out her wash, she'd walk over to the unmarked property line and chat with Pauline about the latest purse snatchings and funerals. Pauline would inevitably be seated in the green plastic chair under her carport, next to the metal tub planted with cactus. Theirs was new friendship, but Willie Belle and Mama had long been friends, more like sisters than sisters-in-law. She even called my mother by her family nickname, "Suster." After Willie Belle moved in next door, they saw each other more often than they had when Brother was alive. On her way home from work at the sheriff's office, Willie Belle might stop by Mama's to check on her, and they began a Saturday ritual of eating dinner at River-Bend Catfish House.

I still telephoned Mama daily, though there seemed to be less necessity now. She usually didn't have much to say, and neither did I.

"What have you been doing?"

"Nothin.'"

"Surely you did something."

"Naw. Nothin.'"

"Did you see Willie Belle?"

She paused. "Yeah. Me'n Willie Belle ate us a pear today."

"You did what?"

"We ate us a de-li-cious pear from Grandma's ole tree. Ripe 'n juicy. Out in the backyard."

Whereas she'd used to sneak over to have a cigarette with Dot Knot, now she was eating pears with Willie Belle. Shortly after Dot died, Mama had stopped smoking.

Then the season began its transformation; spring and summer came early, but fall came late and stayed but briefly. Mama's conversations turned to leaves as all efforts were given over to frenzied raking. Charlene the lawn lady helped Mama gather up the offensive brown carpet, which each night the prolific sycamores deposited anew. They even enlisted the help of Charlene's husband, because leaf clearing was the work of weeks. After their daily sessions, the threesome would come to rest on the front porch, sitting and chatting before the couple departed. There Mama would remain, watching the five o'clock traffic come and go on Calhoun.

One fall evening, while Mama was still on the porch, Willie Belle passed by on her way home from work. Mama often saw her getting in late, because Willie Belle did everything in that office, from filling out arrest cards to sewing the deputies' uniforms. My aunt waved as she passed, and after parking in her carport cut through the Bermuda grass in their adjoining yards. She was dressed in her uniform of dark brown pants and tan shirt, with her shiny brass collar insignias, *MISS.* and *Y.C.S.D.*, for Yazoo County Sheriff's Department. Willie Belle had a tendency to walk straight-legged and with effort, since she was overdue having her knees replaced. But she was moving fast that evening as she came around the corner of the duplex, swinging one leg in front of the other.

Willie Belle also answered the telephone at the sheriff's office, and she was often the first to hear the latest goings-on. My aunt kept official business to herself, but there was news about Grandma's house. She told Mama that another offer had been made and that Pauline was said to be considering it. This prospective buyer didn't want to move the house out into the country, and he was one of the town's most prominent citizens, a veterinarian. Pauline could have no objection on those counts. But he didn't actually want to live in the house; he only planned to put his veterinary there. He also wanted the Nicholas Trust to sell him the vacant lot, which bordered on Willie Belle's new backyard. In fact, he even wanted a strip of Willie Belle's yard, so he could pave it all over and create one long parking area.

To implement his plan, the veterinarian had to get the block's zoning changed from residential to commercial, and Pauline dutifully began making the rounds collecting signatures on a petition. There was no other choice: The family had run out of money to keep Grandma in Martha Coker. If something weren't done, she would have to be moved to a facility directly across Calhoun that accepted Medicaid, a distressing prospect that Pauline referred to as Grandma "havin' to go across the street."

But Grandma's house a veterinary! I envisioned her elegant, square rooms partitioned into cubicles, furnished with examining tables. Clients would sit in the waiting room—Grandma's living room—holding their pets. Dogs and cats would run wild where once her fine furniture had rested. She'd always kept a dog, but would she approve of cats there? We were, Daddy had said, dog people. I'd had a childhood acquaintance who'd taken her horse to this veterinarian: Would there be farm animals at Grandma's, too? I worried about what the veterinarian would do not only to the inside of the house but also to the garden, the old wisteria and hydrangeas and spider lilies.

Not wanting to live next to an expanse of asphalt, Willie Belle objected. Mama signed the petition, though she worried. Not about a parking lot or the sale of Grandma's beloved property, not about change or loss. She worried because for the first time in her life, she was in cahoots with the Nicholases against a member of her own family. "Treesa, Pauline wants me to ask Willie Belle for her signature because she's my kinfolk. But I don't think I can." In the end, Mama never asked Willie Belle to sign, and the veterinarian withdrew his offer. We lost our best chance to sell Grandma's house, and so the old home place continued its vigil.

Of course, I could have made an offer myself. Thirty thousand dollars, an absurdly small amount of money, at least by New York standards, would have bought me the house, the repository of my happiest childhood memories. But I held back; I must have suspected even then what it would still take me years to understand: that I couldn't ever live there. That you could surround yourself with too much memory.

Grandma "went across the street" shortly before her birthday in November. The new nursing home could not have been more different from the peaceful Martha Coker, with all the tranquillity of a bus terminal. Its more diverse and mobile population used a variety of means—wheelchairs, crutches, canes, walkers—to roam about from their harshly lit quarters to the underfurnished dining area and even outside. Grandma was given a room on the ground floor, and for her roommate, a black woman.

Throughout the fall, Grandma had been eating very little and not speaking much. She was the sort of person who had always liked to set goals, and I figured she would try to live for her birthday. She and Pauline celebrated with chocolate cupcakes, and Grandma even ate a few bites. "The nurses and her roommate were marvelous," Pauline told me. "They brought us Cokes." In New York, I waited for Mama's call; it came two days later. After we hung up, I couldn't stop thinking about Grandma, even little things about her. Like how she fixed a piece of toast—slowly, the way she did everything. Pauline said, "She knew who she was until the end."

I did not go home for Grandma's funeral. Not long before, I'd had an accident on a treadmill that had left me with a sprained ankle and a broken arm. No, I didn't go home. Instead, I lay on my back in bed, unable to walk. I could have traveled in a wheelchair, but I chose not to. I preferred to remember. To see her as she was when we'd lived together in the old house, in our happiest of days.

Thirty-one

We went home for Christmas that year, the same as always. By then my arm had healed completely, and my ankle enough so that I could walk with a cane. We traveled through Texas, changing planes and flying west to east, because that was how the airline had routed us from New York. It was a bright sunshiny day, and I could see when we reached Mississippi because there was the great twisting river converging with its largest tributary, the Yazoo, at the port of Vicksburg. I thought about how my great-grandfather George, his wife, Rosa, and my toddler grandfather had landed in this river town before setting out the fifty miles inland to Yazoo City. Nearly a hundred years later, Vicksburg appeared vulnerable amid the countryside, encircled mostly by woods but also by farmland.

East toward Jackson, there were more woods and more fields of picked cotton. I thought of my mother and her nine brothers and sisters, who had once worked fields like these, and of the other sharecroppers, both black and white, and of the slaves before them. If only the plants had been taller, so you didn't have to stoop so low to pick the fiber; if only the bolls hadn't been surrounded by needlelike points and had ripened all at once; if only the fields had not been so dusty, the weather so hot and humid for so much of the year. The land had shaped us all.

Having grown up a sharecropper, Mama had come to believe she wasn't good enough for Daddy's citified family, even though George Nicholas had immigrated in steerage and had covered the land on foot, peddling notions in the small towns of Benton, Midway, and Valley. Eventually, he and Rosa had been able to buy their properties near the railroad tracks in Yazoo City. The grocery store that Grendaddy took over from them was also dependent on the land. "Cottin begin to go to gins," he'd written me the fall I was a sophomore in college. "Things pick up some."

Neither of my sisters came home that Christmas, so Gerry and I ate a lonely holiday dinner with Mama, Cindy, and Erin. Then four days later, we received a phone call that Uncle Sam had died. Once more we assembled in Funeral Parlor A at Stricklin-King, and almost a year after Sam and I had looked on Daddy, I looked on Sam. *If anybody would go to heaven, it would be your daddy, because he was a saint.* Uncle Sam had been the last survivor of that second generation of Nicholas immigrants, the last of Grendaddy's brothers; born six years after my grandfather, he'd lived eighteen years longer. And he'd reminded me so much of Grendaddy, with his foreign looks and accent, even with his aftershave. At his funeral, I spoke with some of Uncle Sam's eight children, and again the Irish priest pounded my arm, asking, "What side of the family are you?" Then Uncle Sam took his place in Glenwood beside Aunt Mildred, near my grandparents.

The day had been raw, and the drafty duplex was cold when we got back from the funeral. Gerry went off to the Toy Room to read under the bedcovers, while Mama huddled in her chair with a blanket and took up her book of word-find puzzles. I lit the gas space heater in the living room, then sat down on the love seat next to her. Mama's head was bowed, and she was absorbed in the grids of letters, with titles like *Come to the Fair!* and *Send in the Clowns!* The table lamp pooled strong yellow light, and I felt an unaccustomed contentment, remembering other dark rooms and their lamplight, and my grandmother's presence. As a child, I had often sat next to Vashti on the settee in the wide hallway of her house, with Grendaddy across from us in his reclining chair. There, during the evenings, under the cozy lamplight in the otherwise darkened room, he would watch his TV shows and smoke his cigar while Grandma worked the puzzles in the Jackson paper.

Much of the day, I'd thought about both my grandparents. For months, I'd been wanting Mama to tell me their secret, which I was sure she knew. Now I began, as I had before, "Grandma said Grendaddy did her dirty. What was she talking about?"

Mama sighed and rested the paperback in her lap. She said simply, "Well, back in the '30s, your grendaddy had an affair." Then she took a good, long look at me, as if judging the effect of her revelation.

But I was too shocked to react, shocked even that Mama had spoken the word. Finally I manage to ask, "Who did he have an affair with?"

She just picked up the puzzle book again and adjusted her glasses. Perhaps she, too, had felt the intimacy of the yellow lamplight, or perhaps Grandma's death had freed her. At last she had divulged my grandparents' secret, but she'd done so grudgingly; now, if she could help it, she would not go into any of the particulars.

But I couldn't let it drop. "How did Grandma find out?" I asked.

She kept on drawing long, lazy circles around the hidden words. Evidently this was a detail she could allow, because she replied, "The garden shed." By way of explanation, she added, "There was a men's robe out yonder in her garden shed."

This was the ancient tool shed that had stood in my grandparents' backyard, where Debbie had once nailed a Girl Scout insignia to the door that we were forbidden to enter. "What was a robe doing in the garden shed?" I asked.

"She gave your grendaddy a robe, and Grandma found it there in a box."

"What color was it?"

Mama finally looked up. "What color was what?"

"The robe."

"I think it was navy."

I could picture a gift box, with a silk navy dressing gown hidden in folds of white tissue. But I couldn't imagine my gentle grandfather wearing it as he lounged in his lover's bedroom. And why would he have hidden it in Grandma's garden shed?

"Then what happened?"

Mama drew a particularly languorous line. "Grandma told him that if he didn't stop seein' that woman she'd divorce him."

"So what did he do?"

She glared at me. *You always did ask too many questions, young'un.* "He stopped. He was Catholic. He couldn't git no divorce."

"How did you find out?"

"Grandma told me. I guess it bothered her, and she wanted somebody to talk to about it."

I was surprised that Grandma had confided in my mother, since I'd never thought they were close. "When did she tell you?" I asked.

"When she was in the nursin' home. But I already knew."

Something else occurred to me. "Mama, did Daddy know?"

She sighed, bigger this time, and lowered the booklet. "Of

course. He was twelve. The whole town knew, Treesa. She was a telephone operator." Then Mama went back to her puzzles and didn't look up again for the rest of the afternoon.

The television was left off, perhaps out of deference to the occasion, and I sat on the love seat as if by myself. If Daddy was twelve at the time, that meant the affair had been revealed in 1938. That was the year that Grendaddy was taking over his parents' store on West Broadway, renaming it the U Save Nicholas Grocery. I had the commemorative photograph of the grand event hanging over my kitchen bookshelves: Grendaddy out of the frame and Grandma off to the side, Daddy in a fancy white suit next to the drink box. Many of the townspeople had turned out; maybe even she'd been there, in the crowd. In those days, everybody knew everyone and everything about everyone. *The whole town knew, Treesa. She was a telephone operator.*

Then the store had failed and opened again as the Nicholas Cash Gro. For decades, Grendaddy had sat day after day on his stool next to the peanut parcher, staring out the plate glass window, waiting for a customer. He'd even sat there by himself on Sundays, when it was almost certain no one would come. And on those long afternoons, sadness had emanated from him like the lingering scent of his cigars.

Grandma was built for complaining, and after she found out about the affair, she would have made his life unendurable. The Old Battle-Axe, Grendaddy had called her, with a whisper and a tight smile. And if she weren't complaining, she would have been nitpicking, everything, even the way he made repairs at the grocery. Now I wondered, had he poked wadded-up bubblegum into the uneven surfaces of the counter and painted them with brown shoe polish just to annoy her?

Yet my grandparents had slept in the bird's-eye maple bed, in the room with the rose-patterned wallpaper, and I'd thought

they'd been happy. As a child, I'd been happy with them, but maybe I'd just confused my happiness with theirs. Had the double bed been only a pretense, a way to preserve her pride? Even when describing his death, Grandma had seemed angry with him. She hadn't given him a funeral Mass, but she'd had her Baptist minister eulogize him from the lectern at Stricklin-King. The family had been shocked, but we'd accepted it as what she wanted. All those Sundays, Grendaddy had tread lightly up the center aisle of St. Mary's to his place in our pew and hadn't taken Communion. Finally, I thought I understood why—and why Grandma hadn't cried at his funeral.

The year the affair was revealed was also the year Daddy got his picture on the front page of the *Yazoo Herald*, when his Soap Box Derby racer crashed into the curb on Broadway. For the rest of his life, he kept the newspaper clipping in its plastic sleeve, tucked into the pages of his Holy Bible. Whenever he'd examined the photo, he'd seemed wistful. Not only had the race been one of his life's unforgettable moments, now I thought that perhaps it was his last innocent moment.

What might Daddy have learned from that watershed year? That he couldn't trust his father, even to provide for them. That his mother might break up their household. The following year, World War II would start in Europe. Back home, Daddy's beloved grandfather George would die. And all these events had taken place during the last years of the Great Depression. Nothing would have ever been the same for Daddy again. The future must have appeared bleak and untrustworthy. He'd put his faith in God, but since he couldn't trust in the future, he'd saved. Saved everything. He began his lifelong hobby of collecting coins, sifting through the change in the store's cash register. He would later add to his collections the car memorabilia and the old black telephones, plastic pimento cheese containers and circus posters, mannequins and mops. And of course, money. Little by little, he'd accumulated his savings, depositing them in not one but both of the town's banks and even under his mattress. *He pinched ever' penny he could, Treesa. He was good at it.*

I could see how years later, as an adult, he would choose to look to the past, back to those happy years before so much had changed. The past was spinning tops and sweet-smelling Christmas trees, and it was the county fair. The past was the Soap Box Derby, that too-brief race down Broadway, the moment before the wheel fell off. When we were young, he would retreat into a child's world, trying to bring us along so that we might love what he loved, value what he valued, be touched by what touched him. He became Cartoon Daddy, a man who did tricks with his hands and let us ride on his back. He was a father obsessed by baby airplanes, monkeys, and the little red tractor in the window of the farm implement store on Highway 49. Just as he idealized his childhood, he idealized ours, so much so that he kept a bakery receipt for Debbie's first birthday cake and created the cigar box keepsakes for each of us.

Yet while he was squirreling away the past, storing it in bureau drawers and under the bed, change was coming, coming at a rate he'd never seen before. He'd reacted the only way he knew, by trying to stop it. He became a sympathizer of the White Citizens' Council to prevent the town from changing. But I was changing, too, asking questions about the birds and the bees—of his father, of all people. At home, he used his verbal clout, the Silent Treatment, and his big weapon, his anger. Now I could see these as ways not only of controlling us but also of trying to protect us. Even the beating he gave me after I cut my thumb opening a can of tuna: Was that his way of keeping from happening to me what had happened to Sol Boy?

We had all been shaped by the memories of only a few

events—Daddy by betrayal and uncertainty, Mama by death and hardship. I'd defined myself by my fights with Daddy. But now I realized the past was richer than these memories, not just fixed in black and white. Sitting on the love seat in the dark living room, I had the unexpected insight that Daddy and I were alike. I'd wanted my dolls to remain on the Pink Bathroom shelves; I'd wanted Grandma's house and her belongings to remain as they always had been. Like Daddy, I'd even become a collector, in my case of antiques and high-priced knickknacks. For both of us, our happiest years had been lived at Grandma's, and for both of us, that happiness had been truncated—his, when he'd learned of the affair; mine, when he'd moved me into the duplex. But why had I chosen to emphasize the difficult memories with Angry Daddy and not the good memories with Cartoon Daddy? Because after we moved, I wasn't open to happiness. I'd never forgiven him.

A few days later, the air became soft and light, with a prospect of spring. I was sitting on the porch in the early afternoon when an old black man hobbled up into our yard. He started talking so fast and with such an accent that at first I couldn't understand him. I thought he was looking for somebody, then I realized he'd been walking by on his way to town and on seeing me had stopped to pay his respects.

"Your daddy, he sho was a good man. When I was in that there hospital and couldn't no more pay my bill, he sho did pay my bill. And after he done that, he brung my family a sack of groceries, he sho did. Brung us a sack of groceries. And didn't expect nothin' in return. He sho was a good man."

Mama must have heard him, because she came outside and stood on the porch. The old black man nodded to her and repeated his story. After he ambled off, I asked her if she knew him, and she told me his name. She said his story didn't surprise her.

Then Mama sat down beside me. "What do you think of this? I got me a price to git my house fixed up."

I turned to look at her. "From who?"

"My cousin Mike. He fixes up houses for a livin'."

"How old is he?" I asked suspiciously.

"Not much older 'n you."

"How much does he want?"

"Nearly ten thousand dollars. But, Treesa, he would do ever'thang. Build me a brick foundation, paint inside and out, lay carpet, put down linoleum, hang sheetrock, remodel the kitchen, even patch the roof."

"Seems like a fair price," I said. "Better than fair. A good price."

"I thought so," she answered.

"So are you going to go ahead with it?"

"With what?"

"Fixing up the house."

"Might as well. I been thinkin' about it."

We sat awhile longer, watching the traffic pass on Calhoun. I thought it was fitting that the old black man had come to pay his respects now and not a year ago. Then, I would have found his story about Daddy impossible to believe. A year ago, I also wouldn't have thought that Mama would ever spend Daddy's money. But now she'd made a decision and announced it quietly. Finally, after thirty-five years, she was free to do what she'd always wanted: fix up the house. She'd mourned Daddy and, I suspected, forgiven him.

A year ago, Mama had said, "Treesa, you don't know your daddy." Now, even after she'd revealed my grandparents' secret,

I realized I couldn't find the answer to Daddy as though he were a solution to one of Mama's puzzles. Maybe I would never know him, but at least I could say that I knew something of what life had done to him. And finally, I could forgive him, too.

Thirty-two

It was March again, and we were all going home for Mama's seventy-first birthday. Late on a humid afternoon, Gerry drove the rented Chevrolet Prizm north on Highway 49. When he stopped at the traffic light on the outskirts of Flora, he gestured toward the circles of fat, gray clouds. "Are they always so dramatic this time of year?"

I nodded, proud of the landscape. It was sky we had here, not skyscrapers. Gerry hadn't ever been in Mississippi during the spring, so he didn't know: March was the beginning of tornado season, when warm, moist Gulf air, heavy as a mantle, collided with cooler, drier air from the west. I searched the unstable sky, remembering a Sunday in February when I'd been a senior in high school. Dozens of tornadoes had struck, destroying the town of Little Yazoo ten miles to our south. Yet Little Yazoo had rebuilt, and its few businesses and churches and houses once again peppered the frontage road.

We got to Yazoo City about five o'clock. Gerry drove down Grand Avenue and made the right at Grandma's corner onto Thirteenth Street. Her purple wisteria was in bloom again, and I thought, *How odd that a house goes on but a person doesn't.* We continued past Uncle Moe's and Aunt Pauline's. Then, just before the intersection at Calhoun, Gerry pulled into our yard—

not onto Bermuda grass but onto a new concrete parking pad wide enough for two cars.

He turned off the motor, and I sat staring at the duplex. I had been home once during the renovation. Mama was fortunate to have hired Mike, her first cousin on the Hood side. He looked like a wild man, with his untidy salt-and-pepper hair and beard, but he treated her respectfully, calling her not "Suster" but "Miz Florence." When I'd visited, Mike had made every room in the house unusable except for Mama's. The furniture from Daddy's bedroom and the Toy Room was piled high in the dining and living rooms, leaving only a narrow passage. Mama was enduring the disruption, but I couldn't. "The mess is one of the reasons your daddy never wanted to fix up this house," she said, as I left after only two days. For months, while the other rooms were renovated, Mama's bedroom remained her oasis, where she read and dined on po' boys from Patenotte's. At the end, Mike tackled her room, which needed the least amount of work.

Gerry got out, but I remained in the rental car. "Come on, aren't you anxious to see it?" he called back.

I did feel anxious, but not in the way he meant. Finally I joined him near the front steps. The floor of the porch was a lustrous gray, and the junk had been carted off, leaving the rocker and straight-backed chair and the table from the Bon Ton. The duplex was painted beige with white trim around the windows. The two overhangs from its previous front doorways remained, but the doors had been neatly covered with clapboards and the stairways removed, so that these protrusions now appeared decorative. There was a slate-gray roof and a new brick foundation.

I stepped onto the porch and opened the screen door, peering through the high fan window. There was Mama in the Bassett. When she saw me, she jumped up to let us in.

We hugged, and she retook her seat, but Gerry and I lingered in front of the television, surveying the room. The wooden floor had been covered with baby-blue carpeting, the walls and ceiling sheetrocked and painted crisp white.

"Wow, Mama, this looks great," Gerry marveled.

"Don't it, though?" she beamed.

She waited while we inspected the other rooms. Cousin Mike had laid the blue carpet in each bedroom, but in the dining room, kitchen, Junk Room, and both bathrooms, he'd put down pretty blue-green linoleum. All the rooms had been sheetrocked with the exception of the kitchen, where Mike had mounted tan paneling flecked with blue. He'd also installed five maple cabinets, butcher-block countertops, and a double aluminum sink. He'd even built a wooden enclosure around the hot water tank. The kitchen's focal point was a large picture window, which framed the hackberry tree in the backyard.

After we finished our tour, Gerry and I took a seat with Mama. I'd never thought the duplex could look this good, but still something was bothering me. Not Gerry. He said, "The house looks fantastic, Mama, but we've got to buy you some decent furniture."

She beamed at him again. Mama had gotten Mike and his helpers to move the high desk with the pull-down front from Grandma's. They'd positioned it in a corner of the dining room in place of the china cabinet, which had been relegated to the Junk Room. Aside from this, the furniture was the same. But Mama had changed the pictures on the walls. In the living room, instead of Daddy's Sacred Heart of Jesus prints, she'd put up Grandma's oil paintings and gold-leaf mirror.

"What about new couches?" Gerry suggested.

Mama nodded eagerly.

"And maybe it's time to replace your TV," he added.

She seemed so happy. Hadn't we gotten what we'd always wanted? The house fixed up. But as I sat listening to Gerry and Mama make plans—tomorrow, they'd shop for the new television—I thought how the duplex had housed our memories, both good and bad. I remembered a photo of Mama taken in the tiny kitchen: She is buttering and flouring pans for a German chocolate cake. Never again would Mama make our Christmas favorites standing over those chewed-up, gummy counters. Never again would we get out of bed on a winter morning and feel our feet touch a cold wooden floor. Now both bathrooms were white. The duplex had been our family; our family had been the duplex. Daddy and Sol would never see these renovations. *A house goes on, but a person doesn't.* Yet as we visited that March afternoon, two days before Mama's birthday, I could feel myself getting used to the changes. I liked the clean white walls, the smooth butcher-block countertops, and the neat maple cabinet fronts. Still it was hard, saying good-bye to who we'd been, leaving Daddy and Sol behind.

The next afternoon, the three of us went to Jackson in the Prizm, with Mama tucked into the backseat. She would have preferred taking the Ford Crown Victoria, but Gerry wasn't as comfortable navigating Mama's big car, which had so much play in the steering wheel that a quarter turn had no effect on its trajectory. We were going to pick up Debbie at the airport, but on the way we would make a detour. Cowboy Maloney was having a sale, and Mama had decided to buy herself a Sony Trinitron.

It was a warm day, so in addition to worrying about how we'd get both the television and Debbie's luggage in the small trunk, I worried about whether Mama could manage the trip. During the past few months, it seemed she'd become more fragile. She was wobbly when she walked, and her calves had a tendency to cramp. One of her knees bothered her, and she said her eyes "weren't right." But she'd visited the Jackson ophthalmologist who was treating Erin, and he'd pronounced her vision sound.

"I don't have what Erin has," Mama had reported to me after her appointment. Once again, I'd sat atop the Mississippi-sewn quilt on my bed, anxiously holding the receiver of the old black telephone. "What's that called again?" she'd asked.

Finally, Erin had received a diagnosis. She had Von Hippel–Lindau syndrome, a rare disease that allows tumors to grow in areas rich with blood vessels—the eyes, brain, spinal cord, and kidneys. She'd been found to have VHL when the ophthalmologist discovered a tiny tumor, a knot of capillaries in her left eye. The disease was genetic, though no one else on our side of the family or Cindy's had been diagnosed with it.

"Treesa, there's no reason to worry," Mama had told me on the phone.

But I did worry—about my mother, my sisters, and myself and about Lisa's daughter, Elizabeth. Would another one of us be found to have VHL? Should we subject ourselves to DNA testing? Be screened for tumors? Some people with VHL were diagnosed as early as their teens, often with eye problems, but others not until middle age. Did VHL explain our family tendency to have high blood pressure and to die young? Was it somehow behind the Hood heart and my brother's leukemia? Finally, I decided to concern myself only with Erin's health, and so far she'd been fine, the tumor in her eye successfully controlled.

We got to Cowboy Maloney's shortly after dinnertime. The

parking lot was nearly full, so Gerry dropped Mama and me at the store's entrance. Cowboy Maloney's had been started in the 1950s by Cowboy and his wife, Dolly Mom, as a lumberyard, but it had grown into a popular electronics and appliance chain. The TV showroom, up a small set of stairs, was a dark enclosure ringed with color televisions, all broadcasting the same program. A salesman introduced himself; he, too, was named Mike, and Mama took an immediate liking to the young black man. She followed him one turn around the displays, then pointed to the Sony.

"I like this one," she told Gerry as he joined us. He examined the medium-sized portable, which had a sharp, true picture, and pronounced it perfect for the living room. The salesman went off to check its availability.

After what seemed a long time, Mike returned, but he was scowling. "Ma'am, I can't find this TV in none of our stores. Do you by any chance want to buy the floor model? It's only been up a week, and I think all the parts is there."

Once more Mama turned to Gerry. "How many parts does a TV have?"

He shrugged.

Then Mike was off again, saying, "I'll go check."

We waited in the showroom, pondering what to do. It was getting late, and we had to leave soon for the airport. Finally, the salesman returned, announcing that everything was there; he'd been worried about the remote control.

"How much would you take off the floor model?" Mama asked him.

We walked to the cashier. Mike bounded up a little set of stairs to an office, where we could see a bearded older man. I wondered, *Was this Cowboy Maloney himself?* The two talked animatedly, and this time when Mike returned, he looked apologetic. "We'd only be able to take off five dollars, ma'am, because the TV is already discounted."

Mama began to question him: Exactly when had the floor model been put up? When did the store open and close each day? How many hours had it been turned on? She was polite but persistent, and I listened in awe while Mike answered her as best he could.

Then she lanced a question at Gerry and me. "Well, what do y'all think?"

Mama seemed to want to take the floor model. But the TV would be her near-constant companion, and suppose a problem developed once she got home? I wasn't sure what to recommend. Gerry also didn't seem to know what to say.

Mama said, "I'll take it."

While she wrote out a check, Mike took the Sony and wrapped it in cellophane. There was no box—that had been the missing part. Then he put the TV on a dolly and pushed it out to the car, which Gerry had pulled up in front of the store.

Mike tried wedging the Sony into the Prizm's trunk while I ran next door to Chuck E. Cheese to buy Mama a diet soda. A few minutes later, Mike still hadn't been able to get the TV to fit. We'd never get to the airport.

Finally Mama said, "Mike, put that thang in the back with me."

She sat on the right side and fastened her seat belt, and Mike placed the TV to her left.

"Y'all come back now," he called, waving us off like old friends.

But as Gerry began to drive away, Mama shouted, "Just a sec!"

He braked sharply. She instructed, "Treesa, fasten the seat belt." I reached back and managed to connect the buckle ends around the TV's widest part.

"Now we're ready," she announced, resting her arm on top of her Sony.

We arrived at the airport just before Debbie's flight landed. We put her small bag in the trunk, but she peered through the rear window at the cellophane-wrapped TV and asked, "Where am I going to sit?"

Mama simply opened the door and motioned her in. As we started off, Debbie asked me how we'd come to buy that particular television.

"We didn't," I told her. "Mama picked it out and paid for it herself."

She redirected her question, but Mama only answered, "Well, I liked it."

Although Mama seemed tired, she was making it fine, sitting quietly in the back, sipping her soda. When we got to Bentonia, I noticed a farm stand on the side of the road, and Gerry made a U-turn on Highway 49. A middle-aged man was sitting under a lean-to, selling boiled peanuts, home-canned tomato relishes, and sweet pickles. While Mama and Debbie remained in the car, we got out to shop. The loquacious fellow bagged our purchases and asked where we were from, and I replied that my mama lived in Yazoo City.

"I know you not from there," he said. "Where you from?"

"New York," I admitted.

He shook his head. "I was in the army for twenty years," he said meaningfully. We paid him, and he promised that the produce was Mississippi grown. "Now if y'all not satisfied with anythin' y'all bought, y'all come back, and I'll make it right."

We climbed into the car, and I put the paper bags at my feet.

"What was he sayin' to y'all?" Mama asked. "It took a long time."

I told her that he'd wanted to know where we were from and that first I'd tried to make him think Yazoo City, but then I'd owned up to New York.

"Naw, y'all is in-between people," she said. "Part southern and part Yankee. And the part that's Yankee is good Yankee." Then she took a slurp from her soda. She'd come a long way, finding her place in the world without Daddy, and she had it figured out for me, too. As we pursued the rolling hills toward Yazoo City, I looked out at the empty land waiting to be planted with cotton and soybeans and corn, and at the kudzu vines covering the trees and telephone poles. It sounded right. Gerry and I didn't have to choose between the North and the South; he could be part southern, and I could be part Yankee.

When we got home to Yazoo City, Lisa and Joel and Elizabeth were slumped in the chairs on the front porch. Lisa was wearing a pair of red-framed sunglasses on top of her head. "Mama, what did you do with the spare key?" she demanded as we ambled up the walkway. "It's not under the *N* on the Little House."

"I know," Mama said. We gathered in front of the door in a semicircle behind her while she dug in her pocketbook for her key ring. "I hid it in a different place."

"But why?" Lisa sighed.

"'Cause I got plans for the Little House."

We trailed her into the living room, and Lisa forgot whatever annoyance she'd felt. She and Debbie took a turn around the duplex, exclaiming at the sheetrock and ceiling tiles and paneling. Then they sat down with us on the corduroy couch and love seat. Elizabeth perched on the carpeted floor, stared at her crazy aunts, and opened a deck of cards for a game of solitaire. Joel and Gerry unloaded the Sony Trinitron and set it up in place of the Zenith, which was taken unceremoniously to the Junk Room. Mama rocked in the Basset, supervising, satisfied that we were home.

It was getting close to suppertime. Debbie was in favor of

taking out pork barbecue from Clancy's. Lisa debated which was better, Clancy's or the Pig Shack. Mama mentioned Stub's. Gerry wanted to go to the Steak House because it seemed the most festive, and everybody agreed. We phoned Miz Bea and made a reservation for six o'clock.

Then I called Cindy and Erin and Willie Belle to ask them over. We visited in the way that southerners do, languidly, enjoying the conversation that seemed to come naturally and was so full of stories. Willie Belle said that in her spare time, she'd started sewing checkered aprons for Palmolive soap bottles, giving them to people around town. "They look just like little squat ladies," she explained, speaking of the bottles, "so I wanted to put little aprons on them." She promised to make one for me and asked what color I'd prefer.

"My soap is green," I said.

She laughed. "What color is your kitchen? I've got to make the apron to match that, not the soap."

I told her light yellow, and she said she had just the fabric. Then I admitted, "But what I really want are brass collar pins from the sheriff's office."

"I have extra brass I can give you. But you can't tell anybody, Treesa."

I promised.

"Do you also want to be made a deputy sheriff?" she asked.

I answered that I did.

"Tomorrow, I'll fix you a laminated card with your name on it, statin' that you're an official deputy. You can keep it in your wallet. But just don't show it to anybody." Elizabeth rolled her eyes.

It was time to go to the restaurant. Mama changed from her tennis shoes into the pointy loafers, and we crowded into two cars and drove north on Highway 49, past Mississippi Chemical, where Sol used to work. We got to the Steak House as the sun was setting over the catfish ponds across the road. The sky was full of clouds, illuminated bands of purple and yellow, skirting a sliver of moon. *Same moon shines on you, shines on me,* Daddy used to say on the telephone.

The Steak House always got the prettiest sunsets, not that you could see them from inside the restaurant, a squat building without many windows. The decor, if you could call it that, was a little like a hunting lodge, with a large stone fireplace and deer heads mounted on the walls. Miz Bea's food was plain and good—not just the steaks, which were served with a wedge of lemon, but also the catfish and redfish and Gulf shrimp and oysters. Each entree came with an iceberg salad and choice of dressing—homemade blue cheese or Kumback Sauce. For appetizers, there were fried pickles, fried cheese, or fried crab claws. The jukebox played Mississippi natives—Elvis and Faith Hill and B. B. King and Muddy Waters. We talked and ate, and when the din got too loud, we just ate. As soon as we finished, we got up to leave, because Miz Bea didn't serve dessert. Instead, we went back to Willie Belle's to eat lazy chocolate cake. I thought then about Brother; I'm sure we all did.

Just after we left, Willie Belle telephoned. "Did y'all know that a tornado was sighted between here and Bentonia?" she asked, worried whether we'd made the hundred feet between the houses safely. Soon there came a downpour, and we gathered around the Sony, trying to find out if we were under a tornado warning. One of the local channels displayed a map of Mississippi, and Lisa insisted that Yazoo was within the watch area, but I didn't see how she could be sure, since the map was such a little thing in the lower left-hand corner. Then, when the lightning strikes intensified and the thunder seemed to rise up from the center of the house, I told her to turn off the new

TV. Immediately after that, Mama retired to her bedroom. The moment had arrived when we had to decide where the rest of us would sleep.

I looked from Debbie to Lisa. "We slept in the Toy Room last night, but we'll move into Daddy's room."

"Then Joel and Elizabeth and I'll take the Toy Room," Lisa said.

"That leaves you with that couch again," I told Debbie.

She shrugged. "It's all the same to me."

Lisa stood up. "Elizabeth and I'll take our turns in the Pink Bathroom first."

Again I looked at my sisters. "Are we going to keep calling it that? After all, it's not pink anymore."

Debbie replied matter-of-factly. "Of course we will. We've always called it that."

Gerry and I said good night to everybody and walked to the entrance of Daddy's bedroom. I tugged on the sticky door, swelled from the humidity. Mama had finally cleaned out the room, but she'd left some pretty things on the taller bureau—an amber oil lamp from Grandma's; Grendaddy's silver pocket watch, which hung from a miniature stand shaped like a grandfather clock; and a photograph of Daddy. The picture, standing in its own cardboard frame, had been taken about the time he'd become a teenager. He is posed on the prickly mauve chair in Grandma's living room; I could make out the gas fireplace and brick mantle behind him and the glass-fronted cabinets with her knickknacks. Dressed in shorts and a matching jacket, he appears fleshy and baby faced. Whatever effect the revelations of his father's affair had on him, it doesn't show in his expression. He's smiling broadly at the camera.

Gerry climbed into bed and pulled up the covers. I opened the top bureau drawer, a little surprised to find that Mama hadn't already gotten there with her black plastic garbage bag. I removed a Perfecto Garcia cigar box and perched on the edge of Daddy's bed. Mama and I hadn't opened this one the last time we'd been together in his room. But just as I was about to examine the keepsakes that I knew would be inside, Lisa called out to me.

I went to the doorway of the Toy Room. My sister was standing next to the window, clutching a quilt, while Elizabeth lay in bed, feigning sleep.

"I just realized, Mama's thrown everything away!"

"I know," I answered. One tiny chair remained in a corner, but now the Toy Room was filled with grown-up furniture, the double bed and a low table and a rocking chair with a red corduroy cushion. Our old toys and games were gone, including my dolls. Betsy McCall, Barbie, Ken, Chatty Cathy, the Tiny Chatty Twins, the bride doll, even Shrinking Violet—all had either been given to Erin or had found their way inside Mama's garbage bag.

"Oh, well," I said to Lisa.

"It's a relief she finally got rid of all that old stuff," she agreed.

I crept back to Daddy's room, where Gerry was asleep. Then I sat down on the bed again and opened Daddy's cigar box. On top was a manila envelope that said in big letters, *IMPORTANT CONTENTS. BLUE PRINT PLANS PER YOUR ORDER.* According to the return address and postmark, the envelope had been mailed from National Plan Service, Inc., Chicago, Illinois, on July 21, 1954. Inside was also a yellowed clipping from the *Jackson Daily News*. It was the drawing of a new home, advertised as having "year-round air-conditioning; sliding doors throughout; all-electric kitchen with birch cabinets; Youngstown dishwasher; beautiful wood-paneled den; concrete patio with barbecue pit; two ceramic tile baths; adequate wiring; and many other outstanding features."

I unfolded the blueprints, three sheets with all the various elevations, fireplace details, foundation and floor plans. I studied them, imagining our family in a house like the one in the drawing. Were these the blue sheets Daddy had flattened out over the Chevrolet's hood on Carter Road all those years ago? Who might we have become if we had lived in that house? Would we have been happier there? Was that all it would have taken, a den and a barbecue pit? After a while, I put everything back inside the envelope. When I turned it over, I recognized Daddy's handwriting, a column of numbers that added up to $11,600. I sighed. He'd wanted something better for us, but he hadn't felt he could provide it. Then I closed the cigar box. Though the storm lasted until dawn, I slept deeply.

The next day, Mama's birthday, was a day of clear light and blue skies. The Sol Boy and Lisa Maria sycamores weren't yet in full leaf, and their gray trunks stood out against a carpet of purple and white onion flowers in the lawn. We spent a quiet morning around the house, but that afternoon we decided to visit the cemetery. About three o'clock, we picked up Erin and drove to the gates of Glenwood.

We walked a winding path past the bend in the road and the large magnolia tree to the Catholic section. Up a small hill was the monument of my great-grandparents George and Rosa, and we stopped so the girls could pick the onion flowers that also grew in profusion over the graves. As they prepared their bouquets, we talked about where we would be buried. Mama said that Gerry and I should be next to the twins, which would put us near George and Rosa. Cindy would be buried next to Sol. Lisa and Debbie said they weren't sure, but they might want to be cremated. We started walking again, toward Sol, my grandparents, and Daddy. Then Mama stood at the place where she would be buried.

"Grandmother, it's silly that you already had your tombstone carved," Elizabeth commented, but when Mama tried to explain to her, she frolicked away toward another patch of flowers.

I reached over to Mama, hugged her close. I saw such a look in her eyes, of sadness and distance. But I knew we could stand the pain, now and to come. It will remain a blur of brightness, of warmth and light, that day in the cemetery when we stood around the graves of those we had loved.

Acknowledgments

Thanks to my early readers, whose continued support sustained me during the seven years ("seven *long* years," Mama would say) it took me to finish the manuscript: André Baltimore, Amy Boorstein, Jill Conner Browne, Beverly Donofrio, William Ferris, Ann Fessler, Chip Gibson, Lindy Hess, Andy Hughes, Caroline Jarboe, Mark McCauslin, JoAnne Prichard Morris, Betty Prashker, Walter and Miriam Schneir, Laurie Stark, Susan Stauber, William Strachan, Lulu Torbet, Jane Treuhaft, Ruth Williams, Steve Yarbrough, and Lane Zachary.

Thank you to the staff at the University Press of Mississippi: my editor, Craig Gill; Ellen D. Goldlust-Gingrich; Shane Gong; Clint Kimberling; John Langston; Leila W. Salisbury; Anne Stascavage; and Steven B. Yates.

A hearty thank you to Deirdre Mullane at the Mullane Literary Agency for managing to be a Renaissance publishing professional, one who reads widely and well, edits with skill and compassion, and agents tirelessly and creatively.

I wish to thank my family: Lisa and Debbie, Joel and Jan, Sol and Cindy, Erin and Elizabeth, Pauline and Willie Belle, Moe and Helen, Brother and Lee, Danny and Melinda, and Mama and Daddy. I love you. Thank you for allowing me to tell your story, too.

And finally, Gerry. Thank you for everything—for encouraging me and for teaching me, but especially for our life together.